International Standardization and Trade Regulation

World Trade Institute Advanced Studies

VOLUME 15

The titles published in this series are listed at *brill.com/wtia*

International Standardization and Trade Regulation

Exploring Linkages between International Standardization Organizations and International Trade Agreements

By

Sebastian Klotz

BRILL | NIJHOFF

LEIDEN | BOSTON

The open access publication of this book has been published with the support of the Swiss National Science Foundation.

The Library of Congress Cataloging-in-Publication Data is available online at https://catalog.loc.gov
LC record available at https://lccn.loc.gov/2023049356

Typeface for the Latin, Greek, and Cyrillic scripts: "Brill". See and download: brill.com/brill-typeface.

ISSN 2405-9331
ISBN 978-90-04-69183-4 (hardback)
ISBN 978-90-04-69184-1 (e-book)
DOI 10.1163/9789004691841

This book is printed on acid-free paper and produced in a sustainable manner.

To Karen, and in loving memory of Marlene and Friedrich Junge

Contents

Acknowledgements

The journey of this book commenced exactly ten years ago. It was the undergraduate research internship under the supervision of Ian Wooton at the University of Strathclyde in Glasgow, Scotland in 2011 that first sparked my interest in international trade and in academic research. Various trade and research related internships, my visit at the Tec de Monterrey in Mexico City, Mexico in 2012, and the graduate programme in International Trade, Finance and Development at the Barcelona Graduate School of Economics in Spain in 2013/2014 solidified my interest in international trade and research. My time at the International Trade Centre in Geneva, Switzerland between 2014 and 2017 under the supervision of Marion Jansen motivated me to pursue further interdisciplinary research on international trade (and standardization), and apply for the doctoral programme at the World Trade Institute (WTI) at the University of Bern, Switzerland.

The doctoral programme at the WTI has been an intense but greatly rewarding period. First and foremost, I would like to thank my supervisor Manfred Elsig who gave me both the flexibility and the guidance which I benefited from immensely during these years. Manfred, a strong advocate of the WTI's interdisciplinary focus, relentlessly pushed me to engage with literature that, with my background in Economics, was foreign to me and which I grew to appreciate tremendously. Here, I would also like to thank Cédric Dupont from the Graduate Institute of International and Development Studies in Geneva, Switzerland for agreeing to be the external examiner of this doctoral thesis.

At the WTI and the University of Bern, I benefited greatly from conversations and advice from Marietta Angeli, Thomas Cottier, Valentino Desilvestro, Ilaria Espa, Octavio Fernández-Amador, Joseph Francois, Irene Garcés Iriarte, Christian Häberli, Michael Hahn, Marc Möller, Ahmadzai Khwaja Muhammad, Doris Oberdabernig, Rodrigo Polanco, Damian Raess, Wanlin Ren, Sean Stacy, Jenny Surbeck, Peter Van den Bossche, Achim Vogt, Patrick Wagner, Simon Wüthrich, and Aydin Yildirim. I would also like to thank Pablo Rahul Das, Sascha Finger, Rebecca Gilgen, Sandra Jospeh, Corinne Karlaganis, Christine Kreis, Markus Obi, Christian Steiger, Sophia Thompson, Patrizia Vernon, and Margrit Vetter for their outstanding administrative support.

For generous financial support, I would like to thank the National Centres of Competence in Research Trade Regulation project (Manfred Elsig) in 2016 and 2017, and the Big Data and Global Trade Law project (Mira Burri) of the Swiss National Science Foundation (SNSF) in 2018 and 2019. I would, in particular, like to thank the SNSF for supporting me with the Doc.Mobility fellowship for my research visit at the Department of Politics and International Relations at the University of Oxford, England in 2020. Furthermore, I would like to thank the University of Bern for supporting me with the Research Promotion Fund in 2018, and the Swiss Network for International Studies for supporting me with the International Organization Research Stipend in 2018.

This support not only allowed me to pursue my doctoral studies at the WTI but also facilitated my participation in a number of international conferences and summer/winter schools which I not only thoroughly enjoyed but which also greatly benefited this book. For their patience and dedication I would like to thank Michael T. Heaney at the St. Gallen Global School in Empirical Research Methods, Switzerland in 2017, Philip Leifeld at the winter school of the European Consortium for Political Research (ECPR) at the University of Bamberg, Germany in 2018, and Balázs Vedres at the ECPR summer school at the Central European University in Budapest, Hungary in 2019.

This book also benefits greatly from the discussions and comments received at the World Trade Forum in Florence, Italy in 2016 (discussant Chad P. Brown), the European International Studies Association in Barcelona, Spain in 2017 (discussant Matthew Louis Bishop), the infamous WTI retreat in Galbino Castle close to Arezzo, Italy in 2017, the ECPR annual conference in Hamburg, Germany in 2018 (discussant Manuel Fischer), the Researching the United Nations conference in Geneva, Switzerland in 2018 (discussant Simon Hug), the ECPR annual conference in Wroclaw, Poland in 2019 (discussant Ronny Patz), the European Political Science Association annual conference in Belfast, Northern Ireland in 2019 (discussant Raymond Hicks), the International Political Economy Society in San Diego, CA, United States, in 2019, the Political Economy of International Organization annual conference in Salzburg, Austria in 2019 (discussants Eric Arias and Peter Rosendorff), and the Swiss Political Science Association annual conferences in 2019 and 2020 (discussant Lukas Linsi and Oliver Westerwinter). I would also like to thank Michael Beer, Awilo Ochieng Pernet, and Martin Müller for facilitating my participation in the 42nd Codex Alimentarius Commission in Geneva, Switzerland in 2019.

The WTI not only supported my doctoral studies in Switzerland but also actively facilitated my research visits abroad. Here, I would like to extend my gratitude to Tim Büthe, whose contributions to the literature not only ignited my interests in international standards but who also kindly hosted my research visit at the Technical University of Munich (TUM), Germany in 2018. Tim not only provided valuable feedback, he also provided me with the opportunity to present my research in his (post-) doctoral colloquium, and to meet my co-author Cindy Chen. In a more informal, but by no means less significant, note I would like to thank Toni Ser, who has not only been my best friend for more than 20 years but who also hosted me on his (and is his flat mates') living room sofa for three months. Without him, the fruitful research visit at TUM would not have been possible. I would also like the WTI and the SNSF for facilitating my research stay at the University of Oxford, England in 2020. While my visit was unfortunately shortened by the global COVID-19 pandemic, I would like to thank Duncan Snidal and Karolina Milemicz for hosting my research visit and for giving me the opportunity to present my work at the joint doctoral colloquium of Nuffield College and University College.

This book benefits immensely from a long list of conversations with current and former staff members of international organizations. For their time and insightful comments I would like to thank Belina Cleeland, William J. Drake, Richard Hill, Lee Ann Jackson, Marion Jansen, Paulo Luciano, João Magalhães, Devin McDaniels, Kazuaki Miyagishima, José Carlos Engra Moreno, Ahmad Mukthar, Roberta Piermartini, Victor do Prado, Olga and Jean-Marc Solleder, Gretchen H. Stanton, Susan Stone, Cristian Ugarte, Reinhard Weissinger, and Christiane Wolff.

During my doctoral studies I had the opportunity to benefit from organizing and/or participating in a number of mentoring programmes. Here, I would like to thank the Association of German International Civil Servants, the Carlo Schmid Network for International Politics and Co-operation, the German Council on Foreign Relations, the Tönissteiner Kreis, and the University of Bern's Faculty of Business, Economics and Social Sciences as well as, in particular, Lutz Güllner, Ghislaine Weder, Klaus-Heinrich Standke, Hans-Dieter Kalscheuer, and Georg Roebling.

Finally, and most importantly, I would like to thank my family, and in particular Alina, Ute and Roger Klotz, and friends for their strong support during this doctoral journey. I am most grateful for the loving support of Karen Gentleman who, at the time of my first research project on international trade in 2011, surely did not know what she signed up for. The long nature walks with her and Clyde not only allowed me to reflect on my research but actually kept me sane during the final period of my doctoral studies.

Figures

Tables

Abbreviations

AOAC	Association of Official Analytical Chemists
AU	African Union
BEUC	European Consumer Organization
BSI	British Standards Institute
CAC	Codex Alimentarius Commission
CCASIA	Codex Coordinating Committee for Asia
CCCPC	Codex Committee on Cocoa Products and Chocolate
CCEXEC	Executive Committee of the Codex Alimentarius Commission
CCFH	Codex Committee on Food Hygiene
CCGP	Codex Committee on General Principles
CCNMW	Codex Committee on Natural Mineral Waters
CCPR	Codex Committee on Pesticide Residues
CCRVDF	Codex Committee on Residues of Veterinary Drugs in Foods
CEN	European Committee for Standardization
CENELEC	European Committee for Electrotechnical Standardization
CETA	Canada-EU Comprehensive Economic and Trade Agreement
CI	Consumers International
Codex	Codex Alimentarius
CPTPP	Comprehensive and Progressive Agreement for Trans-Pacific Partnership
CROP	CropLife International
DESTA	Design of Trade Agreements database
DG	Directorate-General
ECPR	European Consortium for Political Research
EEC	European Economic Community
EU	European Union
FAO	Food and Agriculture Organization of the United Nations
GATT	General Agreement on Tariffs and Trade
GDP	Gross domestic product
GIFAP	Groupement International des Associations Nationales de Fabricants de Produits Agrochimiques
IAEA	International Atomic Energy Agency
IBRD	International Bank for Reconstruction and Development
ICANN	Internet Corporation for Assigned Names and Numbers
ICGMA	International Council of Grocery Manufacturer Associations
ICT	Information and communication technology
IDF	International Dairy Federation
IEC	International Electrotechnical Commission

IEEE	Institute of Electrical and Electronics Engineers
IETF	Internet Engineering Task Force
IGF	Internet Governance Forum
IGO	Inter-governmental organization
IICA	Inter-American Institute for Cooperation on Agriculture
ILSI	International Life Sciences Institute
IMF	International Monetary Fund
IPPC	International Plant Protection Convention
ISA	International Federation of National Standardization Associations
ISDI	International Special Dietary Foods Industries
ISO	International Organization for Standardization
ITC	International Trade Centre
ITU	International Telecommunication Union
MLS	Maximum levels
MRLS	Maximum residue limits
NAFTA	North American Free Trade Agreement
NGO	Non-governmental organization
NSB	National standards body
NTM	Non-tariff measure
OECD	Organization for Economic Co-operation and Development
OIE	International Office of Epizootics
OIE	World Organisation for Animal Health
OIT	Orchestrator – Intermediary – Target
OIV	International Organisation of Vine and Wine
P-A	Principal – Agent
PAHO	Pan American Health Organization
PTA	Preferential trade agreement
RIT	Rule-maker – Intermediary – Target
SNSF	Swiss National Science Foundation
SPS	Sanitary and Phytosanitary Measures
TBT	Technical Barriers to Trade
TC	ISO technical committee
TFAMR	Codex Intergovernmental Task Force on Antimicrobial Resistance
TMB	ISO Technical Management Board
ToTA	Text of Trade Agreements database
TPP	Trans-Pacific Partnership
TRIPS	Trade-Related Aspects of Intellectual Property Rights
TTC	Trade and Technology Council
TTIP	Transatlantic Trade and Investment Partnership
TUM	Technical University of Munich

UN	United Nations
UNCITRAL	United Nations Commission on International Trade Law
UNECE	United Nations Economic Commission for Europe
UNSCC	United Nations Standards Coordinating Committee
US	United States of America
USMCA	United States-Mexico-Canada Agreement
USTR	Office of the United States Trade Representative
WHO	World Health Organization
WIPO	World Intellectual Property Organization
WSIS	World Summit on the Information Society
WTI	World Trade Institute
WTO	World Trade Organization

CHAPTER 1

Introduction

Standards play an important role in the governance of the global economy and, in particular, in the regulation of international trade. Standards help to signal the quality of products and services to consumers and to trading partners, and therefore drive quality-based competition. Standards also enable the compatibility of products and services across countries and, as a result, help to lower trade barriers, and production and transaction costs. Finally, standards help firms to innovate and to benefit from economies of scale. (Blind, 2015; BSI, 2018)

Generally without being noticed, standards affect everybody's daily life.[1] For more than 40 years, for instance, there has been an international standard in place which, in its current form,[2] lays down that "chocolate [...] shall contain, on a dry matter basis, not less than 35% total cocoa solids, of which not less than 18% shall be cocoa butter and not less than 14% fat-free cocoa solids" (CODEX CXS 87, p. 2). Other standards ensure the quality of children toys (ISO 8124), the security of information technology systems (ISO/IEC 27001), or even an internationally accepted way to represent dates and times (ISO 8601). The dimensions of the shipping container, which infamously made the world smaller and the world economy bigger (Levinson, 2016), are also described in a standard (ISO 6346).

As global supply chains have become more complex over the past decades, international standards also became more important to internationally active firms as well as governments. During the COVID-19 pandemic, this importance of international standards has become even more evident, albeit probably not to the general public. There are, for instance, standards for protective gloves and clothing (ISO 374 and ISO 13688), lung ventilators (ISO 10651), and other medical devices (ISO 17510). Other relevant standards provide guidelines on food hygiene to control viruses in food (Codex CXG 79), or on the exchange of information between importing and exporting countries to support the trade in food (Codex CXG 89).

While there exists no universally accepted definition of the term "standard", one often-cited source describes a standard as a "[d]ocument approved by a

1 de Vries (2015) provides an overview of how standards affect different parts of everyday life, resulting in a wide range of academic disciplines studying standardization.

2 This standard was originally adopted in 1981, revised in 2003, and amended in 2016.

recognized body, that provides, for common and repeated use, rules, guidelines or characteristics for products or related processes and production methods, with which compliance is not mandatory" (WTO (1995), Annex 1.2). In contrast to a standard, the term "technical regulation" refers to a "[d]ocument which lays down product characteristics or their related processes and production methods, including the applicable administrative provisions, with which compliance is mandatory" (WTO (1995), Annex 1.1). And indeed, it is generally acknowledged that the compliance with standards is not mandatory, while the compliance with technical regulations is. Importantly, however, the compliance with a standard may be *de jure* voluntary but become *de facto* mandatory if the standard is incorporated into a regulation or a law.[3] The European Union (EU) Directive 93/42/EEC on medical devices, for instance, includes multiple references to standards on transfusion equipment for medical use (ISO 1135-4) (ITC, 2016).

This so-called "legalization" of standards can also be achieved through their incorporation into multilateral trade agreements and preferential trade agreements (PTAs). Multilateral trade agreements are trade agreements upon which countries[4] agree in the World Trade Organization (WTO) based in Geneva, Switzerland. PTAs, by contrast, are trade agreements upon which countries agree bilaterally or plurilaterally outside the realm of the WTO. Two WTO Agreements in which international standards play a particularly important role are the Agreement on Technical Barriers to Trade (TBT Agreement) and the Agreement on the Application of Sanitary and Phytosanitary Measures (SPS Agreement).

The TBT Agreement aims to ensure that technical regulations, standards, and conformity assessment procedures are non-discriminatory and do not create unnecessary obstacles to trade. The SPS Agreement covers all measures whose purpose is to protect human, animal, and plant life or health from pests or diseases, and aims to ensure that such measures do not constitute disguised restrictions on international trade. What is common in both Agreements is that they strongly encourage WTO members to base their national TBT and SPS measures on international standards. Measures that are based on international standards benefit from the presumption of conformity with the TBT and SPS Agreements, and therefore provide safe legal harbourage in WTO disputes.

3 Standards may also become *de facto* mandatory after WTO litigation (Bijlmakers and van Calster, 2015; Lindahl, 2015; Schepel, 2015).

4 The term "country" is used in a broad sense here and in this book in general. Not all WTO members, such as for instance the EU, are countries in a strict sense.

A key difference between the two Agreements is that the SPS Agreement explicitly endorses the Codex Alimentarius (Codex), based in Rome, Italy, as the relevant international organization to develop food safety-related international standards upon which national SPS measures are to be based.[5] The TBT Agreement, by contrast, is less explicit in its endorsement of a standardizing body but arguably gives a certain preference to the International Organization for Standardization (ISO)[6] based in Geneva, Switzerland.

As previously mentioned, international standards also play an important role in countries' PTAs. As of September 2023, 360 PTAs are notified to the WTO and in force. The large majority of these PTAs include detailed provisions or entire chapters on TBT and SPS measures (Espitia et al., 2020; Stone and Casalini, 2020). This is also true when considering both WTO-notified and non-WTO-notified PTAs, which together sum up to over 700 PTAs (Design of Trade Agreements (DESTA) dataset, version 2.0 Düur et al. (2014)). In many of these PTAs, countries agree to base their cooperation in the areas of TBT and SPS on international standards. Many of these PTAs mention Codex in the area of SPS, some mention ISO in the area of TBT (McDaniels et al., 2018).

As the previous discussion indicates, international standards play a central role in the regulation of international trade. The two international standardization organizations ISO and Codex are of particular importance in this context. However, in the political science and international relations literature, ISO and Codex have so far received relatively little scholarly attention. One branch of research has explored the politics of standard-setting in ISO and Codex. Another body of research has investigated the institutional design differences between the WTO's TBT and SPS Agreement. A third branch of literature has analysed the institutional design differences of PTAs' TBT and SPS chapters. While each body of research provides interesting insights into its rather narrowly defined topic, there is, to the best of the author's knowledge, no contribution that brings these branches of literature together.

5 The International Office of Epizootics (OIE) is responsible for the development of international standards, guidelines and recommendations for animal health and zoonoses. The Secretariat of the International Plant Protection Convention (IPPC) in cooperation with regional organizations operating within the framework of the International Plant Protection Convention is responsible for the development of international standards, guidelines and recommendations for plant health. With regards to the SPS Agreement, this book focuses on Codex and not on the OIE and the IPPC.

6 Other relevant standard-setting organizations for the TBT Agreement include the International Electrotechnical Commission (IEC), the International Telecommunication Union (ITU), and Codex.

The objective of this book is to contribute to closing this gap in the literature. More precisely, this book aims to investigate the, so far under-researched, linkages between international standardization organizations, multilateral trade agreements, and preferential trade agreements. In a nutshell, this book posits that the institutional design of multilateral trade agreements affects countries' participation in international standardization organizations. Countries' participation in international standardization organizations, in turn, is expected to affect the institutional design of PTAs. Empirically, this book illustrates that the institutional design of the WTO's TBT and SPS Agreements affects countries' participation in ISO and Codex, respectively. Countries' participation in ISO and Codex, in turn, is shown to respectively affect the institutional design of the TBT and SPS chapters of the PTAs countries sign.

Chapter 2 outlines the concepts and debates which present the foundation for this book. The Chapter first provides a clarification of concepts that are of central importance in this book. In this context, the relevant literature on international regime complexity, regime-shifting and forum-shopping, and institutional design and indirect governance is reviewed.

Based on this, Chapter 2 then discusses the linkage between the multilateral trade policy regime and the international standardization regime. In a nutshell, it is posited that the institutional design of relevant multilateral trade agreements affects countries' incentives to participate in international standardization organizations. More precisely, it is argued that the WTO TBT and SPS Agreements increased countries' political and economic stakes in international standards, limited countries' ability to engage in forum-shopping and/or regime shifting, and ultimately increased countries' incentives to participate more in the standard-setting processes of ISO and Codex. Due to differences in the institutional design of the two WTO Agreements, this positive relationship is expected to be stronger between the SPS Agreement and Codex than between the TBT Agreement and ISO.

Chapter 2 then moves on to explore the linkage between the international standardization regime and the preferential trade policy regime. Here, it is posited that countries' participation in relevant international standardization organizations affects the institutional design of PTAs. More specifically, it is argued that countries which have actively been participating in the standard-setting processes of ISO and Codex, have also been able to shape the design of standards in their political and economic interests. Consequently, countries' participation in the standard-setting processes of ISO and Codex is expected to be positively related to the probability that countries base international cooperation in the areas of TBT and SPS on international standards and, therefore, refer to international standards in the TBT and SPS chapters of their PTAs.

As the previous discussion indicates, ISO and Codex are of central importance in this book. Chapter 3 provides a detailed and comparative account of the two international standardization organizations' history, structure, procedures, and controversies. The Chapter also describes the two original datasets on countries' participation in ISO and Codex that were collected for this book and upon which the empirical Chapters are based.

The dataset on Codex includes information on the participation of 189 governments, 58 inter-governmental organizations (IGOs), and 337 non-governmental organizations (NGOs) in the 880 meetings the 44 standard-setting committees held between Codex's establishment in 1963, and 2019. The overall participation of governments, IGOs, and NGOs is severely positively skewed, meaning that only a small group of actors participates in a large number of standard-setting processes. The United States (US) has been by far the most represented government in Codex. Between 1963 and 2019, the US participated in 89% of the total 880 meetings. Over this period of time, US delegates accounted for eight percent of total delegates. With around 16%, the US also has the largest share of meetings in which it held the position of the chairperson.

The dataset on ISO includes information on the membership of 202 governments[7] in 289 standard-setting committees active between 1987 and 2019. Similarly to the Codex dataset, the membership of governments is severely positively skewed, meaning that only a small group of governments participates in a large number of standard-setting processes. European countries are the most represented country group in ISO. Of the 25 most represented members, 15 are European. The most represented non-European members include China, Russia, Japan, the US, the Republic of Korea, South Africa, Australia, Canada, India, and Iran.

Chapter 4 explores the linkage between the multilateral trade policy regime and the international standardization regime. The institutional design of multilateral trade agreements is the independent variable of interest, and countries' participation in international standardization organizations is the dependent variable of interest. Empirically, the multilateral trade policy

7 Technically, these are national standards bodies that may or may not be part of the government. For simplicity, however, the term "government" is used here since the participation data will also be linked to government-level data such as gross-domestic product, trade, political system, etc. For a detailed discussion, see Chapter 3.

regime is represented by the WTO's TBT and SPS Agreements. The international standardization regime is empirically represented by the two international standardization organizations Codex and ISO.

The principal proposition of this Chapter is that countries' incentives to actively participate in international standardization organizations partly depend on the institutional design of relevant multilateral trade agreements. More precisely, it is argued that the WTO TBT and SPS Agreements increased countries' political and economic stakes in international standards, limited countries' ability to engage in forum-shopping and/or regime shifting, and ultimately increased countries' incentives to participate more in the standard-setting processes of ISO and Codex. Due to differences in the institutional design of the two WTO Agreements, this positive relationship is expected to be stronger between the SPS Agreement and Codex than between the TBT Agreement and ISO.

The empirical analysis of the Chapter provides supportive evidence for this argument. Based on panel event studies as well as a set of Poisson regressions, negative binomial regressions, and ordinary least square regressions, the Chapter finds a positive and statistically significant association between countries' obligations under the TBT and SPS Agreements, and their participation in the international standard-setting processes of ISO and Codex, respectively. This association is found to be stronger and statistically more robust for the SPS Agreement and Codex than for the TBT Agreement and ISO. The Chapter concludes by discussing a number of caveats and by pointing out avenues for future research.

Chapter 5 explores the linkage between the international standardization regime and the preferential trade policy regime. Countries' participation in international standardization organizations is the independent variable of interest, and the institutional design of preferential trade agreements is the dependent variable of interest. Empirically, the international standardization regime is represented by the two international standardization organizations Codex and ISO. The preferential trade policy regime is empirically represented by the TBT and SPS chapters of 200 PTAs signed between the WTO's establishment in 1995, and 2016.

The principal proposition of this Chapter is that countries' participation in international standardization organizations affects the institutional design of the PTAs countries sign. More precisely, it is argued that the more countries have participated in the international standard-setting processes of ISO and Codex, the more they have been able to shape the design of standards in their political and economic interests, and the more likely they are to refer to international standards in the TBT and SPS chapters of their PTAs, respectively.

Since, however, only the SPS Agreement explicitly endorses a particular international standardization organization, this positive relationship is expected to be stronger for Codex and SPS chapters than for ISO and TBT chapters.

The empirical analysis of this Chapter, based on a set of ordered probit regressions and probit regressions, provides mixed evidence for this argument. Surprisingly, countries' participation in the international standard-setting processes in Codex is negatively, and statistically significantly, associated with the probability of countries referring to international standards in the SPS chapters of their PTAs. The association between countries' participation in the international standard-setting processes of ISO is found to be positively, but not statistically significantly, related to the probability that TBT chapters base cooperation on international standards. The Chapter concludes by discussing a number of caveats and by pointing out avenues for future research.

CHAPTER 2

Concepts and Debates

It is widely acknowledged in the literature that the international regime complex of trade policy is characterized by the multilateral trade policy regime, represented by the World Trade Organization (WTO) and its Agreements, and the preferential trade policy regime, represented by preferential trade agreements (PTAs). The literature also recognizes the existence of a dialectical relationship between the two trade policy regimes, in which they mutually affect each other. The institutional design of the WTO's Agreements influences the institutional design of PTAs, and *vice versa*. Within the preferential trade regime, there are considerable institutional design spillovers among PTAs. (Figure 1, thin arrows)

While there is a large body of literature on the international regime complex of trade policy, far less is known about the trade regimes' interaction with other regimes. One regime that is closely linked to the multilateral and preferential trade policy regimes, but so far has received little scholarly attention, is the international standardization regime. Indeed, multilateral and preferential trade agreements strongly encourage countries to base their regulations on international standards as a means of facilitating trade.

The principal objective of this book is to explore these under-researched linkages between international trade regulation and international standardization organizations. The central proposition is that, in the area of non-tariff measures, the international standardization regime, represented by the International Organization for Standardization (ISO) and the Codex Alimentarius (Codex), presents an indirect link between the multilateral and the preferential trade policy regime. In Chapter 4, it is posited that the institutional design of the WTO's Agreement on Technical Barriers to Trade (TBT Agreement) and the Agreement on the Application of Sanitary and Phytosanitary Measures (SPS Agreement) matters for countries' participation in ISO and Codex, respectively. In Chapter 5, it is posited that countries' participation in ISO and Codex, in turn, respectively matters for the institutional design of the TBT and SPS chapters of the PTAs countries sign. (Figure 1, bold arrows)

Understanding this international regime complex has important implications for other trade-related areas, such as e-commerce, in which multilateral and preferential negotiations are ongoing, and in which standardization is becoming increasingly politicized.

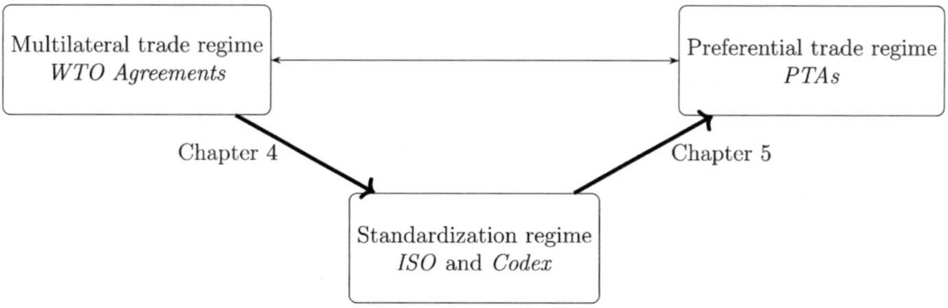

FIGURE 1 Schematic overview of international regime linkages
AUTHOR'S ILLUSTRATION

The following Sections synthesize the related literature and, based on this, present the concepts (Section 2.1) and debates (Section 2.2) which are of central importance to this book. Section 2.3 focuses on the link between the multilateral trade policy regime and the international standardization regime, and presents the foundation for the empirical Chapter 4. Section 2.4 discusses the link between the international standardization regime and the preferential trade policy regime, and presents the foundation for the empirical Chapter 5.

2.1 Clarification of Concepts

2.1.1 *Bodies, Institutions, and Organizations*

Many of the literature contributions outlined in this Section refer to the terms of "international bodies", "international institutions", and "international organizations". While these terms are often used interchangeably in the literature, it is useful to distinguish and clarify them here.

"[I]nstitutions [are defined] as persistent and connected sets of rules that prescribe behavioral roles, constrain activity, and shape expectations" (Keohane, 1988, p. 386) or as "explicit arrangements, negotiated among international actors, that prescribe, proscribe, and/or authorize behaviour" (Koremenos et al., 2001, p. 762).

International organizations are characterized by "[…] centralization (a concrete and stable organizational structure and an administrative apparatus managing collective activities) and independence (the authority to act with a degree of autonomy, and often with neutrality, in defined spheres" (Abbott and Snidal, 1998, p. 9).

An international body "[…] broadly signif[ies] some entity to which states have granted authority to make decisions or take actions" (Bradley and Kelley,

2008, p. 6) — the concept is therefore broader than that of an international organization.

For clarity, in this book the term "international institution" broadly refers to rules, whereas the terms "international bodies" and "international organizations" refer to entities (Simmons and Martin, 2012),[1] and are used interchangeably. More precisely, international institutions are empirically represented by multilateral and preferential trade agreements, while the international organizations/bodies are empirically represented by international standardization organizations.

2.1.2 *Multilateral and Preferential Trade Agreements*

By definition, multilateral trade agreements are trade agreements agreed upon by three or more parties. In this book, and more commonly, multilateral trade agreements refer to the trade agreements agreed upon by the members of the WTO and its predecessor the General Agreement on Tariffs and Trade (GATT). Most of the WTO Agreements were signed at the Marrakesh ministerial meeting in 1994 and are the result of the 1986–1994 Uruguay Round negotiations. The particular focus of this book lies on the TBT Agreement and the SPS Agreement.

The GATT/WTO Agreements provide an explicit link between multilateral and preferential trade agreements, and therefore between the multilateral and preferential trade policy regimes. Indeed, Article XXIV of the GATT permits WTO members to form PTAs as long as the PTAs cover substantially all trade between members, result in significant trade liberalization among members, and do not raise tariffs on non-members. PTAs may be agreed upon between two or more parties, and entail different degrees of economic integration. In a free trade area, for instance, parties agree to eliminate barriers on substantially all trade. In a customs union, parties agree to enter a free trade area as well as apply a common external tariff. Parties may also establish a common market, in which they enter into a customs union and, in addition, allow the free flow of factors of production. The highest degree of economic integration is achieved in an economic union, in which parties establish a common market and, in addition, coordinate their fiscal and/or monetary policies. (Mansfield and Milner, 2012)

In the past decades, the number of PTAs increased dramatically. As of September 2023, 360 PTAs are notified to the WTO and in force. Since 2016, all

1 When referring to other literature contributions, the original terminology of the author(s) will be used.

WTO members have at least one PTA in force. The origin of this new "regionalism", or rather "preferentialism" since many PTAs are cross-regional, is often associated with the signing of the Treaty on the European Union — Maastricht Treaty in 1992 and the North American Free Trade Agreement (NAFTA) in 1993 (Mansfield and Milner, 1999). Countries sign PTAs for a number of domestic and international economic (Baier and Bergstrand, 2004) and political (Manger, 2009) reasons.[2] The slow progress of multilateral trade negotiations is generally considered to be one of the most important international drivers. (Baldwin, 1993; Mansfield and Reinhardt, 2003; Hoekman, 2014; Cottier et al., 2015; Lewis, 2023)

Multilateral and preferential trade agreements are strongly intertwined as their institutional designs build upon one another in a dialectical process. Indeed, PTAs build upon the common law of the multilateral WTO Agreements and, in turn, multilateral rules are often derived from PTAs (Cottier et al., 2015; Lewis, 2023).[3] Not only do PTAs refer to WTO Agreements, they also adopt considerable parts of the legal texts (Allee et al., 2017b). More precisely, many PTAs refer to existing WTO Agreements but partly further extend trade cooperation (WTO plus, WTO+). Other areas, such as for instance labour standards and e-commerce, go beyond the current WTO mandate altogether (WTO extra, WTO-X) (Horn et al., 2010). Furthermore, PTAs differ not only in the scope of issue areas covered but also in their legal depth (Düur et al., 2014; Hofmann et al., 2019), flexibility (Rosendorff and Milner, 2001; Baccini et al., 2015a), and enforcement (Allee and Elsig, 2014).

Albeit these differences in institutional design, there are certain PTA templates which have diffused particularly successfully over the past years, following a certain hub-and-spoke nature. There is, for instance, a significant transatlantic divide with regards to PTA design between the United States (US) and the European Union (EU) — not least with regards to standardization in TBT and SPS (Horn et al., 2010, 2011; WTO, 2011; Lester and Barbee, 2013; Egan and Pelkmans, 2015; Baccini et al., 2015b; Elsig and Klotz, 2019). These templates have diffused through the PTA network as third countries replicate sizeable parts of legal text into their PTAs (Allee and Lugg, 2016; Allee et al., 2017a; Allee and Elsig, 2019; Peacock et al., 2019).

2 For a comprehensive literature overview, see Baccini (2019).

3 Burri (2023) explores this dialectical relationship in the increasingly important field of digital trade regulation.

2.2 Review of Global Governance Debates

2.2.1 *International Regimes*

A central concept that captures this dialectical relationship between multilateral and preferential trade agreements is "international regime complexity". The literature widely recognizes "[i]nternational regimes [...] as principles, norms, rules, and decision-making procedures around which actor expectations converge in a given issue-area" (Krasner, 1983, p. 185).[4] Building upon this, "[i]nternational regime complexity refers to the presence of nested, partially overlapping, and parallel international regimes that are not hierarchically ordered" (Alter and Meunier, 2009, p. 13).[5] A more recent definition refers to "[i]nternational regime complexity [as] international political systems of global governance that emerge because of the coexistence of rule density and regime complexes" (Alter and Raustiala, 2018, p. 329).

This coexistence of rule density and regime complexes can lead to legal inconsistencies, rule ambiguity, and the fragmentation of international law (Raustiala and Victor, 2004; Alter and Meunier, 2009). In the case of parallel regimes, these inconsistencies may be due to the lack of formal or direct substantive overlap, where different regimes are not coordinated, and are maintained by different sets of actors in distinct fora (Raustiala and Victor, 2004; Alter and Meunier, 2009). In the case of overlapping and nested regimes,[6] the inconsistencies and ambiguities may be built in strategically to accommodate countries' diverging preferences (Raustiala and Victor, 2004; Alter and Meunier, 2009; Drezner, 2009).

Two ways in which countries may exploit legal inconsistencies and ambiguities are "forum-shopping" and "regime-shifting". Forum-shopping aims to achieve a single desired outcome within a given regime (Busch, 2007; Helfer, 1999, 2004, 2009; Alter and Meunier, 2009). Regime-shifting, by contrast, is a power-based rather than law-based, iterative, longer-term strategy designed to reshape the global structure of rules (Steinberg, 2002; Helfer, 2004, 2009; Alter and Meunier, 2009). One often-cited empirical case of regime-shifting refers to

4 For critical views on international regimes and their definition, see, for instance, Strange (1982), de Senarclens (1993), Hurrell (1993), and Kingsbury (1998).

5 This definition builds upon an earlier definition of a regime complex as "a collective of partially overlapping and nonhierarchical regimes" (Raustiala and Victor, 2004, p. 277). For a recent study on how to measure institutional overlap in global governance, see Haftel and Lenz (2022).

6 In overlapping regimes, multiple institutions have authority over an issue but agreements are not mutually exclusive or subsidiary to another. In nested regimes, institutions are embedded within each other in concentric circles. (Alter and Meunier, 2009).

the successful efforts of the US and the EU to shift the negotiations on intellectual property matters from the World Intellectual Property Organization (WIPO) to the WTO through the negotiation of the Agreement on Trade-Related Aspects of Intellectual Property Rights (TRIPS) (Steinberg, 2002; Raustiala and Victor, 2004; Helfer, 2004, 2009; Alter and Meunier, 2009; Marx, 2010).

The previous Sections outline a number of concepts and definitions that are of central importance in this book. This discussion also highlights some of the inconsistencies in which definitions and concepts are used in the literature.[7] Alter and Raustiala (2018), for instance, define "[a] regime complex [as] a compound institution composed of elemental institutions" (p. 332) but then refer to organizations (the World Health Organization) and regimes (the African Union's initiative to address HIV/AIDS) as examples. Similarly, the definition of institutions "as persistent and connected sets of rules that prescribe behavioral roles, constrain activity, and shape expectations" (Keohane, 1988, p. 386) is remarkably close to the definition of regimes as "as principles, norms, rules, and decision-making procedures around which actor expectations converge in a given issue-area" (Krasner, 1983, p. 185). And indeed, "[t]he word "institution" has now largely replaced "regime" in the scholarly [international relations] IR literature" (Simmons and Martin, 2012, p. 328). More recent contributions (Abbott and Faude, 2022) further argue that today's world politics are neither governed by individual institutions nor by regime complexes composed of formal interstate institutions but rather by so-called "hybrid institutional complexes" which comprise heterogeneous, infra-state, public-private and private transnational institutions, both formal and informal.

As previously noted, in this book "international organizations/bodies" refer to entities (e.g. Codex and ISO) and "international institutions" refer to rules (e.g. the WTO TBT and SPS Agreements, and TBT and SPS chapters of PTAs) which together characterize international regimes (international trade regulation and international standardization), and international regime complexity (the relationship between international trade regulation and the work of international standardization organizations).

2.2.2 *Indirect Governance*

A central concept related to the evolution of regime complexity is "legalization" (Raustiala and Victor, 2004), defined as "[…] a particular form of institutionalization, [which] represents the decision in different issue-areas to impose international legal constraints on governments" (Goldstein et al., 2000, p. 386).

7 See Alter (2022) and EilstrupSangiovanni and Westerwinter (2022) for a recent and comprehensive review of this debate.

The concept of legalization is characterized by the three components of obligation, precision, and delegation.[8] "Obligation means that states or other actors are bound by a rule or commitment or by a set of rules or commitments. Specifically, it means that they are legally bound by a rule or commitment in the sense that their behavior thereunder is subject to scrutiny under the general rules, procedures, and discourse of international law, and often of domestic law as well. Precision means that rules unambiguously define the conduct they require, authorize, or proscribe. Delegation means that third parties have been granted authority to implement, interpret, and apply the rules; to resolve disputes; and (possibly) to make further rules" (Abbott et al., 2000, p. 401).

The concept of legalization is closely related to the concepts of "soft law" and "hard law". Whereas soft law characterizes legal norms that do not effectively compel compliance, hard law refers to a system with a relatively high expectation of compliance. The enhanced legalization of a legal system may be described as a transition from a soft law to a hard law system. (Abbott, 1997) As will be discussed in more detail in the following Sections, both the multilateral and the preferential trade policy regime are argued to have undergone such transition. (Abbott, 1997, 2000; Abbott and Snidal, 2000; Goldstein and Martin, 2000; Ansell and Vogel, 2006; Shaffer and Pollack, 2013)

Of the three components of legalization, delegation is of particular importance in this book. In addition to the definition provided above (Abbott et al., 2000), delegation may also be defined as "a conditional grant of authority from a principal to an agent that empowers the latter to act on behalf of the former" (Hawkins et al., 2006, p. 7) or a "grant of authority by two or more states to an international body to make decisions or take actions" (Bradley and Kelley, 2008, p. 2). The types of authority that countries may grant include legislative, adjudicative, regulatory, monitoring and enforcement, agenda-setting, research and advice, policy implementation, and redelegation (Bradley and Kelley, 2008). Moreover, delegation may be measured according to the three categories of agent services (bargaining, monitoring, compliance, enforcement), agent resources (size of budget, size of staffing), and agent autonomy (staffing autonomy, financial autonomy, management autonomy, principal obligations) (Brown, 2010).

In the more recent literature, delegation is conceptually distinguished from another type of indirect governance — orchestration. While delegation is based on principal-agent (P-A) theory, orchestration is based on the Orchestrator-Intermediary-Target (OIT) model. In the case of delegation, the

---

8 For a critical discussion of the concept of legalization, see, for instance, Finnemore and Toope (2001) and Goldstein et al. (2001).

principal grants authority to an agent to influence the target. In the case of orchestration, the orchestrator enlists the intermediary to influence the target. (Abbott et al., 2015, 2016) More precisely, in the case of delegation, the governor grants authority to the agent *ex ante* and then manages the agent in a hierarchical way *ex post*. In the case of orchestration, by contrast, the governor enlists authority to the intermediary *ex ante* and then manages the intermediary in a non-hierarchical way *ex post*. (Abbott et al., 2020) In other words, while delegation provides the governor hard control over the agent, orchestration provides the governor 'only' with soft power over the intermediary (Abbott et al., 2015). In both types of indirect governance, the governor (principal or orchestrator) relies on a third party (agent or intermediary) to reap benefits related to expertise, agenda setting, credible commitment, access to targets, monitoring, adjudication, and legitimacy. In practice, the two types of indirect governance often overlap and the difference between them becomes more of a continuum than a sharp distinction. (Abbott et al., 2016)

A generalization of the OIT model is presented in the RIT model (Abbott et al., 2017), where the "orchestrator" is replaced by the "rule-maker" or "regulator" (Lytton, 2017). In the RIT model, particular importance is given to the role of the intermediaries conceptualized as "regulatory actors with the capacity to affect, control, and monitor the relations between rule-makers and rule-takers via their interpretations of standards and their role in the increasingly institutionalized process of monitoring, verification, auditing, and certification" (Levi-Faur and Starobin, 2014, p. 21). (Abbott et al., 2017; Havinga and Verbruggen, 2017; Jordana, 2017; Koenig-Archibugi and Macdonald, 2017) Indeed, intermediaries can affect each of the five stages of the regulatory process: agenda-setting, negotiation, implementation, monitoring, and enforcement (Abbott and Snidal, 2009).

2.2.3 *Institutionalisms*

Broadly speaking, there are three schools of thought on the origins and consequences of institutional design — or three "institutionalisms" (Hall and Taylor, 1996). There exists a rich body of literature as well as comprehensive literature reviews on rational choice institutionalism (Milner, 1998; Snidal, 2002, 2012; Pollack, 2006), historical institutionalism (Fioretos, 2011; Fioretos et al., 2016; Rixen and Viola, 2016), and sociological institutionalism (Finnemore, 1996; Finnemore and Sikkink, 2001) as well as on the comparison between the three (Hall and Taylor, 1996; Immergut, 1998; Schmidt, 1999; Campbell, 2004; Katznelson and Weingast, 2005; Fioretos, 2011; Rixen and Viola, 2016; Farrell, 2018). Dominant features according to which the three schools of thought can be differentiated include their substantive focus, temporality, source of preferences, theory of action, conception of history, unintended consequences, the role of ideas, the role of material forces, the understanding of constraints on actions, as well as key mechanisms of institutional reproduction, and key sources of incremental and radical change (Fioretos, 2011, p. 374). While it is out of the scope of this Section to discuss these features in detail, a brief discussion of the three institutionalisms helps to provide some theoretical context for the following Chapters.

Rational choice institutionalists argue that "[i]nstitutions, as sets of rules, shape incentives in a particular society. Organizations, as collective actors, pursue their self-interest within a given set of rules, perhaps changing those rules in the process" (Farrell, 2018, p. 29).[9] Indeed, the concept of individual goal-seeking under certain constraints plays an important role in rational choice institutionalism. More precisely, rational choice institutionalism pays particular attention to the relevant actors, their goals, their abilities, and their constraints. One seminal contribution on the rational design of international institutions (Koremenos et al., 2001, pp. 781–782), for instance, bases its conjectures on the assumptions of rational choice (states and other international actors act for self-interested reasons and design institutions to advance their interests), the shadow of the future (the value of future gains is sufficiently strong to support cooperation), transaction costs (costs involved in establishing and participating in international institutions), and risk aversion (states and other international actors are risk-averse when it comes to creating or modifying international institutions). While rational choice institutionalism is fairly flexible as to who the actors are, what goals and abilities they have, and what constraints they face, importance is placed on the simplification and the generalization of the analysis. As a result, however, critics of the rational choice approach lament an excessive use of mathematical formalization as well as the difficulty to test theoretical arguments empirically. (Snidal, 2002, 2012) Other critics of the rational choice approach (Duffeld, 2003; Thompson, 2010; Copelovitch and Putnam, 2014)[10] lament that limited attention is paid to path dependency and institutional context.

Some of these critiques are addressed by historical institutionalism. "In contrast to rational choice scholars, who tended either to see institutions as structures producing an equilibrium, or as that equilibrium itself, historical institutionalists thought of institutions in terms of processes of change, with

9 Farrell (2018) builds here on North (1990). See also Koremenos et al. (2001) and the authors' presumption that "*states use international institutions to further their own goals, and they design institutions accordingly*" (Koremenos et al., 2001, p. 762).

10 See Koremenos and Snidal (2003) for a direct response to Duffield (2003).

no necessary end point". (Farrell, 2018, p. 32) In a nutshell, historical institutionalism seeks "to understand the processes by which institutions change or do not change, rather than to focus on comparative statics that compare an institution in time t_1 and time t_2" (Rixen and Viola, 2016, p. 10). Some historical institutionalists see institutions as structures which are relatively stable over the long run, whereas others regard institutions as processes (rules, procedures, or policies) which do change over time (Farrell, 2018). Of particular importance are the concepts of path dependence, sequencing, critical junctures, and unintended consequences. While scholars agree that path dependency goes beyond "history matters" (Mahoney, 2000; Pierson, 2000; Rixen and Viola, 2016), there exists no single definition. One often-cited contribution, defines path dependency as "that what happened at an earlier point in time will affect the possible outcomes of a sequence of events occurring at a later point in time" (Sewell, 1996, p. 262). A critical juncture may present the initial contingent event that leads to path dependence. Early definitions consider critical junctures "as periods of significant change, which typically occur in distinct ways in different countries (or other units of analysis), and which are hypothesized to produce distinct legacies" (Collier and Collier, 1991, p. 29). More recent contributions define critical junctures "as relatively short periods of time during which there is a substantially heightened probability that agents' choices will affect the outcome of interest" (Capoccia and Kelemen, 2007, p. 348). Sequencing presents another important concept in the historical institutionalism literature. "[S]elf-reinforcing sequences [are] characterized by the formation and long-term reproduction of a given institutional pattern" (Mahoney, 2000, p. 508) and therefore conceptually associated to the economic concept of increasing returns. Closely related are reactive sequences, defined as "chains of temporally ordered and causally connected events" (Mahoney, 2000, p. 509). Finally, scholars of historical institutionalism emphasize the importance of gradual and incremental changes to institutional design (Streeck and Thelen, 2005) which may result in unintended consequences (Fioretos, 2011; Rixen and Viola, 2016; Farrell, 2018). Importantly for this book, and in particular for Chapter 4, the WTO's establishment in 1995 and the subsequently stalled trade negotiations are an often-cited empirical case of a critical juncture with unintended consequences (Barton et al., 2006; Goldstein and Steinberg, 2009).

"Sociological institutionalism starts from the premise that institutions are organizing myths" (Farrell, 2018, p. 35). Indeed, in contrast to rational choice institutionalists and historical institutionalists who emphasize the structural and constraining features of institutions, sociological institutionalists focus on the social and cognitive features of institutions. While rational choice institutionalism is interested in the way in which different actors and their interests shape institutions, sociological institutionalism predicts that similarities between international institutions are caused by impersonal social forces as well as by global trends and culture. (Keohane, 1988; Finnemore, 1996; Meyer et al., 1997) In a sense, sociological institutionalism is more focused on explaining the continuity rather than the change of institutions (Farrell, 2018). Indeed, a central argument of sociological institutionalism is that, over time, international institutions converge on similar procedures and approaches through different isomorphic processes (DiMaggio and Powell, 1983). Coercive isomorphism, for instance, results from pressures by other, more powerful, actors such as other organizations or states. Mimetic isomorphism describes a process in which organizations model themselves on other organizations to reduce uncertainty. Normative pressures present a third source of isomorphic organizational change and are often associated with the professionalization of organizations. (DiMaggio and Powell, 1983)

One way to summarize the three "institutionalisms" (Hall and Taylor, 1996), is that rational choice institutionalism follows the "logic of interests", historical institutionalism the "logic of path dependence", and sociological institutionalism the "logic of appropriateness" (Schmidt, 1999). The three institutionalisms differ in a number of features (Fioretos, 2011, p. 374) but also share commonalities. Furthermore, "[i]n recent years, institutional theorizing in international relations and comparative politics has become much less sectarian and more inclusive methodologically. Once sharply drawn boundaries among historical institutionalists, Realists, Liberal Institutionalists, and others have begun to soften and blur" (Jupille et al., 2013, p. 4). While it is not the ambition of this book to empirically assess the three institutionalisms, they do provide valuable theoretical context for Chapter 4 which discusses the historical context as well as the actors and interests that shaped the institutional design of the WTO TBT and SPS Agreements.

Having clarified the concepts and debates that are of central importance in this book, the next two sections develop the principal arguments that present the foundation for the empirical Chapters 4 and 5.

2.3 Multilateral Trade Agreements and International Standardization

This Section outlines the linkage between the multilateral trade policy regime and the international standardization regime. Here, and in Chapter 4, the institutional design of multilateral trade agreements is the independent variable of interest, and countries' participation in international standardization organizations is the dependent variable of interest. The principal proposition is that countries' incentives to actively participate in international standardization organizations partly depend on the institutional design, more precisely the degree of legalization, of related multilateral trade agreements.

To begin with, it is important to recognize that in a world of sovereign countries with different histories, cultures, and political and legal backgrounds, it is inevitable, and legitimate, that rules, laws, and regulations vary across countries. This regulatory heterogeneity, however, may present an impediment to international trade. Indeed, firms which export to different countries face a number of associated adjustment costs. First, internationally active firms incur information costs associated with the time and effort spent on identifying specific rules and regulations applicable to different countries and markets. Second, internationally active firms face specification costs when they tailor their production processes to different country-specific rules and regulations. Third, internationally active firms face conformity assessment costs if they are obliged to demonstrate their compliance with the applicable country-specific rules and regulations. (Karttunen, 2020)

International standards can help to reduce these costs. In contrast to laws and regulations, international standards are not legally binding. However, legally binding laws and regulations may be, and often are (Fliess et al., 2010), based on international standards. In other words, international standards are *de jure* voluntary but *de facto* become legally binding when they are incorporated into laws and regulations.[11] Internationally active firms therefore have an incentive to adapt their production processes according to international standards to reap the benefits associated with better compatibility, lowered transactions costs, and larger economies of scale (Heires, 2008) but also to be compliant with future laws and regulations based on international standards.

Standards can also function as strategic tools (de Vries, 2006; Delimatsis, 2015b; Larouche and van Overwalle, 2015; Chu, 2020) and competitive devices (Heires, 2008) for industrial promotion (Victor, 2000) with which actors can exploit the presence of asymmetric information and organizational differences (Delimatsis, 2015c; Mavroidis and Wolfe, 2017). Indeed, technological innovation usually precedes standardization and different previously existing standards compete for becoming the international standard to which harmonization will take place. This may result in adjustment costs and conflicts of interest of the distributional consequences of those costs. (Krasner, 1991; Braithwaite and Drahos, 2000; Mattli and Büthe, 2003; Heires, 2008; Büthe, 2010; Blind, 2015; Delimatsis, 2015c; Mattli and Seddon, 2015; Berman, 2017)

11 Standards may also become *de facto* mandatory after WTO litigation (Bijlmakers and van Calster, 2015; Lindahl, 2015; Schepel, 2015).

To summarize, "[m]any times, (voluntary) standards are the precursors of domestic (mandatory) technical regulations. Even though standards are adopted mainly through soft-law processes by non-state actors, these actors aspire to capitalise on their success and see the initially non-binding norms they champion transformed into hard law to gain rents from first mover advantages through expedited enforcement. Thus, because stakes are high, strategic behaviour is sometimes observable. The more important standardisation becomes, the fiercer is the competition for increased influence in [standardization organizations]" (Delimatsis, 2015a, p. 8).[12]

As a consequence, internationally active firms have strong economic incentives to actively participate in international standard-setting processes to influence the design of standards in their interest, to minimize their adjustment costs, and to maximize the benefits from improved access to international markets. State actors also have strong incentives to actively participate and to shape the international standard-setting processes. From an economic point of view, governments have an incentive to influence international standards in the interest of their domestic industries, and to promote their international competitiveness. From a political point of view, governments have strong incentives to shape international standards according to their regulatory philosophies. (Post, 2005; Veggeland and Borgen, 2005; Pollack and Shaffer, 2009; Halabi, 2015) The EU and the US, for instance, are well-known for their divergent views on the precautionary principle and their attempts to diffuse their regulatory preferences (Vogel, 2012; Bergkamp and Kogan, 2013).

Arguably the most effective and efficient way to exert influence on international standard-setting processes is to actively participate in the relevant international standardization organizations. (Hüller and Maier, 2006; Weiler, 2012; Schroeder et al., 2012; Bailer and Weiler, 2015; Halliday et al., 2013; Bailer, 2017; Onderco, 2019) "To put it bluntly: you have to play to win. Those who actively participate in the technical work — directly or indirectly — have many more opportunities to shape the scope and the specific content of the standard than those who only comment at the enquiry stage or later. Effective participation in turn should require early and good information, so as to allow stakeholders to determine the implications of a proposed new standard for their products [...] and to influence the technical specification accordingly" (Büthe and Mattli, 2010b, p. 466). Indeed, "[t]here is a likelihood that participating industries will provide information that tilts standards towards their interests, to the detriment of their competitors" (Berman, 2017, p. 116). Of course, participation is not a perfect

12 Delimatsis (2015a) builds here on contributions of O'Connel (2000) and Besen and Farrell (1994).

proxy for actual influence. However, conversely it is unlikely that actors can exert any influence without participating (Hüller and Maier, 2006).

The principal proposition of this Section, and Chapter 4, is that in the international regime complex of trade policy and standardization, actors' incentives to participate in international standardization organizations are partly driven by the institutional design of related multilateral trade agreements. More precisely, it is argued that actors' incentives to participate in international standardization organizations depend on the degree of legalization of related multilateral trade agreements.

Consider first delegation as one of the three components of legalization (Abbott et al., 2000). The more explicitly a related multilateral trade agreement delegates the authority to develop international standards to a particular organization, the larger are the incentives of actors to actively participate in the standard-setting processes of this specific organization. Indeed, the explicit delegation to a particular international standardization organization reduces actors' ability to engage in forum-shopping and/or regime-shifting, and therefore increases actors' incentive to focus on the participation in the endorsed organization. From a historical institutionalism point of view, such delegation may be seen as a critical juncture because it potentially locks-in actors to a particular organization's standards and subsequently results in path dependence.[13] As discussed above, delegation can be conceptually distinguished from orchestration (Abbott et al., 2015, 2016, 2020). In this case, the multilateral trade agreement enlists rather than grants the authority to develop certain international standards to an organization. Whether the type of indirect governance is delegation or orchestration is of secondary importance here, which is why the more general term of "endorsement" will be used to describe the way in which multilateral trade agreements reference international standardization organizations.

The previously described increase in actors' incentives to participate in the standard-setting processes of an international standardization organization due to an explicit endorsement in a related multilateral trade agreement is particularly strong if the multilateral trade agreement obliges countries to base their national regulations on the international standards developed by this specific organization. This obligation, a second component of legalization (Abbott et al., 2000), essentially upgrades the organization's standards from being *de jure* voluntary to being *de facto* legally binding (Veggeland and Borgen, 2005; Ansell and Vogel, 2006; Livermore, 2006; Avant et al., 2010; Prakash and

13 For a similar argument on the role of lock-in and path dependence in technological innovation, see Cecere et al. (2014).

Potoski, 2010; Arcuri, 2015; Delimatsis, 2015a) or, in other words, from a soft(er) to a hard(er) law system (Abbott and Snidal, 2000; Büthe, 2008; Shaffer and Pollack, 2013).

As a consequence, actors' economic and political stakes in this organization's standards increase (Stewart and Johanson, 1998; Smythe, 2009; Pollack and Shaffer, 2009; Büthe and Harris, 2011; Büthe, 2008, 2009, 2015) and potential distributional conflicts become more significant (Braithwaite and Drahos, 2000; Victor, 2000; Sklair, 2002; Livermore, 2006; Alemanno, 2007; Smythe, 2009; Clapp and Fuchs, 2009; Fuchs and Kalfagianni, 2010). This reinforces actors' incentives to actively participate in the standard-setting processes of this particular international organization, and to shape the design of the standards in their political and economic interests.

In Chapter 4, this general line of reasoning translates into the following, more specific, proposition. The multilateral WTO SPS Agreement, which entered into force in 1995, strongly encourages (obligation) WTO members to base their national SPS-related measures on international standards. The SPS Agreement also explicitly endorses (delegation/orchestration of authority) the Codex Alimentarius as *the* organization to develop the international standards upon which national food safety measures shall be based (Bradley and Kelley, 2008; Büthe, 2008, 2009, 2015; Abbott et al., 2015; Elsig, 2015; Dupont and Elsig, 2017). By contrast, the WTO TBT Agreement, which also entered into force in 1995, does not explicitly endorse any organization as the relevant standard-setter for TBT-related international standards.

This has two implications. First, while the TBT Agreement leaves room for countries to engage in forum-shopping and/or regime-shifting, this is not, or at least less so, the case for the SPS Agreement. Second, while the SPS Agreement increases actors' political and economic stakes by essentially upgrading Codex standards from being *de jure* voluntary to being *de facto* legally binding (Veggeland and Borgen, 2005; Ansell and Vogel, 2006; Livermore, 2006; Avant et al., 2010; Prakash and Potoski, 2010; Arcuri, 2015), or from a soft(er) to a hard(er) law system (Abbott and Snidal, 2000; Büthe, 2008; Shaffer and Pollack, 2013), this is not the case for the TBT Agreement. Even though ISO is generally regarded as one, if not *the*, TBT-related international standardization organization (Bernstein and Hannah, 2008; Büthe, 2010; Büthe, 2010; Büthe and Mattli, 2010b,a; Jansen, 2012a,b; Delimatsis, 2015c,b; Elsig, 2015; Lindahl, 2015; Mavroidis and Wolfe, 2017), its standards are not explicitly endorsed by the TBT Agreement and therefore remain voluntary. In line with the argument outlined above, it is therefore expected that the SPS Agreement significantly increases actors' incentives to actively participate in the standard-setting processes of Codex. The TBT Agreement, by contrast, is expected to have less of an effect on actors' incentives to participate in the standard-setting processes of ISO.

2.4 International Standardization and Preferential Trade Agreements

This Section outlines the linkage between the international standardization regime and the preferential trade policy regime. Here, and in Chapter 5, countries' participation in international standardization organizations is the independent variable of interest, and the institutional design of preferential trade agreements is the dependent variable of interest. The principal proposition is that countries' participation in international standardization organizations affects the institutional design of the preferential trade agreements countries sign.

As discussed in the previous Section, firms have strong incentives to adapt their production processes in compliance with international standards in order to reap benefits associated with better compatibility, lowered transactions costs, and larger economies of scale (Heires, 2008). In this section, and in Chapter 5, it is argued that actors have a particularly strong incentive to comply with international standards that are designed in their political and economic interest and with which compliance can be achieved at a low adjustment cost. To push this thought further, firms have a particularly strong incentive to comply with international standards that they developed in the first place as this would minimize their adjustment costs associated with compliance. The incentive structure is similar for governments which represent the interests of their domestic industries. Indeed, governments have strong incentives to promote international standards which are aligned with their domestic industries' interests or, even more so, which were set by their domestic industries in the first place.

In essence, actors have strong incentives to comply with international standards. However, actors may also have considerably divergent views on which international standards to comply with. In a game theoretical sense this set-up is akin to a "Battle of Sexes" (Abbott and Snidal, 2001) in which players have an incentive to coordinate but due to distributional conflicts disagree on the outcome of coordination.

In the international regime complex of trade policy, countries may choose to coordinate and cooperate through signing preferential trade agreements. Indeed, countries use PTAs to negotiate and agree with trading partners on measures that facilitate international trade among themselves. In this context, international standards play an important role. To reduce firms' costs associated with the regulatory heterogeneity of the PTA members, the PTA members may agree on coordination and cooperation based on international standards. Rather than having to adapt their production processes to the rules and regulations of each PTA member country, firms may adapt their production processes to international standards to be able to export and import between the PTA member countries.

As suggested above, agreeing on cooperation based on international standards may be the easier part. More difficult, however, is to agree on the international standards upon which to base cooperation. In line with the previous discussion, it is argued in this Section, and in Chapter 5, that PTA members have an incentive to agree on cooperation based on the international standards which are designed in their political and economic interests or, even more so, which have been designed by them in the first place.

Consider the hypothetical example of country A and country B. Assume that country A has been extensively involved in the standard-setting processes of organization X and therefore managed to design organization X's standards in alignment with its domestic (industries') standards. By contrast, country B has not been involved in the standard-setting processes of organization X and, as a consequence, organization X's standards are considerably different to country B's domestic (industries') standards. If country A and B enter PTA negotiations, both countries have incentives to base their cooperation on international standards to reduce the previously discussed trade-impeding costs related to regulatory heterogeneity. However, they are likely to have different views on which international standards cooperation should be based on. Country A has strong incentives to promote organization X's standards as the international standards upon which country A and country B should base cooperation. Country B, by contrast, has little incentive to agree on basing cooperation on organization X's standards because the adjustment of country B's standards to organization X's standards would incur considerable costs and ultimately put country B (and its industries) at a competitive disadvantage.

As outlined in the previous Section, the most effective and efficient way in which actors can influence international standards in their interest is to actively participate in the relevant standardization organizations (Hüller and Maier, 2006; Weiler, 2012; Schroeder et al., 2012; Bailer and Weiler, 2015; Halliday et al., 2013; Bailer, 2017; Onderco, 2019). It can therefore be expected that, in PTA negotiations, a country which has been actively participating in a certain standardization organization is more likely to promote this organization's standards as a basis for cooperation than a country that has not been participating in this organization's standard-setting processes. In other words, the institutional design of PTAs is argued to partly depend on the PTA members' participation in the relevant international standardization organizations.

In Chapter 5, this general line of reasoning translates into the following, more specific, proposition. The more PTA members have participated in the standard-setting processes of Codex and ISO, the more likely they are to have successfully designed Codex and ISO standards in their political and economic interests, and the more likely they are to refer to the two organizations' standards as a basis for cooperation in the area of SPS and TBT, respectively. This relationship, however, is expected to be stronger for Codex and SPS than for ISO and TBT. Indeed, since, as discussed in detail in the previous Section, the WTO SPS Agreement explicitly endorses Codex as *the* relevant international standardization organization in the area of food safety, countries' participation in Codex is expected to have a significant impact on the institutional design of the SPS chapters of the PTAs countries sign. By contrast, since the TBT Agreement does not explicitly and exclusively endorse ISO as the relevant international standardization organization in the area of TBT, the impact of countries' participation in ISO is expected to have less of an effect on the institutional design of the TBT chapters of the PTAs countries sign.

2.5 Interim Conclusion

This Chapter outlines the concepts and debates that present the foundation for the empirical Chapters 4 and 5. The principal objective of this book is to explore indirect linkages between the international standardization regime, and the multilateral trade policy regime and the preferential trade policy regime. While the direct and dialectical relationship between the multilateral trade policy regime and the preferential trade policy regime is well understood in the literature, the indirect relationship between the international trade policy regime and the international standardization regime has so far received little scholarly attention. The objective of this book is to contribute to closing this research gap.

The linkage between the multilateral trade policy regime and the international standardization regime is the focus of Chapter 4. The principal proposition of this Chapter is that the institutional design of multilateral trade agreements affects countries' incentives to participate in relevant international standardization organizations. More precisely, it is posited that the WTO TBT and SPS Agreements increased countries' incentives to participate in the international standard-setting processes of ISO and Codex, respectively. Due to differences in institutional design between the TBT and SPS Agreement, this positive relationship is expected to be stronger for the SPS Agreement and Codex than for the TBT Agreement and ISO.

The linkage between the international standardization regime and the preferential trade policy regime is the focus of Chapter 5. The principal proposition of this Chapter is that countries' participation in relevant international standardization organizations affects the institutional design of PTAs. More precisely, it is posited that countries' participation in ISO and Codex respectively affects the institutional design of TBT and SPS chapters in countries' PTAs. Due to differences of institutional design between the WTO TBT and SPS Agreement, this positive relationship is expected to be stronger for Codex and SPS chapters than for ISO and TBT chapters.

CHAPTER 3

International Standardization Organizations

The Codex Alimentarius (Codex) and the International Organization for Standardization (ISO) are at the centre of this book. The participation of countries in these two international standardization organizations presents the dependent variable in Chapter 4, and the principal independent variable in Chapter 5. This Chapter provides an introduction into both organizations as well as a number of descriptive insights into the two novel datasets upon which the empirical analyses of the subsequent Chapters are based.

3.1 The Codex Alimentarius

3.1.1 *History*

Codex was established in 1963 by the Food and Agriculture Organization of the United Nations (FAO) and the World Health Organization (WHO). The official history of Codex is outlined on the organization's website and the (less official) politics behind its establishment and its evolution are well-documented in the literature (Braithwaite and Drahos, 2000; Masson-Matthee, 2007; Arcuri, 2015). This Section provides a brief summary of these developments and an overview of Codex's general principles and organizational characteristics.

The Codex Alimentarius is a collection of internationally adopted food standards and related texts presented in a uniform manner.[1] These food standards aim at protecting consumers' health and ensuring fair practices in food trade — two goals that some observers regard as potentially competing (Lin, 2011). Codex standards cover processed, semi-processed and raw foods and include provisions in respect of food hygiene, food additives, residues of pesticides and veterinary drugs, contaminants, labelling and presentation, methods of analysis and sampling, and import and export inspection and certification. As of September 2023, Codex lists 233 standards, 85 guidelines, and 56 codes

1 The collection of food standards and related texts adopted by the Codex Alimentarius Commission is known as the Codex Alimentarius. For simplicity, the term "Codex Alimentarius (Codex)" is used in this thesis to refer to the organization. The term "Codex Alimentarius Commission (CAC)" is used in this thesis to refer to Codex's plenary session, discussed later in this section.

of practice.[2] Since its establishment, Codex has also developed thousands of maximum levels (MLs) for food additives and maximum residue limits (MRLs) for pesticide residues.

Codex standards are voluntary in nature and need to be translated into national legislation or regulations in order to be enforceable (Codex, 2020). There is broad agreement among scholars and legal practitioners, however, that the legal status of Codex standards was upgraded from *de jure* voluntary to *de facto* legally binding when in 1995 the World Trade Organization (WTO) explicitly endorsed Codex as the relevant international organization to develop international standards for food safety against which national measures and regulations are evaluated (Rosman, 1993; Dawson, 1995, 1997; Garrett et al., 1998; Braithwaite and Drahos, 2000; Horton, 2001; Boutrif, 2003; Poli, 2004; Post, 2005, 2006; Ansell and Vogel, 2006; Livermore, 2006; Büthe, 2008, 2009, 2015; Pollack and Shaffer, 2009; Smythe, 2009; Büthe and Harris, 2011; Pernet, 2015).

In a joint publication with the WTO (FAO and WTO, 2017), one of Codex's parent organizations — the FAO — describes Codex as "the world's pre-eminent international food-standard-setting body [...]" (p. 14) and "[...] the single most important international reference point for food standards." (p. 15). The origins of Codex date back to 1903 and the work of the International Dairy Federation (IDF). The IDF developed standards for milk and milk products, presented an important catalyst for the foundation of Codex, and remains an influential actor in Codex to this day. After World War II, several regional fora were established, notably the Latin American Food Code (1949) and the Codex Alimentarius Europaeus (1958). To promote wider participation, the Council of the Codex Alimentarius Europaeus proposed to the FAO (founded in 1945) to take over the standardization work that had commenced (Masson-Matthee, 2007). This proposal was supported by the United States (US), which together with other non-participating states had become increasingly nervous about the trade implications of European agenda-setting in the area of food safety (Braithwaite and Drahos, 2000). The establishment of the Joint FAO/WHO Food Standards Programme and the development of the Codex Alimentarius was decided upon by the decision-making bodies of the FAO in 1961 and the WHO in 1963.

As Codex was established by two international organizations, legally speaking it cannot be considered to be a new and autonomous international

2 For simplicity, in this thesis the term "standard" is used to refer to Codex standards, guidelines and codes of practice. Under the World Trade Organization, Codex standards, guidelines and codes of practice have the same legal status.

organization which has its own legal personality (Masson-Matthee, 2007). More practically speaking, Codex is akin to an inter-governmental organization or inter-governmental body.[3] In the political science and international relations literature, Codex has been referred to as an intergovernmental body (Abbott and Snidal, 2001), an hybrid inter-governmental-private administration (Kingsbury et al., 2005), a trans-governmental regulatory network (Lang and Scott, 2009), an inter-governmental organization with informal characteristics (Duquet and Geraets, 2012), a quasi-regulatory network (Newman and Zaring, 2013), and a trans-national legal order (Büthe, 2015). In the context of its close relationship with the WTO, discussed in detail in Chapter 4, Codex has even been described as a satellite organization of the WTO legal system (Poli, 2004) and a quasi-legislator (Alemanno, 2007; Marceau and Trachtman, 2014).

3.1.2 *Structure*

The diversity in terminology surrounding Codex is related to its subsidiary character and the composition of involved actors from governments, inter-governmental organizations (IGOs) and non-governmental organizations (NGOs). Codex is composed of the Codex Alimentarius Commission (CAC), the Executive Committee (CCEXEC), General Subject Committees, Commodity Committees, *ad hoc* Intergovernmental Task Forces and Coordinating Committees (Table 1, Appendix). These organizational elements are supported by a relatively small Secretariat which comprises a Rome-based team of professional and technical officers and support staff (18 staff members as of September 2023). The CAC is the plenary body of Codex and is responsible for all matters regarding the implementation of the Joint FAO/WHO Food Standards Programme, most relevantly the adoption of Codex standards. Membership in the CAC is open to all Member Nations and Associate Members of the FAO and the WHO. Meanwhile, the CCEXEC is the executive organ of the CAC and responsible for the general orientation, strategic planning, and programming of the work of the CAC. Finally, the Secretariat is the administrative arm of the CAC. It provides coordination and liaison services across Codex Committees in addition to being responsible for the publication of standards.

The subsidiary bodies — the General Subject Committees, the Commodity Committees, the *ad hoc* Intergovernmental Task Forces and the Regional Coordinating Committees — are in charge of the development and elaboration

---

3 The concept of "international body" is broader than that of "international organization". International bodies need not have or may only temporarily have a concrete and stable organizational structure and a supportive administrative apparatus (Abbott and Snidal, 1998; Bradley and Kelley, 2008). See Chapter 3.

of standards. The General Subject Committees develop so-called horizontal standards which are applied transversely to all products and product categories and cover issues related to hygienic practice, labelling, additives, inspection and certification, nutrition and residues of veterinary drugs and pesticides. The Codex Committee on Food Hygiene (CCFH), hosted by the US, for example, developed the Guidelines on the Application of General Principles of Food Hygiene to the Control of Viruses in Food.

The Commodity Committees, by contrast, develop so-called vertical standards which define the physical and chemical characteristics of specific products. Examples of such standards include standards for quinoa, frozen fish, avocados and (seven different types of) cheese. The Standard for Chocolate and Chocolate Products (CODEX STAN 87–1981, p. 2), developed by the Codex Committee on Cocoa Products and Chocolate (CCCPC) hosted by Switzerland, for instance, lays down that "Chocolate […] shall contain, on a dry matter basis, not less than 35% total cocoa solids, of which not less than 18% shall be cocoa butter and not less than 14% fat-free cocoa solids."

The *ad hoc* Intergovernmental Task Forces are only established for a limited period of time to develop standards in specific issue areas. As of September 2023, only the *ad hoc* Joint FAO/WHO Committee of Government Experts on the Code of Principles Concerning Milk and Milk Products is active.

Finally, there are six Regional Coordinating Committees that develop regional standards or global standards for products of interests to a specific region. The six regions include Africa, Asia, Europe, Latin America and the Caribbean, the Near East, and North America and the South West Pacific. The Coordinating Committee for Asia (CCASIA), for instance, developed a Regional Code of Hygienic Practice for Street-Vended Foods in Asia.

3.1.3 *Procedures*

Codex standards are set in a 8-step procedure. This procedure attempts to balance legitimacy and efficiency concerns by providing the opportunity for consultation with a broad spectrum of stakeholders while, at the same time, allowing urgent standards to be set on a 'accelerated' procedure. In a nutshell, a standard proposal is reviewed by the CCEXEC and compared against the criteria and priorities established by the CAC in step 1. In step 2, the draft text is prepared and circulated to Members and all interested parties for comment in step 3. The draft and the comments are reviewed at the subsidiary committee level at step 4 and, if necessary, a new draft is prepared. In step 5, the CAC reviews the progress made and agrees on whether the draft should go to finalization. At this stage, the draft is also endorsed by the relevant General Subject Committees so that it is consistent with Codex general standards. In step 6 and

7, the approved draft is sent again to the members and all interested parties for comment and finalization by the relevant subsidiary committee. After a final round of comments, the CAC adopts the draft as a formal Codex text in step 8.

There are two ways in which this procedure could be fast tracked. First, the CAC may decide to initiate an 'accelerated' procedure at step 1 if there is urgency to adopt a standard. In this case, the standard-setting procedure adopts the standard in question at step 5. A second option is for the CAC to decide to omit step 6 and 7 and to proceed with the adoption of the standard at step 8. The accelerated procedure tends to be initiated for reasons related to new scientific information, urgent problems related to trade or public health or the revision or up-dating of existing standards. The omission of step 6 and 7, in contrast, often results from the fact that a general consensus has already been achieved at step 5 and makes further discussion unnecessary. (Masson-Matthee, 2007; Codex, 2018, 2019; Cheng, 2019)

3.1.4 *Controversial Topics*

Consensus-based decision-making plays indeed an important role in Codex. The Procedural Manual of Codex states that "[t]he [Codex Alimentarius] Commission shall make every effort to reach agreement on the adoption or amendment of standards by consensus. Decisions to adopt or amend standards may be taken by voting only if such efforts to reach consensus have failed" (Codex, 2019, p. 18). While the Procedural Manual provides advice on the facilitation of consensus, the term "consensus" is not defined. It is generally agreed, however, that consensus does not necessarily require unanimity (FAO, 2020). Votes on the elaboration of standards (decided by a majority of votes cast) or changes to the procedural rules of Codex (decided by a two-thirds majority of the votes cast) occurred relatively rarely[4] during Codex's almost-60 year history. Votes

4 An analysis of the Codex Alimentarius Commission (CAC) reports identifies the following votes: CAC 6 (1969): Amendments to the Rules of Procedure of the Commission; Governing Paragraph for the FAO/WHO Committee of Government Experts on the Codex of Principles concerning Milk and Milk Products; Honey; Margarine; Maximum Water Content. CAC 7 (1970): Report of the Codex Committee on Food Additives; Report to the FAO conference on rule VI.3 of the Rules of Procedure of the Codex Alimentarius Commission. CAC 14 (1981): International Code of Marketing of Breastmilk Substitutes. CAC 16 (1985): Consideration of recommendations of the Joint FAO/WHO expert consultation on residues of veterinary drugs in foods. CAC 18 (1989): Proposed Procedure for the Elaboration of Codex Maximum Residue Limits for Veterinary Drugs. CAC 19 (1991): Maximum Residue Limits for Estradiol-17 β, Progesterone, Testosterone and Zeranol. CAC 20 (1993): Status of the FAO/WHO Committee of Government Experts on the Code of Principles concerning Milk and Milk Products. CAC 21 (1995): Draft Maximum Limits for 5 Growth Hormones at Step 8; Draft Maximum Residue Limits for Bovine Somatotropins at Step 8. CAC 22 (1997): Draft Guidelines for the

that do occur, however, are often very close and can have considerable economic and political consequences for industries and governments.

The safety of meat produced with growth-promoting hormones is a well-known case which illustrates this point. The topic had been a long-standing controversy between the EU and the US. In a nutshell, the EU opposed the adoption of the "Draft MRLs for 5 Growth Hormones at Step 8" and attempted to adjourn the debate during the 21st meeting of the CAC in 1995. As no consensus was achieved, a vote on the adjournment was held in which 28 countries[5] voted in favour of adjournment, 31 countries[6] voted against adjournment, and five countries[7] abstained. The majority of countries voted to proceed by the use of a secret ballot, as was requested by the US. As a result of the secret ballot, the CAC adopted the Draft MRLs with 33 votes in favour, 29 votes opposed, and seven abstentions. In the same CAC meeting, the EU did manage to adjourn the adoption of the "Draft MRLs for Bovine Somatotropins at Step 8" by calling a vote in which 33 countries[8] were in favour of adjournment,

Design, Operation, Assessment and Accreditation of Food Import and Export Inspection and Certification Systems; Draft Maximum Residue Limits for Bovine Somatotropin (BST); Draft Revised Standard for Natural Mineral Waters. CAC 26 (2003): Proposed Amendments to the Rules of Procedure; Proposed Amendments to the Rules of Procedure concerning the Membership of Regional Economic Integration Organizations. CAC 28 (2005): Amendments to current Rules III and IV.1 concerning the enlargement of the Executive Committee and current Rule XIII on matters related to budget and expenses; Amendments to current Rule IV.2 concerning the enlargement of the Executive Committee and the functions of the Executive Committee and consequential amendments to current Rule X; Amendment to current Rule VIII.5 Observers; Amendment to current Rule V. Sessions on the right to address the Chair. CAC 29 (2006): Amendments concerning the duration of terms of office of the Members of the Executive Committee. CAC 30 (2007): Amendments concerning the role of coordinators and members elected on a geographical basis; Draft Revised Standard for Emmental (C-9). CAC 34 (2011): Draft MRLs for Ractopamine. CAC 35 (2012): Draft MRLs for ractopamine (pig and cattle tissues: muscle, liver, kidney and fat).

5 Algeria, Austria, Belgium, Cyprus, Denmark, Finland, France, Germany, Greece, India, Iraq, Ireland, Italy, Kenya, Latvia, Malta, Netherlands, Norway, Poland, Portugal, Romania, Russian Federation, Slovak Republic, Spain, Sweden, Switzerland, Turkey, United Kingdom.

6 Australia, Botswana, Brazil, Canada, Chile, China, Costa Rica, Egypt, Ghana, Hungary, Indonesia, Islamic Republic of Iran, Israel, Japan, Lebanon, Malaysia, Mexico, New Zealand, Nigeria, Paraguay, Peru, Philippines, Qatar, Republic of Korea, Saudi Arabia, Singapore, South Africa, Sudan, Tanzania, Thailand, United States of America.

7 Burkina Faso, Cuba, Uganda, Senegal, Zimbabwe.

8 Algeria, Austria, Belgium, Burkina Faso, Cameroon, Cyprus, Denmark, Finland, France, Germany, Greece, Guinea, Hungary, India, Ireland, Islamic Republic of Iran, Italy, Latvia, Lebanon, Lithuania, Luxembourg, Malta, Netherlands, Norway, Poland, Portugal, Republic of Korea, Romania, Russia, Slovak Rep, Spain, Sweden, Switzerland.

31 countries[9] against adjournment, and six countries[10] abstained. The EU's opposition to growth hormone-treated beef resulted in the so-called Beef Hormone Controversy, involving two WTO dispute settlement cases,[11] which the EU lost against the US and Canada and which will be discussed in further detail in Chapter 4.

Another controversial topic was the adoption of the "Draft Revised Standard for Natural Mineral Waters", for which the 22nd CAC meeting in 1997 could not achieve consensus. In short, the Draft Revised Standard (prepared by the Codex Committee on Natural Mineral Waters (CCNMW) hosted by Switzerland) was closely aligned with an existing European Regional Standard that required Natural Mineral Water to be bottled at the emergence of the source without transportation. Other countries, in particular Japan and the US, opposed this Draft Revised Standard and considered it to be a barrier to international trade. After intense discussions, 33 countries[12] voted in favour of adoption, 31 countries[13] voted against the adoption, and ten countries[14] abstained.

It is interesting to note that until this point, the EU was not actually a full member of Codex but participated as an observing IGO and acted through its member countries. To become a full member, the Rules of Procedure concerning the Membership of Regional Economic Integration Organizations had to be amended and a vote took place in the 26th CAC meeting in 2003. Of the

---

9 Argentina, Australia, Brazil, Canada, Cape Verde, Chile, China, Cuba, Egypt, Ghana, Indonesia, Iraq, Israel, Japan, Kenya, Malaysia, Mexico, New Zealand, Nigeria, Pakistan, Peru, Saudi Arabia, Singapore, South Africa, Sudan, Tanzania, Thailand, Uganda, USA, UK, Zimbabwe.

10 Botswana, Ecuador, Lesotho, Philippines, Senegal, Tunisia.

11 DS26: European Communities – Measures Concerning Meat and Meat Products (Hormones); DS48: European Communities – Measures Concerning Meat and Meat Products (Hormones).

12 Austria, Belgium, Burundi, Cameroon, Côte d'Ivoire, Croatia, Cyprus, Denmark, Estonia, Finland, France, Germany, Greece, Hungary, Ireland, Italy, Lithuania, Luxembourg, Mozambique, Netherlands, Norway, Peru, Poland, Portugal, Romania, Slovakia, Spain, Sweden, Switzerland, Tunisia, Turkey, United Kingdom, Uruguay.

13 Argentina, Australia, Botswana, Brazil, Canada, Chile, China, Costa Rica, Dominican Republic, Egypt, Guatemala, India, Indonesia, Japan, Kenya, Malaysia, Mexico, Morocco, New Zealand, Nigeria, Philippines, Republic of Korea, Russian Federation, Saudi Arabia, Singapore, South Africa, Thailand, Uganda, United Arab Emirates, United States of America, Viet Nam.

14 Algeria, Cuba, El Salvador, Lebanon, Mauritius, Nicaragua, Senegal, Sudan, Swaziland, Zimbabwe.

85 votes cast, 73 countries[15] voted in favour of the amendment, 12 countries[16] (including the US) voted against the amendment, and 13 countries[17] abstained. Since then, the EU is the only full member organization of Codex. Prior to Codex Committee meetings, the EU is requested to submit a document in which it clarifies the division of competence between itself as a member and the EU member states. If a vote occurs on a topic in which the EU has competence, its number of votes is equal to the number of EU member states present at the time the vote is taken. By some observers, the EU's push for full membership was interpreted as an increased importance given to Codex standardization and a considerable increase in the EU's bargaining power (Poli, 2004).

Since the 35th CAC meeting in 2012, no vote had to be taken. This last case concerned, yet again growth-promoting hormones and more precisely, the "Draft MRLs for ractopamine (pig and cattle tissues: muscle, liver, kidney and fat)". The majority of countries voted in favour of a secret ballot. As 136 votes were cast, a majority of 69 votes was required to adopt the Draft MRLs. The secret ballot resulted in exactly 69 votes in favour, 67 votes against, and seven abstentions. While the US regretted that no consensus could be found and a vote had to be taken, it was pleased about the adoption of the Draft MRLs. The EU, in contrast, recorded its strong opposition to the adoption of the Draft MRLs as well as its disappointment of the CAC not being able to resolve the issue by consensus.

While these cases illustrate some of the food safety-related disagreements between countries, and in particular between the EU and the US, they are likely to be only the tip of the iceberg. More fundamentally, the EU and the US are known to have different opinions with respect to consumer risk preferences and consumer perceptions, the role of non-science issues and the precautionary principle in regulatory decision-making, and the need to label and impose traceability requirements for food derived from biotechnology. (Poli,

15 Argentina, Austria, Bahrain, Bangladesh, Barbados, Belgium, Bolivia, Botswana, Brazil, Bulgaria, Canada, Chile, Colombia, Congo (Republic of), Cuba, Czech Republic, DPR Korea, Denmark, Egypt, El Salvador, Eritrea, Finland, France, Germany, Greece, Guinea, Haiti, Hungary, Iceland, India, Indonesia, Iran, Ireland, Italy, Japan, Jordan, Republic of Korea, Kuwait, Lesotho, Madagascar, Mali, Mauritius, Mexico, Morocco, Netherlands, New Zealand, Nicaragua, Nigeria, Pakistan, Panama, Peru, Philippines, Poland, Portugal, Romania, Russian Federation, Saudi Arabia, Syria, Slovak Republic, South Africa, Spain, Sweden, Switzerland, Thailand, Tunisia, Turkey, Uganda, United Kingdom, United Republic of Tanzania, Vietnam, Yemen, Zambia, Zimbabwe.

16 Antigua and Barbuda, Costa Rica, Dominica, Dominican Republic, Kenya, Malaysia, Paraguay, Qatar, Senegal, Singapore, United States of America, Venezuela.

17 Algeria, Angola, Armenia, Australia, Cameroon, China, Georgia, Guatemala, Mozambique, Namibia, Norway, Sudan, United Arab Emirates.

2004; Roberts and Unnevehr, 2005; Post, 2005, 2006; Drezner, 2007; Pollack and Shaffer, 2009; Büthe, 2008, 2009; Scarbrough, 2005; Büthe and Harris, 2011) In particular the votes on growth-promoting hormones are argued to be really about a general decision on whether only 'sound science' should govern the decision-making or whether 'other legitimate factors' should also be taken into consideration (Arcuri, 2015).

3.1.5 *Data Collected*

Since the explicit endorsement of Codex through the WTO's Agreement on the Application of Sanitary and Phytosanitary Measures (SPS Agreement) in 1995, analysed in detail in Chapter 4, Codex has received considerable attention in the political science and international relations literature. So far, however, there is no systematic study of the participation of governments, IGOs, and NGOs in Codex.[18] In an attempt to close this gap, data on the participation of governments, IGOs and NGOs was collected from the reports of all 880 meetings of the 44 Codex Committees (Table 1, Appendix) between 1963 and 2019. This original dataset includes the number of delegates from 189 governments, 58 IGOs, and 337 NGOs. The dataset also includes information on the country location of each meeting and the nationality of the chairperson of each of the 880 meetings. All Committee reports, including the list of participants, are publicly available on the Codex Alimentarius website. Since the reports span over a period of almost 60 years, their quality and structure differ considerably. Indeed, while some of the early reports are image files of typewritten documents converted into PDF files, recent documents are of high quality and well structured. Given these issues, the information was extracted manually.

This Section describes some of the patterns of governments', IGOs', and NGOs' participation in Codex. The data on governments' participation is the foundation of the empirical analyses conducted in Chapter 4 and Chapter 5. While only full members (government delegations) can decide and vote in Codex, IGOs, and NGOs play an important role in the standard-setting procedures. Indeed, Codex encourages IGOs and NGOs to apply for observer status, to attend Committee meetings, and to communicate their views at every stage of the standard-setting process. While the participation of IGOs and NGOs is discussed here, the data is not employed in the empirical analyses of Chapter 4 and Chapter 5. A principal challenge is that while the participation

18 The most comprehensive study (Veggeland and Borgen, 2005) to date focuses on the participation of governments, IGOs and NGOs in the Codex Alimentarius Committee (CAC) and the Codex Committee on General Principles (CCGP) for the years between 1985 and 2003.

of governmental delegations can be linked to economic (gross domestic product, trade flows) and political (political system) indicators, this is not the case for IGOs and NGOs. The following descriptive analysis of their participation does, however, provide insights into the role of IGOs and NGOs in the standard-setting processes of Codex.

3.1.5.1 Participation of Members

Codex experienced a steep increase in membership directly after its creation in 1963 (Figure 2, Appendix). Since the early 1970s, the membership continued to grow gradually. Driven by the increased membership, Codex also experienced an increase in members' participation in the standard-setting processes (Figure 3, Appendix). Again, members' participation grew rapidly in the organization's early years and then levelled between the 1970s and early 1990s. With the establishment of the WTO in 1995, Codex members increased their participation drastically — a development that is the focus of Chapter 4. Between 1995 and 2007, members' participation in Codex more than doubled. Since then, members' participation first levelled and, most recently, declined considerably. When assessing members' total participation between 1963 and 2019, it becomes clear that participation is severely positively skewed, meaning most members only participate in a small number of meetings, and that only a few members participate in a lot of standard-setting meetings (Figure 4, Appendix).

The number of delegates sent by members is, of course, highly correlated to the number of standard-setting meetings the members attend. Unsurprisingly then, the picture is similar for members' participants (Figure 5 and Figure 6, Appendix). Considering members' participation and participants in direct comparison still provides an interesting overview (Figure 7 and Figure 8, Appendix). The US is by far the most represented Codex member. Between 1963 and 2019, the US participated in 787 of the total 880 meetings (89%). Over this period of time, US delegates accounted for eight percent of total delegates. Other highly represented members include Germany, Japan, Thailand, France, Canada, and the Netherlands as well as increasingly Brazil and China. The under-representation of developing countries in Codex is widely acknowledged (Veggeland and Borgen, 2005; Jansen, 2010; Pernet, 2015) and a Codex Trust Fund was established in 2003 to support countries in building strong, solid, and sustainable national capacity to engage in Codex (Codex, 2020). The under-representation of developing countries also becomes apparent when considering the distribution of countries which chaired the standard-setting meetings since 1963. With around 16%, the US also has the largest share of meetings in which it held the position of the chairperson (Figure 9, Appendix).

3.1.5.2 Participation of Observers

As of September 2023, 60 IGOs, 159 NGOs and 16 United Nations (UN) organizations and bodies are registered as Codex observers. The participation of NGOs increased in the first years of Codex's existence but then remained stable until the mid-1990s. Between 1995 and 2000, NGOs' participation more than doubled before returning to the pre-1995 level (Figure 10, Appendix). Similarly to the Codex members, the participation of IGOs varies greatly, and is severely positively skewed (Figure 11, Appendix). The analysis of the number of delegates NGOs send to participate in Codex meetings draws a similar picture (Figure 12 and Figure 13, Appendix). Until 2003, the EU participated as an IGO and was by far the most represented IGO in the Codex standard-setting processes (Figure 14, Appendix). Other well-represented IGOs include the World Organisation for Animal Health (OIE), the International Organisation of Vine and Wine (OIV), the WTO, the International Atomic Energy Agency (IAEA), the African Union (AU), Pan American Health Organization (PAHO), the Inter-American Institute for Cooperation on Agriculture (IICA), the Organisation for Economic Co-operation and Development (OECD), and the United Nations Economic Commission for Europe (UNECE) (Figure 15, Appendix).

The second, and in the literature more controversially discussed, group of observers are NGOs. Private actors and industry representatives are often argued to participate in Codex member delegations (rather than as observers), lobby Codex members (as observers), and submit information for scientific assessments that suits their interests (Braithwaite and Drahos, 2000; Peters et al., 2009; Clapp and Fuchs, 2009; Fuchs and Kalfagianni, 2010; Jackson and Jansen, 2010; Lasalle-de Salins, 2011; Halabi, 2015; Berman, 2017). Consumer voices, in contrast, are claimed to be under-represented at Codex (Suppan, 2004). Between 1963 and 2019, a total number of 337 NGOs participated at Codex. The data collected on NGOs confirms some of the previously outlined observations. Industry representatives do indeed at times participate in Codex member delegations. In some instances, a certain company might even provide delegates to different Codex Member delegations. In the 19th meeting of the CAC in 1991, for instance, Coca-Cola representatives were part of the delegations of Canada, Germany, Nigeria, and the US. It is important to point out, however, that Codex encourages its members to include industry representatives in their national delegations as they possess valued technical knowledge and expertise and, in the end, have to implement the standards. While NGOs are not required to disclose their sector in the list of participants (industry, academia, research, consumer, etc.), an internet search of the 337 NGOs suggests that around 70% of NGOs have close industry ties.

Similarly to IGO observers, NGOs' participation in Codex was relatively stable until the mid-1990s. Between 1995 and 2005, however, NGO participation more than doubled (Figure 16 and Figure 18, Appendix). The large majority of NGOs only participates in a small number of meetings (Figure 17 and Figure 19, Appendix). As previously indicated, the International Dairy Foundation (FILIDF, Figure 20, Appendix) has been a particularly active observer at Codex since the beginning. Other well-represented NGOs include the Groupement International des Associations Nationales de Fabricants de Produits Agrochimiques (GIFAP), CropLife International (CROP), the International Life Sciences Institute (ILSI), the International Council of Grocery Manufacturer Associations (ICGMA), the Association of Official Analytical Chemists (AOAC), and the International Special Dietary Foods Industries (ISDI). Consumers International (CI) and ISO were also represented at a fairly high number of Codex Committee meetings and sent a considerable number of delegates (Figure 21, Appendix).

While some NGOs participate in many different committees, others focus on certain Committees but send large numbers of delegates. In the 50th meeting of the Codex Committee on Pesticide Residues (CCPR) in 2018, for instance, CropLife International presented the largest delegation with 46 attending representatives. The second largest delegation in this meeting was the US with 14 delegates, three of which represented companies that are members of CropLife International. Again, the overall participation of NGOs surged in the early and mid-1990s.

3.2 The International Organization for Standardization

3.2.1 *History*

ISO is a Geneva-based independent, non-governmental international organization founded in 1947. As of September 2023, ISO has a membership of 169 national standards bodies (NSBs). Around half of the NSBs are part of their government, while the other half are non-governmental standards bodies. The latter are the most representative standardization organization in their respective country. (ISO, 2020b)

This composition of ISO's membership, in addition to the important role played by the more than 1000 (as of September 2023) registered partner organizations, has caused political science and international relations scholars to refer to ISO as a mixed private-governmental organization (Abbott, 2003), a private body (Kingsbury et al., 2005), a trans-national private network (Heires,

2008), a private-sector standard-setter (Mattli and Woods, 2009), a global private standard-setting body (Büthe and Mattli, 2010a), a trans-national private regulator (Cafaggi, 2012), a non-governmental organization with informal characteristics (Duquet and Geraets, 2012), an emergent normative order with normative authority (Lindahl, 2015), and a non-governmental, mainly industry-driven, international standard-setter (Delimatsis, 2015b).

ISO's history is closely related to some of the NSBs, in particular the British Standards Institute (BSI) founded 1901. During the early 20th century, scientists and engineers discussed standardization matters at inter-governmental conferences and international exhibitions. At the International Electrical Congress in St. Louis in 1904, participants decided to establish an international body which could continue and expand their standardization work. Only two years later, the International Electrotechnical Commission (IEC) was created in London. A representative of the BSI, Charles Le Maistre, was in charge of the IEC's office. This initial link between the BSI and the IEC presented the foundation of BSI's influential position which it still holds today. In 1911, the IEC established its first technical committee (IEC/TC-1) to deal with all matters related to terminology and definitions in the electrotechnical domain. ISO's predecessor, the International Federation of National Standardization Associations (ISA), was created in 1926. In contrast to the IEC, the ISA did not develop new standards but focused only on the exchange of information between NSBs. After the ISA ceased to function during the World War II, the BSI pushed for a new body. The United Nations Standards Coordinating Committee (UNSCC) was created in 1944 under the directorship of BSI's Charles Le Maistre. Imminently after the UNSCC creation, however, the discussion turned to creating a more permanent successor organization. ISO was formed in a series of meetings in 1945 and 1946, and came officially into existence in 1947. The IEC became an autonomous technical division of ISO. (Murphy and Yates, 2009)

During the early years of its existence, ISO was a largely European organization. In the 1960s, for instance, Australia, Canada, India, Israel, and the US were the only major non-European countries in ISO. As briefly discussed below, and in more detail in Chapter 4 and Chapter 5, the influence of European countries would remain strong to this day. During this time, ISO began to make deliberate efforts to stop the duplication of standards with NSBs, reduce the time required to develop standards, and cooperate more efficiently with the European Economic Community (EEC) and similar regional bodies as well as with the General Agreement on Tariffs and Trade (GATT). This strategy was successful and ISO gained a *de facto* monopoly on setting industrial standards in many sectors that it still has today. (Murphy and Yates, 2009)

3.2.2 *Structure*

Since its creation, ISO has expanded its scope considerably and developed over 23,000 international standards. ISO standards govern everything from medical devices (ISO 13485), and testing and calibration laboratories (ISO/IEC 17025); to quality (ISO 9000), energy (ISO 50001), and environmental (14000) management; and the format of date and time (ISO 8601). ISO is also active in the area of food safety management (ISO 22000), where is cooperates closely with Codex (ISO, 2017).

A central element of ISO's organizational structure is the Council. The Council has direct responsibility over the ISO President's Committee, the Council Standing Committees, the Advisory Groups, and the Policy Development Committees. The Council is also responsible for the Secretariat, which has around 150 members of staff. The Technical Management Board (TMB) also reports to the Council. The TMB is responsible for the more than 300 technical committees (TCs) which lead the standard development (Table 2, Appendix). The rotating membership to the Council is open to all members. The Council reports to the General Assembly, which meets once a year.

3.2.3 *Procedures*

The level of access and influence of the members over the ISO system depends on whether they are full members, correspondent members, or subscriber members. A full membership allows members to participate and vote in ISO technical and policy meetings. Correspondent members attend ISO technical and policy meetings as observers. Subscriber members keep up to date on ISO's work but cannot participate in it.

The ISO standard-setting procedure is organized in six stages. In the Proposal Stage, a new standard proposal is submitted for a three-month vote to the full-members of the relevant TC. A simple majority of members must approve the proposal, and at least five members must actively support it and nominate a project leader. In the Preparatory Stage, a working group is set up by the TC to prepare a standard draft. Once consensus is achieved among the experts, the draft is forwarded to the second consensus-building phase. Consensus is defined by ISO as a "[g]eneral agreement, characterized by the absence of sustained opposition to substantial issues by any important part of the concerned interests and by a process that involves seeking to take into account the views of all parties concerned and to reconcile any conflicting arguments" (ISO, 2012, p. 36). The ISO Directives state explicitly that consensus need not imply unanimity. In the Committee Stage, all full members of the TC have the opportunity to comment and to vote on the draft standard. Once consensus is reached, the text is finalized. In the Enquiry Stage, the draft is circulated to all full members of ISO for voting and comment within a period of three months. All full members are eligible to vote and all members of the relevant TC are obliged to vote. The text is approved if a two-thirds majority of the relevant TC members is in favour, and not more than one-quarter of the total number of votes cast are negative. The final draft is circulated to all full ISO members for a final two-month Yes/No vote under the same criteria as in the Enquiry Stage. Once the final draft is approved, the text is sent to the Secretariat which publishes the international standard.

While only full members are allowed to vote during the standard-setting procedure, it is important to point out that, in addition to the subscriber and correspondent members, more than 700 organizations in cooperation are listed on ISO's website which indirectly influence the standard development.

3.2.4 *Controversial Topics*

Similarly to Codex, ISO began to receive increased scholarly attention with the establishment of the WTO in 1995. While ISO was not explicitly endorsed as a relevant international standardizing body in the WTO's Agreement on Technical Barriers to Trade (TBT Agreement), it is widely understood that ISO is *the* key international standardization body for TBT-related matters, as discussed in further detail in Chapter 4 (Bernstein and Hannah, 2008; Büthe, 2010; Büthe, 2010; Büthe and Mattli, 2010b,a; Jansen, 2012a,b; Delimatsis, 2015c,b; Elsig, 2015; Lindahl, 2015; Mavroidis and Wolfe, 2017).

Some countries, in particular the US, would beg to differ. Indeed, the previously mentioned dominance of European countries in ISO has been a contentious transatlantic issue for years (Mattli, 2001a,b; Abbott, 2003; Büthe and Witte, 2004; Drezner, 2004, 2007; Graz and Hauert, 2014; Graz, 2019). In this "standards war", the US accuses the European countries of hijacking the ISO standardization process, and attempting to establish EU standards as global standards (Murphy and Yates, 2009). The US laments that, as a result of the Vienna and Frankfurt Agreements, European standards are adopted in fast-track, which limits the opportunities for non-European stakeholders to contribute to the development of the standards at an early stage (Abbott, 2003; USTR, 2020).

The Vienna Agreement, signed in 1991, is a cooperation agreement between ISO and the European Committee for Standardization (CEN) which aims to prevent the duplication of effort and to reduce time when preparing standards. As is criticized by the US, CEN explicitly states that "[w]herever appropriate priority is given to cooperation with ISO provided that international standards meet European legislative and market requirements and that non-European global players also implement these standards" (CEN/CENELEC, 2020).

The Frankfurt Agreement from 2016 confirms the long-standing cooperation between IEC and the European Committee for Electrotechnical Standardization (CENELEC) which dates back to the Dresden Agreement signed in 1996. As a result of this close cooperation, almost to 80% of CENELEC standards are identical to or based on IEC publications (CEN/CENELEC, 2020).

As will be discussed in further detail in Chapter 4 and Chapter 5, the US is keen to limit the importance of ISO standards given their perceived European bias. The US, for instance, stresses that the TBT Agreement does not explicitly refer to ISO and that any standard developed in accordance with the TBT Committee principles (WTO, 2000) concerning transparency, openness, impartiality and consensus, relevance and effectiveness, coherence, and developing country interests is to be considered an international standard. The EU, in contrast, underlines the importance of ISO standards in some of its preferential trade agreements. (Abbott, 2003; McDaniels et al., 2018; USTR, 2020)

The widely acknowledged power asymmetries between the EU and the US in ISO are due to the organization's history and the fundamentally different standardization systems on both sides of the Atlantic. Partly due to differences in their national economic structures (Tate, 2003; Winn, 2009), the US standardization system is often described as atomistic and market-oriented, while the EU system is centralized and hierarchical (Abbott, 2003; Mattli and Büthe, 2003; Heires, 2008; Büthe and Mattli, 2011). The ISO system is institutionally more complementary to the EU system (Büthe and Mattli, 2011), which provides the EU with a first-mover advantage (Mattli, 2001b,a). The following Section outlines the data collected on ISO and provides a descriptive analysis which largely confirms the transatlantic asymmetries discussed above.

3.2.5 *Data Collected*

Since the mid-1990s, ISO received increased attention in the political science and international relations literature. Most studies, with the notable exception of Morikawa and Morrison (2004) and Lim and Prakash (2018), are based on case studies on individual standards such as ISO 14001 (Environmental management) (Kollman and Prakash, 2001; Potoski and Prakash, 2005b,a; Prakash and Potoski, 2006a,b, 2007) or ISO 9000 (Quality management) (Casper and Hancké, 1999; Guler et al., 2002). Other contributions focus on selected technical committees such as ISO TC 228 (Tourism) and ISO TC 229 (Nanotechnologies) (Graz and Hauert, 2019).

A major challenge is that data on members' participation in ISO is only partly publicly available. One reason might be the large amount of meetings that take place. ISO claims that "every working day of the year, around twenty six technical meetings take place somewhere in the world" ISO (2020a). More likely, however, the transparency requirements are simply different for a NGO like ISO than for an UN-related body like Codex. ISO's website does provide transparent and detailed information members' TC membership as well as partner organizations' liaisons with TCs. However, in contrast to Codex, this data is not publicly available at the TC meeting level. Furthermore, the ISO website only provides information on the current status of members and cooperation organizations but not on their engagement over the almost 70 year long history of the organization. Even studies on members' ISO membership, which can vary yearly between no membership, full-, subscriber-, or correspondent membership, only appeared relatively recently (Lim and Prakash, 2018).

The empirical analyses conducted in Chapter 4 and Chapter 5 are based on an original dataset which was kindly shared by an ISO staff member, and which includes information on NSBs' membership in almost 300 TCs between 1987 and 2019 (Table 2, Appendix).

3.2.5.1 Participation of Members

Since ISO's creation in 1947, its membership has gradually increased (Figure 22, Appendix). In particular during the mid-1990s, around the time of the WTO creation, more and more NSBs joined ISO. While only 88 NSBs were ISO members in 1990, this number almost doubled by now. With the increased membership, overall participation in the TCs also grew considerably over time (Figure 23, Appendix). The extent to which members participate in TCs, however, varies considerably. The distribution of member's TC participation is severely positively skewed, meaning that only a small group of members participates in a large number of different TCs (Figure 24, Appendix). Of the 25 most represented members, 15 are European. The most represented non-European members include China, Russia, Japan, the US, the Republic of Korea, South Africa, Australia, Canada, India, and Iran. (Figure 25, Appendix) The distribution of the secretariats of the almost 300 TCs, paints a similar picture. Only 31 members actually hold secretariats, thirteen of these are European. Germany holds 43 TC secretariats, followed by the US (39 secretariats), and China (33 secretariats). With 18 TC secretariats, Japan presents another important non-European member in this list. (Figure 26, Appendix)

3.2.5.2 Participation of Cooperation Organizations

As previously indicated, European countries play an important and active role in ISO. Overall, the participation of ISO's registered cooperation organizations is positively skewed, indicating that only few cooperation organization are involved in a high number of TCs (Figure 27, Appendix). The European Commission is by far the most represented cooperation organization (Figure 28, Appendix). The Top 5 cooperation organizations also include the World Customs Organization (WCO), the United Nations Economic Commission for Europe (UNECE), the WHO, and the International Organization of Legal Metrology (OIML). While ISO has been criticized for the low representation of consumer organizations (Farquhar, 2005), it is interesting to that the Top 25 list of cooperation organizations also includes the European Environmental Citizens Organisation for Standardisation (ECOS (Environment)) and the European Association for the Co-ordination of Consumer Representation in Standardization (ANEC).

3.3 Interim Conclusion

This Chapter provides a detailed historical account on Codex and ISO. The two organizations share similarities but also have considerable differences with regards to their history, their structure, and their procedures. Both organizations experienced an increase in the participation of countries around the time in which the WTO was created, and in which the WTO TBT and SPS entered into force. This linkage between the multilateral trade policy regime and the international standardization regime, between multilateral trade agreements and international standardization organizations, will be empirically analysed in Chapter 4.

This Chapter also indicates certain transatlantic tensions between the EU and the US. In Codex, the US is the most represented, and arguably the most influential, actor. For the EU, by contrast, some international standards developed in Codex, such as for instance standards related to growth hormone-treated meat, are problematic. In ISO, the opposite appears to be the case. European countries have been the most represented, and arguably the most influential, actors in ISO. For the US, this European dominance in ISO has presented a challenge for decades. Overall, the transatlantic asymmetry in participation in the two international standardization organizations appears to be more eminent in ISO (Figure 29, Appendix) than in Codex (Figure 30, Appendix). The transatlantic divide between the EU and the US will be discussed in more detail in Chapter 5.

3.4 Appendices

TABLE 1 Codex: Committees

Type	Abbreviation	Name	Active from	Active until
Commission	CAC	Codex Alimentarius Commission	1964	Currently
Executive Committee	CCEXEC	Executive Committee of the Codex Alimentarius Commission	1964	Currently
General Subject	CCCF	Contaminants in Foods	2007	Currently
	CCFA	Food Additives	2007	Currently
	CCFH	Food Hygiene	1964	Currently
	CCFICS	Food Import and Export Inspection and Certification Systems	1992	Currently
	CCFL	Food Labelling	1965	Currently
	CCGP	General Principles	1965	Currently
	CCMAS	Methods of Analysis and Sampling	1965	Currently
	CCNFSDU	Nutrition and Foods for Special Dietary Uses	1966	Currently
	CCPR	Pesticide Residues	1966	Currently
	CCRVDF	Residues of Veterinary Drugs in Foods	1986	Currently
	CCFAC	Food Additives and Contaminants	1964	2006
Commodity	CCCPL	Cereals, Pulses and Legumes	1980	Currently
	CCFFV	Fresh Fruits and Vegetables	1988	Currently
	CCFO	Fats and Oils	1964	Currently
	CCPFV	Processed Fruits and Vegetables	1964	Currently
	CCSCH	Spices and Culinary Herbs	2014	Currently
	CCCPC	Cocoa Products and Chocolate	1963	2001
	CCFFP	Fish and Fishery Products	1966	2015
	CCMMP	Milk and Milk Products	1994	2010
	CCMPH	Meat Hygiene	1972	2005
	CCNMW	Natural Mineral Waters	1966	2008
	CCS	Sugars	1964	2000
	CCVP	Vegetable Proteins	1980	1989
	CCIE	Edible Ices	1974	1976
	CCM	Meat	1965	1973
	CCPMPP	Processed Meat and Poultry Products	1966	1990
	CCSB	Soups and Broths	1975	1977
	CXTO	Joint CODEX/IOOC Meeting on the Standardization of Table Olives	1971	1973

TABLE 1 Codex: Committees (*cont.*)

Type	Abbreviation	Name	Active from	Active until
ad hoc Intergovernmental Task Forces	CGECPMMP	Joint FAO/WHO Committee of Government Experts on the Code of Principles Concerning Milk and Milk Products	1958	1990
	GEFJ	Joint ECE/Codex alimentarius groups of experts on standardization: Fruit Juices	1964	1990
	GEQFF	Joint ECE/Codex alimentarius groups of experts on standardization: Quick Frozen Foods	1965	1980
	TFAF	Ad Hoc Intergovernmental Task Force on Animal Feeding	2000	2013
	TFAMR	Ad hoc Codex Intergovernmental Task Force on Antimicrobial Resistance	2007	Currently
	TFFBT	Ad Hoc Intergovernmental Task Force on Food Derived from Biotechnology	2000	2007
	TFFJ	Ad Hoc Intergovernmental Task Force on Fruit and Vegetable Juices	2000	2004
	TFPHQFF	Ad hoc Codex Intergovernmental Task Force on the Processing and Handling of Quick Frozen Foods	2008	2008
Coordinating Committees	CCAFRICA	Coordinating Committee for Africa	1974	Currently
	CCASIA	Coordinating Committee for Asia	1977	Currently
	CCEURO	Coordinating Committee for Europe	1965	Currently
	CCLAC	Coordinating Committee for Latin America and the Caribbean	1976	Currently
	CCNASWP	Coordinating Committee for North America and South West Pacific	1990	Currently
	CCNE	Coordinating Committee for Near East	2001	Currently

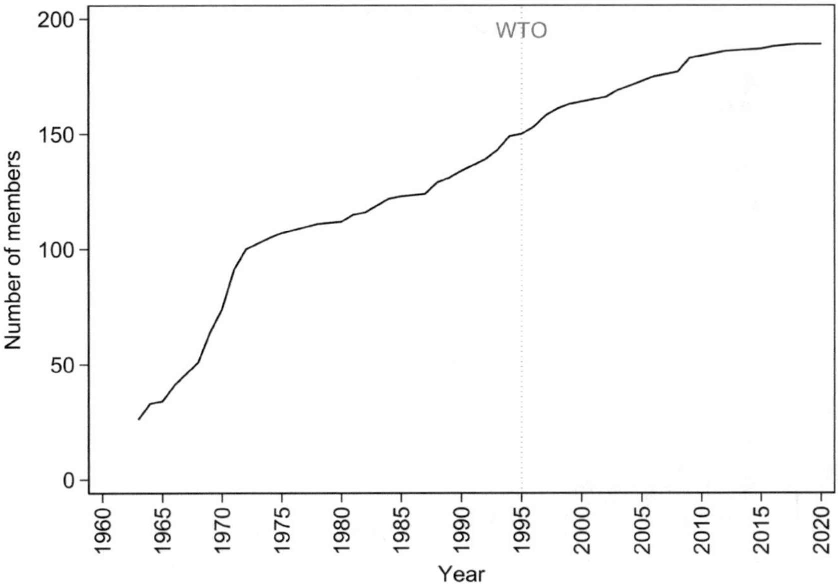

FIGURE 2 Codex membership, 1963–2019
AUTHOR'S ILLUSTRATION

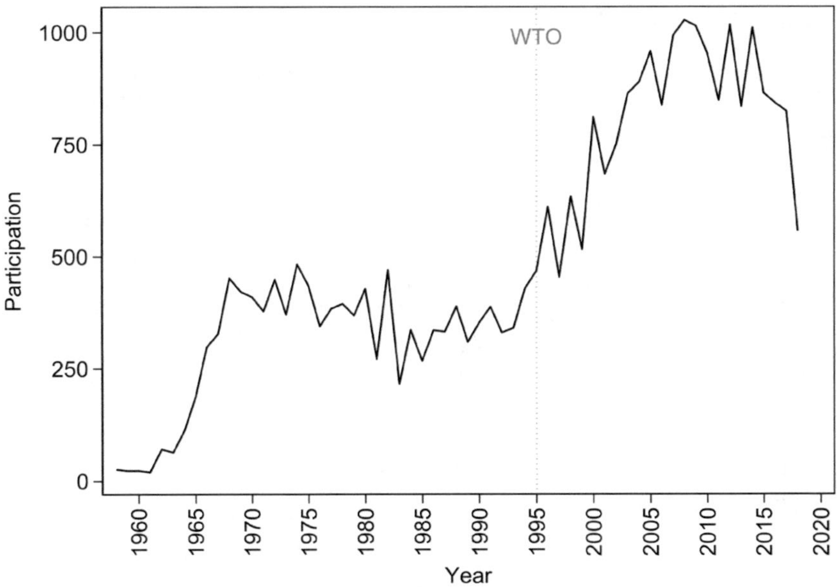

FIGURE 3 Codex member participation, 1963–2019
AUTHOR'S ILLUSTRATION

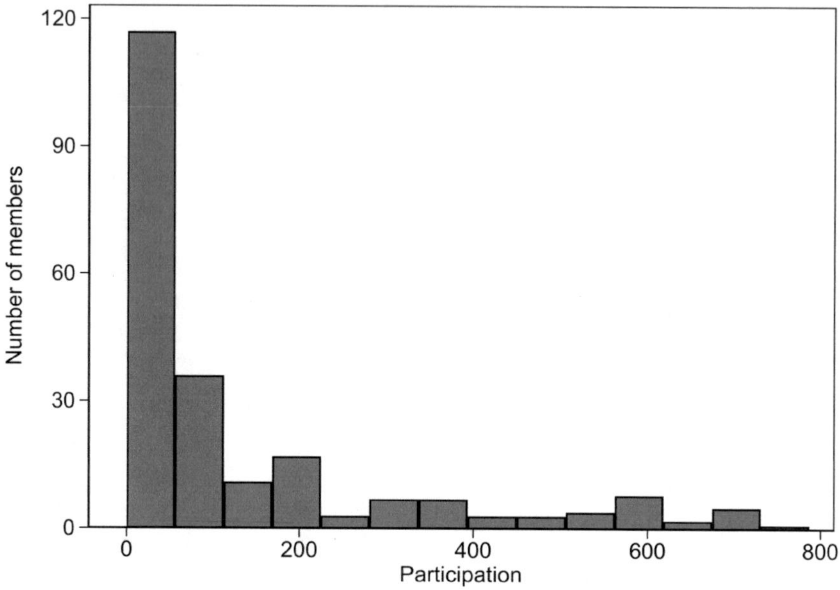

FIGURE 4 Distribution of Codex member participation, 1963–2019
AUTHOR'S ILLUSTRATION

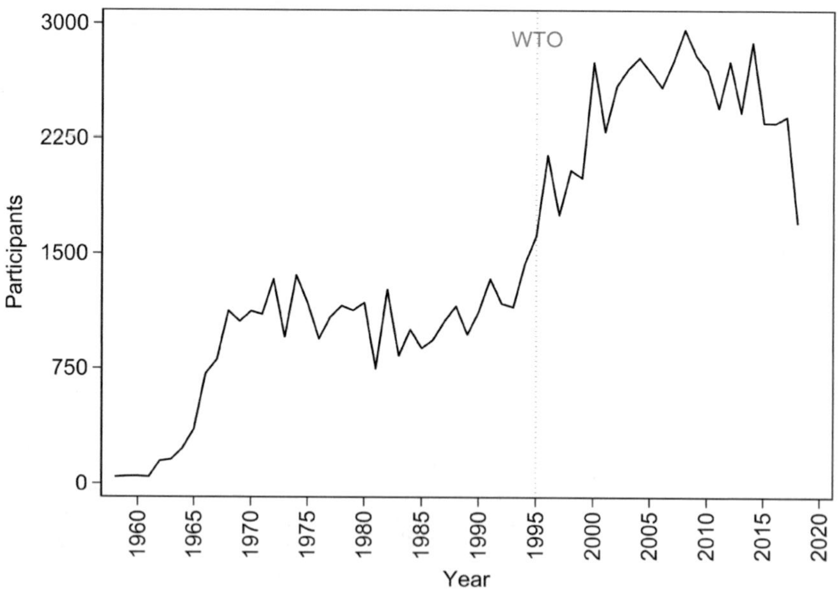

FIGURE 5 Codex member participants, 1963–2019
AUTHOR'S ILLUSTRATION

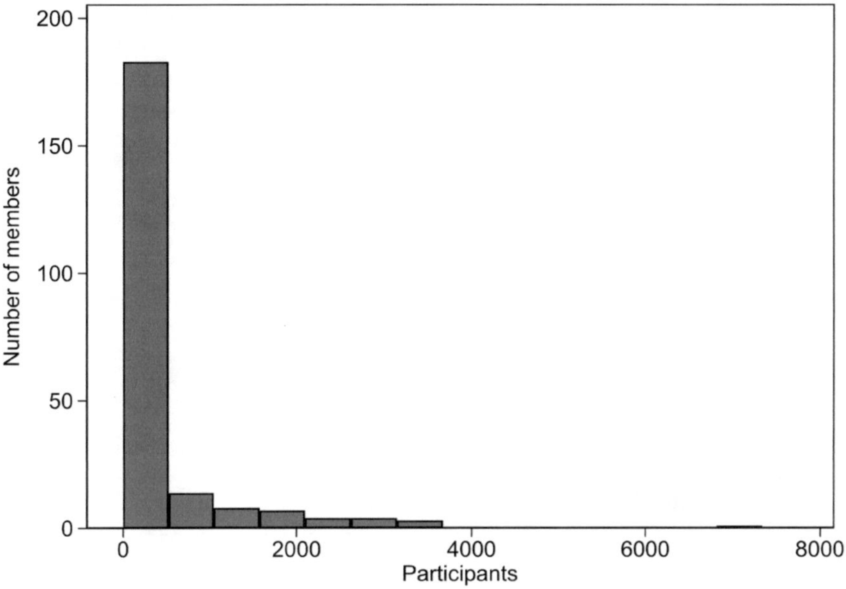

FIGURE 6 Distribution of Codex member participants, 1963–2019
AUTHOR'S ILLUSTRATION

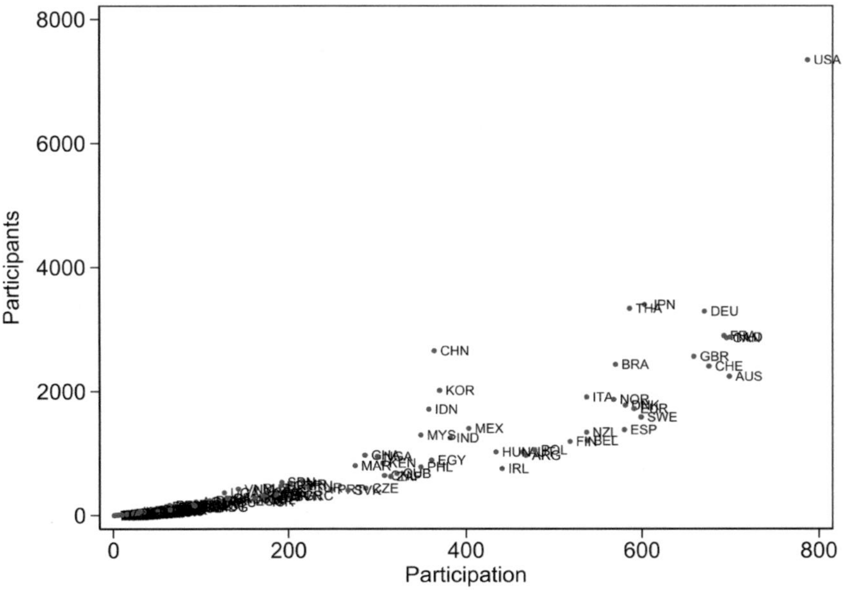

FIGURE 7 Codex member participation and participants, 1963–2019
AUTHOR'S ILLUSTRATION

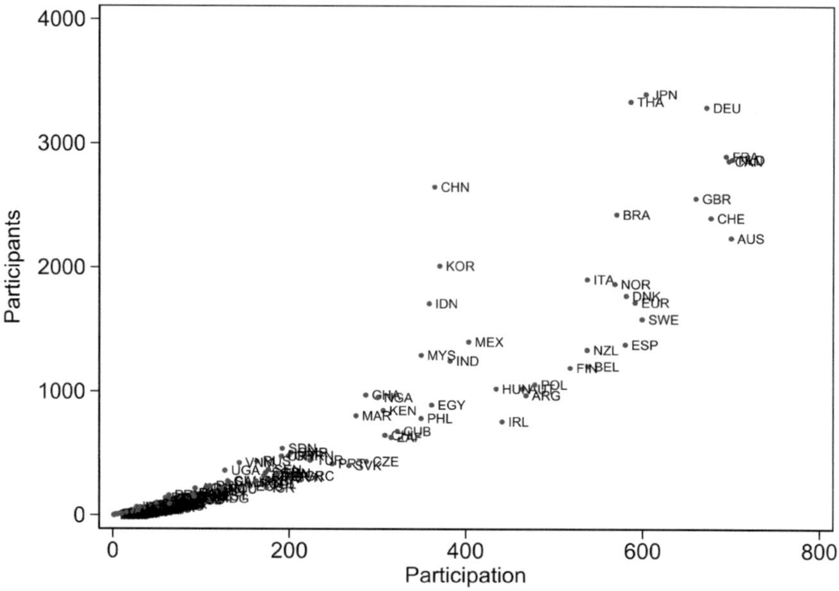

FIGURE 8 Codex member participation and participants (without the US), 1963–2019
AUTHOR'S ILLUSTRATION

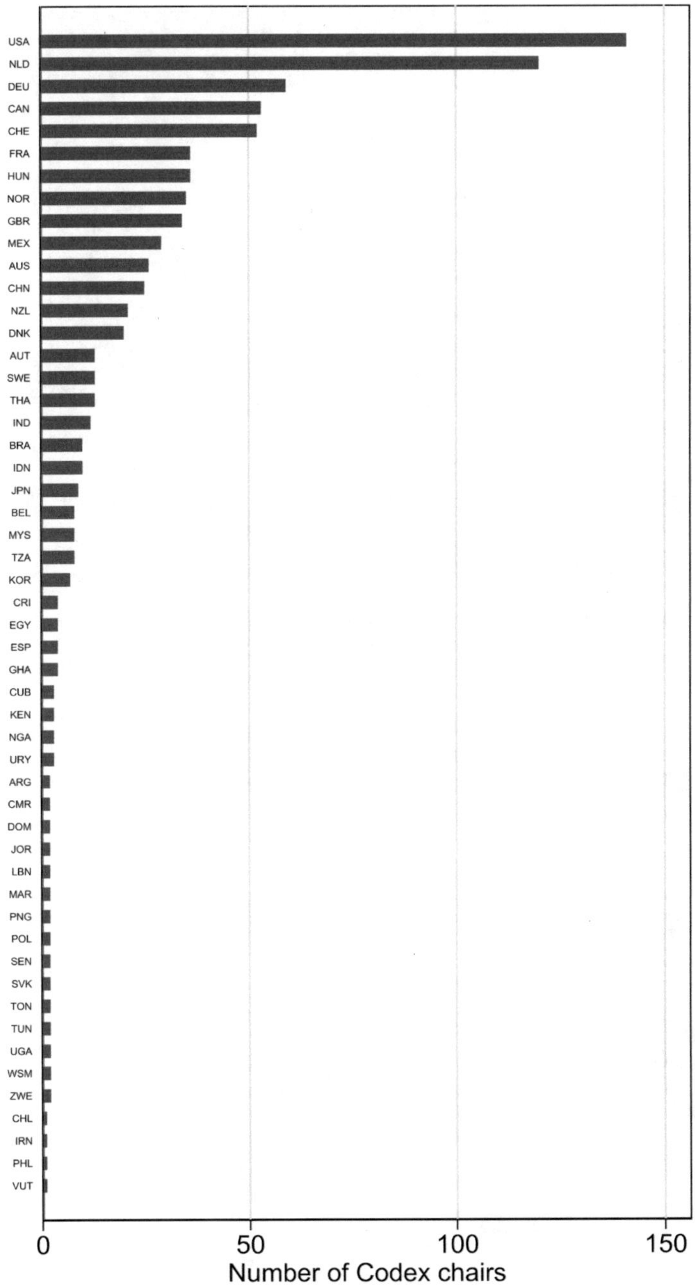

FIGURE 9 Codex chairs, 1963–2019
AUTHOR'S ILLUSTRATION

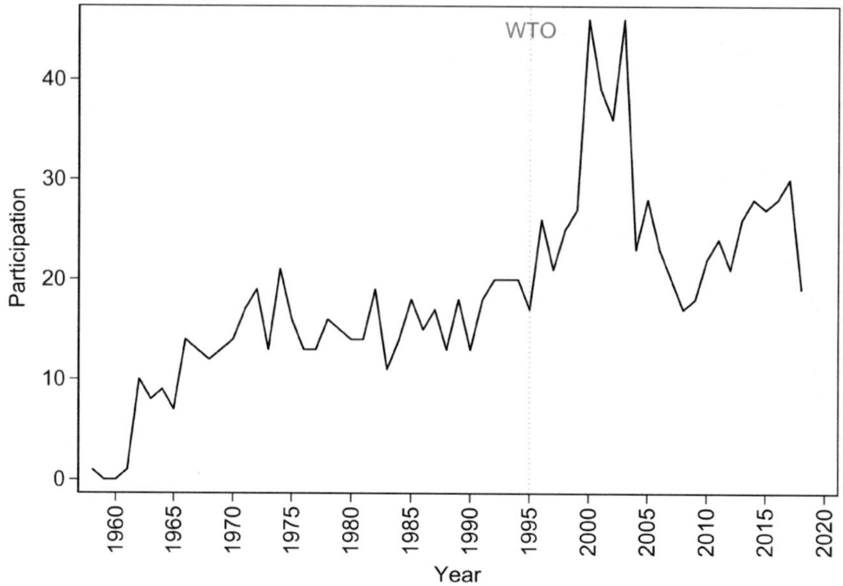

FIGURE 10 Codex IGO observer participation, 1963–2019
AUTHOR'S ILLUSTRATION

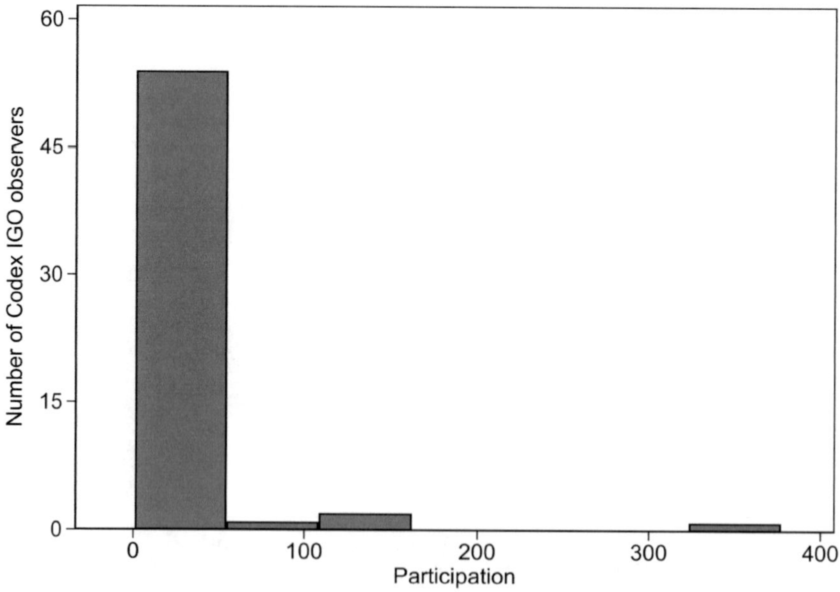

FIGURE 11 Distribution of Codex IGO observer participation, 1963–2019
AUTHOR'S ILLUSTRATION

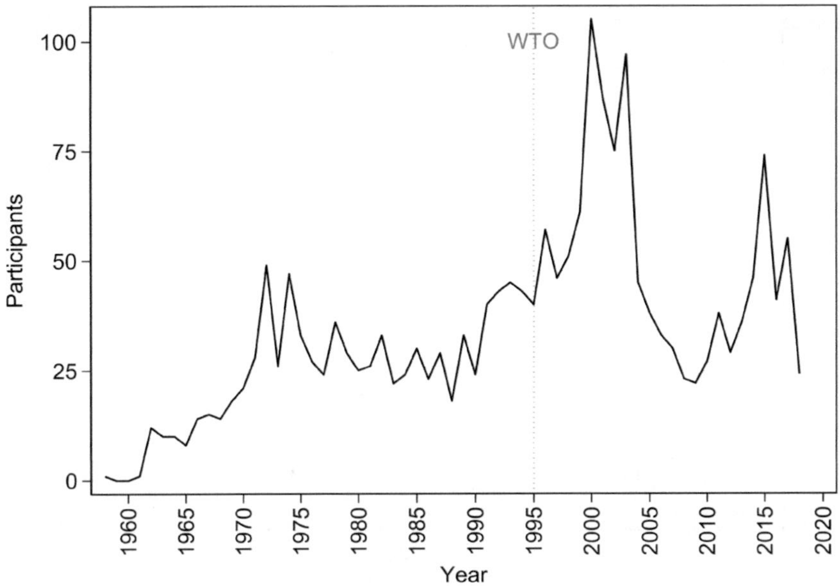

FIGURE 12 Codex IGO observer participants, 1963–2019
AUTHOR'S ILLUSTRATION

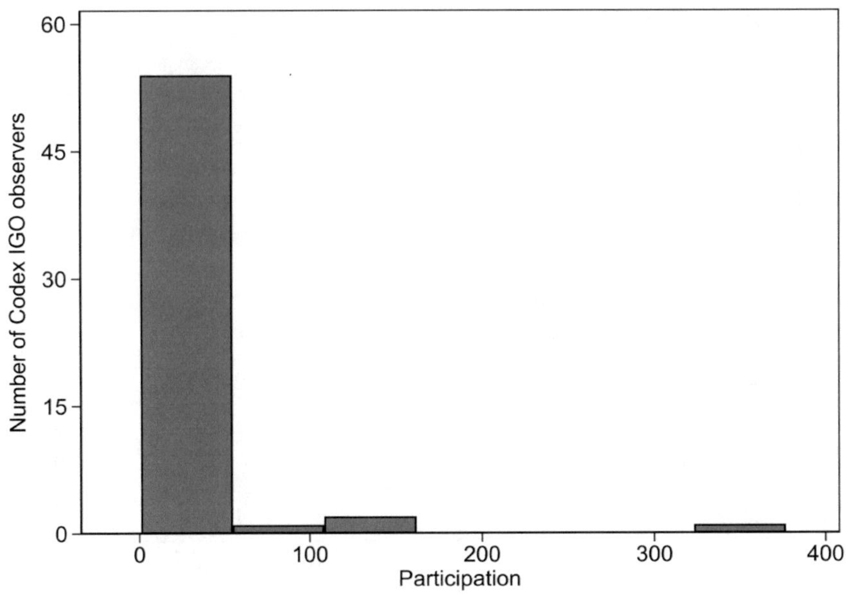

FIGURE 13 Distribution of Codex IGO observer participants, 1963–2019
AUTHOR'S ILLUSTRATION

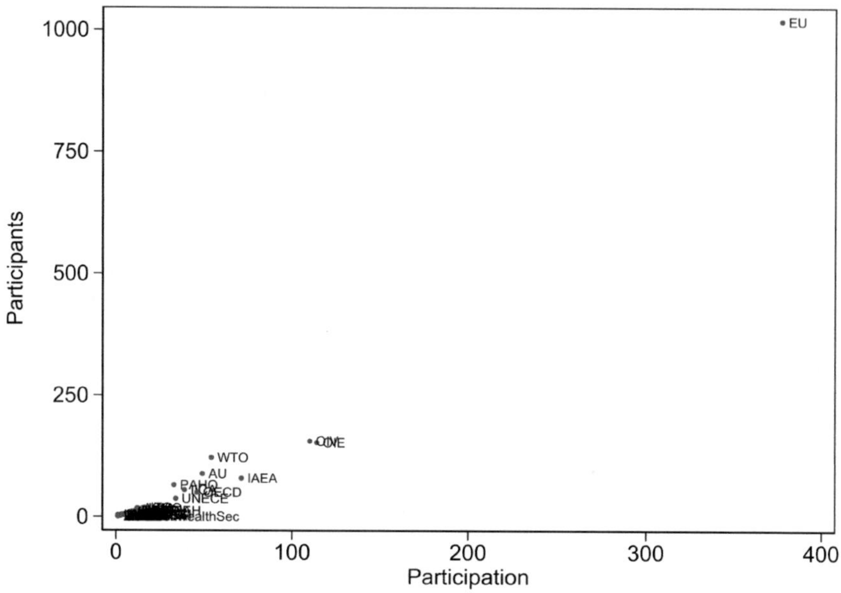

FIGURE 14 Codex IGO observer participation and participants, 1963–2019
AUTHOR'S ILLUSTRATION

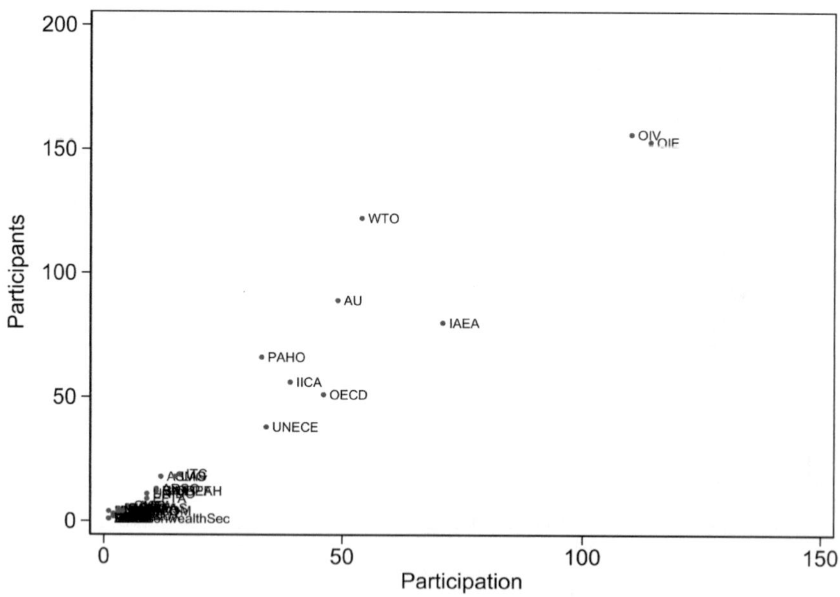

FIGURE 15 Codex IGO observer participation and participants (without the EU), 1963–2019
AUTHOR'S ILLUSTRATION

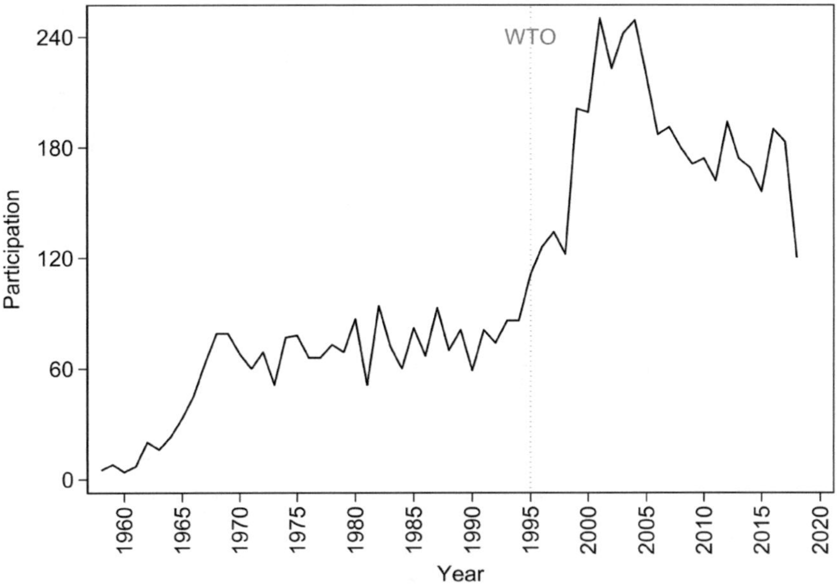

FIGURE 16 Codex NGO observer participation, 1963–2019
AUTHOR'S ILLUSTRATION

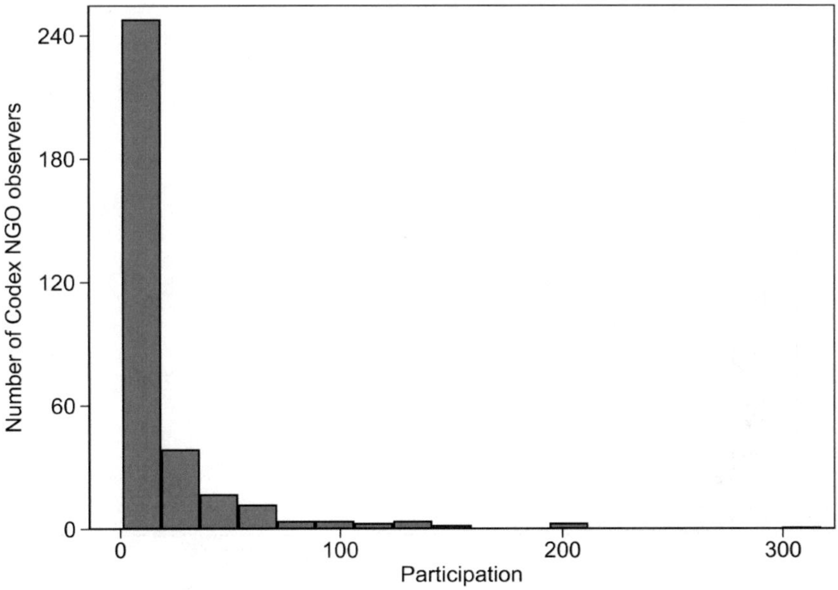

FIGURE 17 Distribution of Codex NGO observer participation, 1963–2019
AUTHOR'S ILLUSTRATION

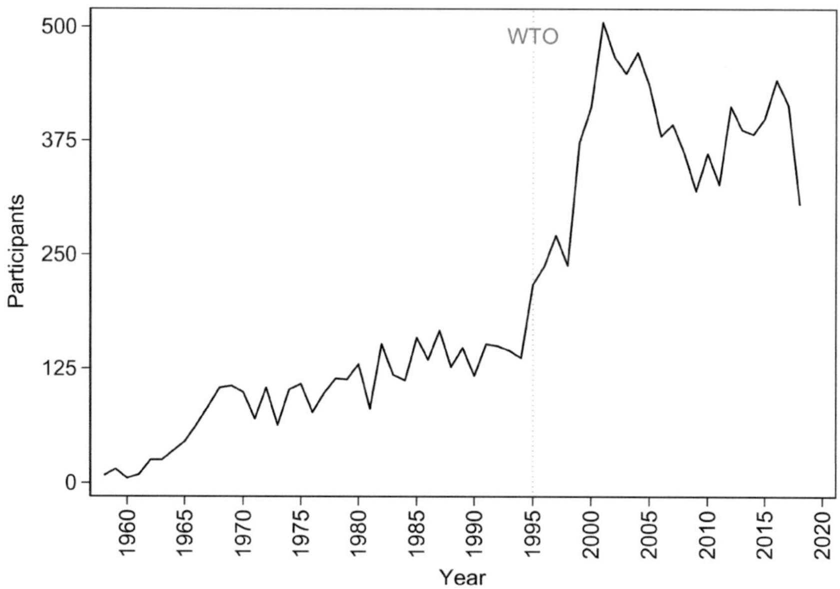

FIGURE 18 Codex NGO observer participants, 1963–2019
AUTHOR'S ILLUSTRATION

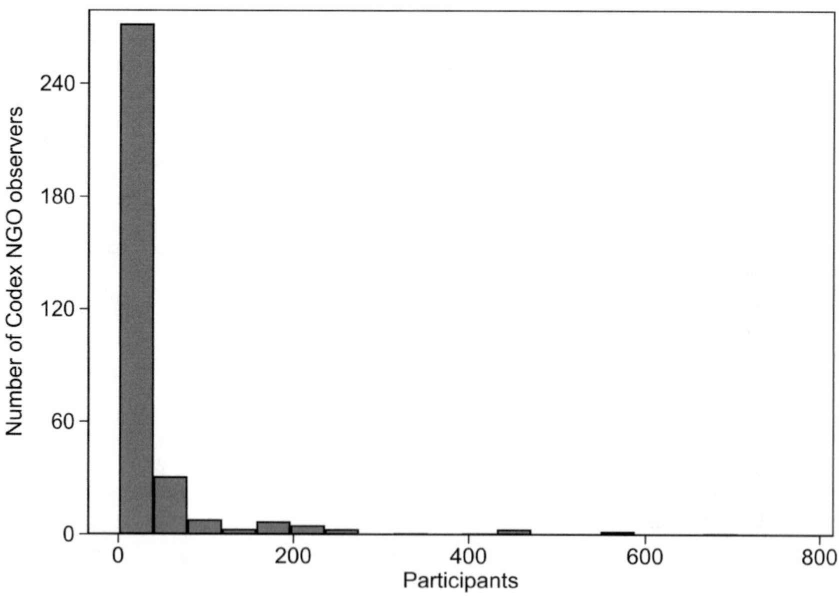

FIGURE 19 Distribution of Codex NGO observer participants, 1963–2019
AUTHOR'S ILLUSTRATION

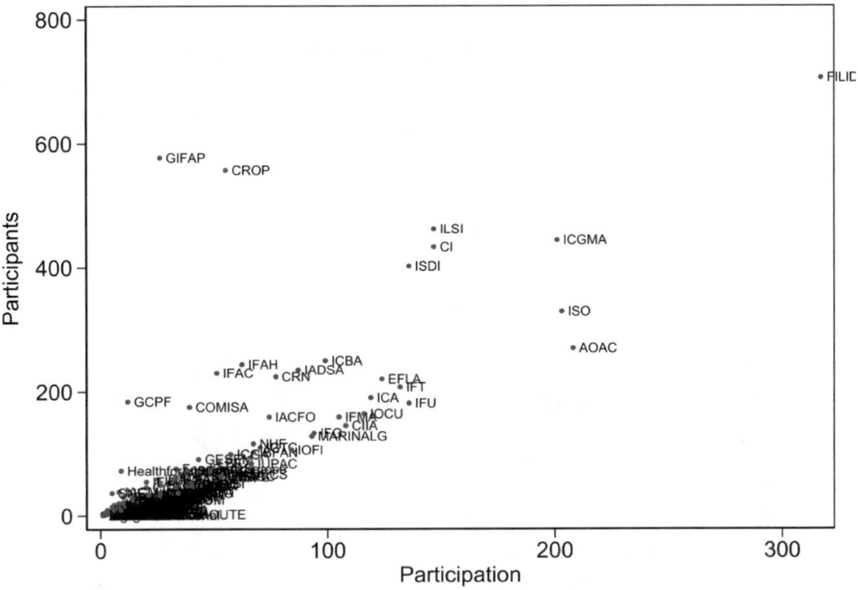

FIGURE 20 Codex NGO observer participation and participants, 1963–2019
AUTHOR'S ILLUSTRATION

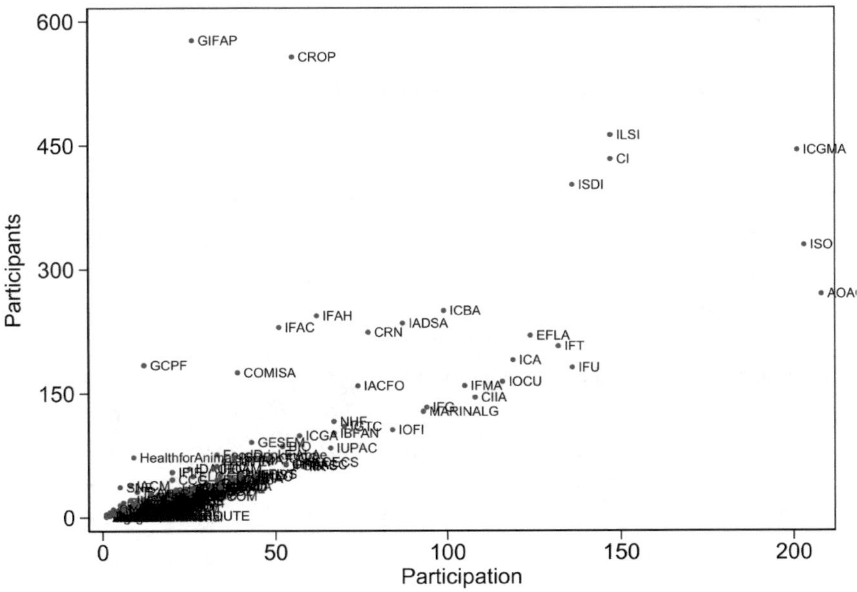

FIGURE 21 Codex NGO observer participation and participants (without FILIDF), 1963–2019
AUTHOR'S ILLUSTRATION

TABLE 2 ISO: Committees

Reference	Title	Active since	Data available since
ISO/IEC JTC 1	Information technology	1987	1987
ISO/IEC JPC 2	Joint Project Committee — Energy efficiency and renewable energy sources — Common terminology	2009	2009
ISO/TC 1	Screw threads	1947	1987
ISO/TC 2	Fasteners	1947	1987
ISO/TC 4	Rolling bearings	1947	1987
ISO/TC 5	Ferrous metal pipes and metallic fittings	1947	1987
ISO/TC 6	Paper, board and pulps	1947	1987
ISO/TC 8	Ships and marine technology	1947	1987
ISO/TC 10	Technical product documentation	1947	1987
ISO/TC 11	Boilers and pressure vessels	1947	1987
ISO/TC 12	Quantities and units	1947	1987
ISO/TC 14	Shafts for machinery and accessories	1947	1987
ISO/TC 17	Steel	1947	1987
ISO/TC 18	Zinc and zinc alloys	1947	1987
ISO/TC 19	Preferred numbers	1947	1987
ISO/TC 20	Aircraft and space vehicles	1947	1987
ISO/TC 21	Equipment for fire protection and fire fighting	1947	1987
ISO/TC 22	Road vehicles	1947	1987
ISO/TC 23	Tractors and machinery for agriculture and forestry	1952	1987
ISO/TC 24	Particle characterization including sieving	1947	1987
ISO/TC 25	Cast irons and pig irons	1947	1987
ISO/TC 26	Copper and copper alloys	1947	1987
ISO/TC 27	Solid mineral fuels	1947	1987
ISO/TC 28	Petroleum and related products, fuels and lubricants from natural or synthetic sources	1947	1987
ISO/TC 29	Small tools	1947	1987
ISO/TC 30	Measurement of fluid flow in closed conduits	1947	1987
ISO/TC 31	Tyres, rims and valves	1947	1987
ISO/TC 33	Refractories	1947	1987
ISO/TC 34	Food products	1947	1987
ISO/TC 35	Paints and varnishes	1947	1987
ISO/TC 36	Cinematography	1947	1987
ISO/TC 37	Language and terminology	1947	1987
ISO/TC 38	Textiles	1947	1987

TABLE 2 ISO: Committees (*cont.*)

Reference	Title	Active since	Data available since
ISO/TC 39	Machine tools	1947	1987
ISO/TC 41	Pulleys and belts (including veebelts)	1947	1987
ISO/TC 42	Photography	1947	1987
ISO/TC 43	Acoustics	1947	1987
ISO/TC 44	Welding and allied processes	1947	1987
ISO/TC 45	Rubber and rubber products	1947	1987
ISO/TC 46	Information and documentation	1947	1987
ISO/TC 47	Chemistry	1947	1987
ISO/TC 48	Laboratory equipment	1947	1987
ISO/TC 51	Pallets for unit load method of materials handling	1947	1987
ISO/TC 52	Light gauge metal containers	1947	1987
ISO/TC 54	Essential oils	1947	1987
ISO/TC 58	Gas cylinders	1947	1987
ISO/TC 59	Buildings and civil engineering works	1947	1987
ISO/TC 60	Gears	1947	1987
ISO/TC 61	Plastics	1947	1987
ISO/TC 63	Glass containers	1947	1987
ISO/TC 65	Manganese and chromium ores	1947	1987
ISO/TC 67	Materials, equipment and offshore structures for petroleum, petrochemical and natural gas industries	1947	1987
ISO/TC 68	Financial services	1948	1987
ISO/TC 69	Applications of statistical methods	1948	1987
ISO/TC 70	Internal combustion engines	1949	1987
ISO/TC 71	Concrete, reinforced concrete and pre-stressed concrete	1949	1987
ISO/TC 72	Textile machinery and accessories	1949	1987
ISO/TC 74	Cement and lime	1950	1987
ISO/TC 76	Transfusion, infusion and injection, and blood processing equipment for medical and pharmaceutical use	1951	1987
ISO/TC 77	Products in fibre reinforced cement	1951	1987
ISO/TC 79	Light metals and their alloys	1953	1987
ISO/TC 81	Common names for pesticides and other agrochemicals	1953	1987

TABLE 2 ISO: Committees (*cont.*)

Reference	Title	Active since	Data available since
ISO/TC 82	Mining	1955	1987
ISO/TC 83	Sports and other recreational facilities and equipment	1955	1987
ISO/TC 84	Devices for administration of medicinal products and catheters	1956	1987
ISO/TC 85	Nuclear energy, nuclear technologies, and radiological protection	1956	1987
ISO/TC 86	Refrigeration and air-conditioning	1957	1987
ISO/TC 87	Cork	1957	1987
ISO/TC 89	Wood-based panels	1957	1987
ISO/TC 91	Surface active agents	1958	1987
ISO/TC 92	Fire safety	1958	1987
ISO/TC 93	Starch (including derivatives and by-products)	1958	1987
ISO/TC 94	Personal safety – Personal protective equipment	1959	1987
ISO/TC 96	Cranes	1960	1987
ISO/TC 98	Bases for design of structures	1960	1987
ISO/TC 100	Chains and chain sprockets for power transmission and conveyors	1960	1987
ISO/TC 101	Continuous mechanical handling equipment	1961	1987
ISO/TC 102	Iron ore and direct reduced iron	1961	1987
ISO/TC 104	Freight containers	1961	1987
ISO/TC 105	Steel wire ropes	1962	1987
ISO/TC 106	Dentistry	1962	1987
ISO/TC 107	Metallic and other inorganic coatings	1962	1987
ISO/TC 108	Mechanical vibration, shock and condition monitoring	1963	1987
ISO/TC 109	Oil and gas burners	1963	1987
ISO/TC 110	Industrial trucks	1963	1987
ISO/TC 111	Round steel link chains, chain slings, components and accessories	1963	1987
ISO/TC 112	Vacuum technology	1964	1987
ISO/TC 113	Hydrometry	1964	1987
ISO/TC 114	Horology	1964	1987
ISO/TC 115	Pumps	1964	1987
ISO/TC 116	Space heating appliances	1964	1987

TABLE 2 ISO: Committees (*cont.*)

Reference	Title	Active since	Data available since
ISO/TC 117	Fans	1964	1987
ISO/TC 118	Compressors and pneumatic tools, machines and equipment	1965	1987
ISO/TC 119	Powder metallurgy	1966	1987
ISO/TC 120	Leather	1966	1987
ISO/TC 121	Anaesthetic and respiratory equipment	1966	1987
ISO/TC 122	Packaging	1966	1987
ISO/TC 123	Plain bearings	1967	1987
ISO/TC 126	Tobacco and tobacco products	1968	1987
ISO/TC 127	Earth-moving machinery	1968	1987
ISO/TC 128	Glass plant, pipeline and fittings	1968	1987
ISO/TC 129	Aluminium ores	1968	1987
ISO/TC 130	Graphic technology	1969	1987
ISO/TC 131	Fluid power systems	1969	1987
ISO/TC 132	Ferroalloys	1969	1987
ISO/TC 133	Clothing sizing systems — size designation, size measurement methods and digital fittings	1969	1987
ISO/TC 134	Fertilizers, soil conditioners and beneficial substances	1969	1987
ISO/TC 135	Non-destructive testing	1969	1987
ISO/TC 136	Furniture	1969	1987
ISO/TC 137	Footwear sizing designations and marking systems	1970	1987
ISO/TC 138	Plastics pipes, fittings and valves for the transport of fluids	1970	1987
ISO/TC 142	Cleaning equipment for air and other gases	1970	1987
ISO/TC 144	Air distribution and air diffusion	1970	1987
ISO/TC 145	Graphical symbols	1970	1987
ISO/TC 146	Air quality	1971	1987
ISO/TC 147	Water quality	1971	1987
ISO/TC 148	Sewing machines	1971	1987
ISO/TC 149	Cycles	1971	1987
ISO/TC 150	Implants for surgery	1971	1987
ISO/TC 152	Gypsum, gypsum plasters and gypsum products	1971	1987
ISO/TC 153	Valves	1971	1987

TABLE 2 ISO: Committees (*cont.*)

Reference	Title	Active since	Data available since
ISO/TC 154	Processes, data elements and documents in commerce, industry and administration	1972	1987
ISO/TC 155	Nickel and nickel alloys	1973	1987
ISO/TC 156	Corrosion of metals and alloys	1974	1987
ISO/TC 157	Non-systemic contraceptives and STI barrier prophylactics	1974	1987
ISO/TC 158	Analysis of gases	1974	1987
ISO/TC 159	Ergonomics	1974	1987
ISO/TC 160	Glass in building	1974	1987
ISO/TC 161	Controls and protective devices for gas and/or oil	1974	1987
ISO/TC 162	Doors, windows and curtain walling	1975	1987
ISO/TC 163	Thermal performance and energy use in the built environment	1975	1987
ISO/TC 164	Mechanical testing of metals	1975	1987
ISO/TC 165	Timber structures	1976	1987
ISO/TC 166	Ceramic ware, glassware and glass ceramic ware in contact with food	1976	1987
ISO/TC 167	Steel and aluminium structures	1977	1987
ISO/TC 168	Prosthetics and orthotics	1977	1987
ISO/TC 170	Surgical instruments	1977	1987
ISO/TC 171	Document management applications	1978	1987
ISO/TC 172	Optics and photonics	1978	1987
ISO/TC 173	Assistive products	1978	1987
ISO/TC 174	Jewellery and precious metals	1978	1987
ISO/TC 175	Fluorspar	1978	1987
ISO/TC 176	Quality management and quality assurance	1979	1987
ISO/TC 177	Caravans	1979	1987
ISO/TC 178	Lifts, escalators and moving walks	1979	1987
ISO/TC 179	Masonry	1980	1987
ISO/TC 180	Solar energy	1980	1987
ISO/TC 181	Safety of toys	1980	1987
ISO/TC 182	Geotechnics	1981	1987
ISO/TC 183	Copper, lead, zinc and nickel ores and concentrates	1983	1987
ISO/TC 184	Automation systems and integration	1983	1987

TABLE 2 ISO: Committees (*cont.*)

Reference	Title	Active since	Data available since
ISO/TC 185	Safety devices for protection against excessive pressure	1983	1987
ISO/TC 186	Cutlery and table and decorative metal hollow-ware	1983	1987
ISO/TC 188	Small craft	1984	1987
ISO/TC 189	Ceramic tile	1985	1987
ISO/TC 190	Soil quality	1985	1987
ISO/TC 191	Animal (mammal) traps	1985	1987
ISO/TC 192	Gas turbines	1988	1988
ISO/TC 193	Natural gas	1988	1988
ISO/TC 194	Biological and clinical evaluation of medical devices	1988	1988
ISO/TC 195	Building construction machinery and equipment	1989	1989
ISO/TC 196	Natural stone	1989	1989
ISO/TC 197	Hydrogen technologies	1990	1990
ISO/TC 198	Sterilization of health care products	1990	1990
ISO/TC 199	Safety of machinery	1991	1991
ISO/TC 201	Surface chemical analysis	1991	1991
ISO/TC 202	Microbeam analysis	1991	1991
ISO/TC 203	Technical energy systems	1991	1991
ISO/TC 204	Intelligent transport systems	1992	1992
ISO/TC 205	Building environment design	1992	1992
ISO/TC 206	Fine ceramics	1992	1992
ISO/TC 207	Environmental management	1993	1993
ISO/TC 208	Thermal turbines for industrial application (steam turbines, gas expansion turbines)	1993	1993
ISO/TC 209	Cleanrooms and associated controlled environments	1993	1993
ISO/TC 210	Quality management and corresponding general aspects for medical devices	1994	1994
ISO/TC 211	Geographic information/Geomatics	1994	1994
ISO/TC 212	Clinical laboratory testing and in vitro diagnostic test systems	1994	1994
ISO/TC 213	Dimensional and geometrical product specifications and verification	1996	1996

TABLE 2 ISO: Committees (*cont.*)

Reference	Title	Active since	Data available since
ISO/TC 214	Elevating work platforms	1996	1996
ISO/TC 215	Health informatics	1998	1998
ISO/TC 216	Footwear	1998	1998
ISO/TC 217	Cosmetics	1998	1998
ISO/TC 218	Timber	1998	1998
ISO/TC 219	Floor coverings	1999	1999
ISO/TC 220	Cryogenic vessels	1999	1999
ISO/TC 221	Geosynthetics	2000	2000
ISO/TC 222	Personal financial planning	2000	2000
ISO/TC 223	Societal security	2000	2000
ISO/TC 224	Service activities relating to drinking water supply, wastewater and stormwater systems	2001	2001
ISO/TC 225	Market, opinion and social research	2002	2002
ISO/TC 226	Materials for the production of primary aluminium	2004	2004
ISO/TC 227	Springs	2004	2004
ISO/TC 228	Tourism and related services	2005	2005
ISO/TC 229	Nanotechnologies	2005	2005
ISO/PC 230	Project Committee: Psychological assessment	2005	2005
ISO/PC 231	Project Committee: Brand valuation	2005	2005
ISO/TC 232	Education and learning services	2007	2007
ISO/PC 233	Project Committee: Cleaning services	2007	2007
ISO/TC 234	Fisheries and aquaculture	2007	2007
ISO/PC 235	Project Committee: Rating services	2007	2007
ISO/PC 236	Project Committee: Project Management	2007	2007
ISO/PC 237	Project committee: Exhibition terminology	2007	2007
ISO/TC 238	Solid biofuels	2007	2007
ISO/PC 239	Project Committee: Network services billing	2007	2007
ISO/PC 240	Product recall	2007	2007
ISO/TC 241	Road traffic safety management systems	2008	2008
ISO/TC 242	Energy Management	2008	2008
ISO/PC 243	Consumer product safety	2008	2008
ISO/TC 244	Industrial furnaces and associated processing equipment	2008	2008
ISO/PC 245	Cross-border trade of second-hand goods	2008	2008
ISO/PC 246	Project committee: Anti-counterfeiting tools	2008	2008

TABLE 2 ISO: Committees (*cont.*)

Reference	Title	Active since	Data available since
ISO/TC 247	Fraud countermeasures and controls	2008	2008
ISO/PC 248	Sustainability criteria for bioenergy	2008	2008
ISO/TC 249	Traditional Chinese medicine	2009	2009
ISO/PC 250	Project committee: Sustainability in event management	2009	2009
ISO/TC 251	Asset management	2010	2010
ISO/PC 252	Natural gas fuelling stations for vehicles	2010	2010
ISO/PC 253	Treated wastewater re-use for irrigation	2010	2010
ISO/TC 254	Safety of amusement rides and amusement devices	2010	2010
ISO/TC 255	Biogas	2010	2010
ISO/TC 256	Pigments, dyestuffs and extenders	2010	2010
ISO/TC 257	Evaluation of energy savings	2010	2010
ISO/TC 258	Project, programme and portfolio management	2011	2011
ISO/PC 259	Outsourcing	2011	2011
ISO/TC 260	Human resource management	2011	2011
ISO/TC 261	Additive manufacturing	2011	2011
ISO/TC 262	Risk management	2011	2011
ISO/TC 263	Coalbed methane (CBM)	2011	2011
ISO/TC 264	Fireworks	2011	2011
ISO/TC 265	Carbon dioxide capture, transportation, and geo-logical storage	2011	2011
ISO/TC 266	Biomimetics	2011	2011
ISO/TC 267	Facility management	2011	2011
ISO/TC 268	Sustainable cities and communities	2012	2012
ISO/TC 269	Railway applications	2012	2012
ISO/TC 270	Plastics and rubber machines	2012	2012
ISO/PC 271	Compliance management systems	2012	2012
ISO/TC 272	Forensic sciences	2012	2012
ISO/PC 273	Customer contact centres	2012	2012
ISO/TC 274	Light and lighting	2012	2012
ISO/TC 275	Sludge recovery, recycling, treatment and disposal	2013	2013
ISO/TC 276	Biotechnology	2013	2013
ISO/PC 277	Sustainable procurement	2013	2013
ISO/PC 278	Anti-bribery management systems	2013	2013
ISO/TC 279	Innovation management	2013	2013

TABLE 2 ISO: Committees (*cont.*)

Reference	Title	Active since	Data available since
ISO/PC 280	Management consultancy	2013	2013
ISO/TC 281	Fine bubble technology	2013	2013
ISO/TC 282	Water reuse	2013	2013
ISO/TC 283	Occupational health and safety management	2013	2013
ISO/PC 284	Management system for private security operations — Requirements with guidance	2013	2013
ISO/TC 285	Clean cookstoves and clean cooking solutions	2013	2013
ISO/TC 286	Collaborative business relationship management	2013	2013
ISO/TC 287	Sustainable processes for wood and wood-based products	2013	2013
ISO/PC 288	Educational organizations management systems — Requirements with guidance for use	2013	2013
ISO/TC 289	Brand evaluation	2014	2014
ISO/PC 290	Online reputation	2014	2014
ISO/TC 291	Domestic gas cooking appliances	2014	2014
ISO/TC 292	Security and resilience	2014	2014
ISO/TC 293	Feed machinery	2014	2014
ISO/PC 294	Guidance on unit pricing	2015	2015
ISO/TC 295	Audit data services	2015	2015
ISO/TC 296	Bamboo and rattan	2015	2015
ISO/TC 297	Waste collection and transportation management	2015	2015
ISO/TC 298	Rare earth	2015	2015
ISO/TC 299	Robotics	2015	2015
ISO/TC 300	Solid Recovered Fuels	2015	2015
ISO/TC 301	Energy management and energy savings	2015	2015
ISO/PC 302	Guidelines for auditing management systems	2015	2015
ISO/PC 303	Guidelines on consumer warranties and guarantees	2015	2015
ISO/TC 304	Healthcare organization management	2015	2015
ISO/PC 305	Sustainable non-sewered sanitation systems	2015	2015
ISO/TC 306	Foundry machinery	2016	2016
ISO/TC 307	Blockchain and distributed ledger technologies	2016	2016
ISO/PC 308	Chain of custody — General terminology and models	2016	2016
ISO/TC 309	Governance of organizations	2016	2016
ISO/PC 310	Wheeled child conveyances	2016	2016

TABLE 2 ISO: Committees (*cont.*)

Reference	Title	Active since	Data available since
ISO/PC 311	Vulnerable consumers	2017	2017
ISO/TC 312	Excellence in service	2017	2017
ISO/TC 313	Packaging machinery	2017	2017
ISO/TC 314	Ageing societies	2017	2017
ISO/PC 315	Indirect, temperature-controlled refrigerated delivery services — land transport of parcels with intermediate transfer	2018	2018
ISO/PC 316	Water efficient products — Rating	2018	2018
ISO/PC 317	Consumer protection: privacy by design for consumer goods and services	2018	2018
ISO/PC 318	Community scale resource oriented sanitation treatment systems	2018	2018
ISO/TC 319	Karst	2018	2018
ISO/TC 321	Transaction assurance in E-commerce	2018	2018
ISO/TC 322	Sustainable finance	2018	2018
ISO/TC 323	Circular economy	2018	2018
ISO/TC 324	Sharing economy	2019	2019
ISO/PC 325	Sex toys — Design and safety requirements for products in direct contact with genitalia, the anus, or both	2019	2019

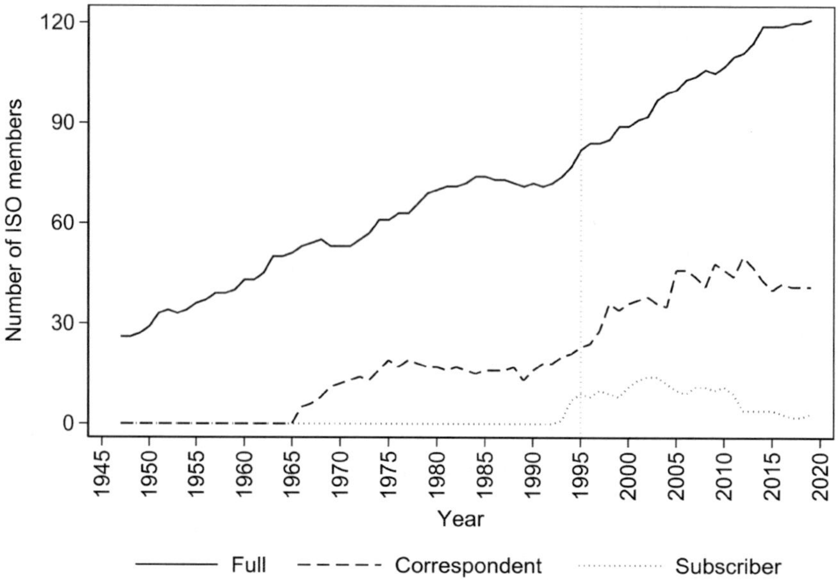

FIGURE 22 ISO membership, 1947–2019
AUTHOR'S ILLUSTRATION

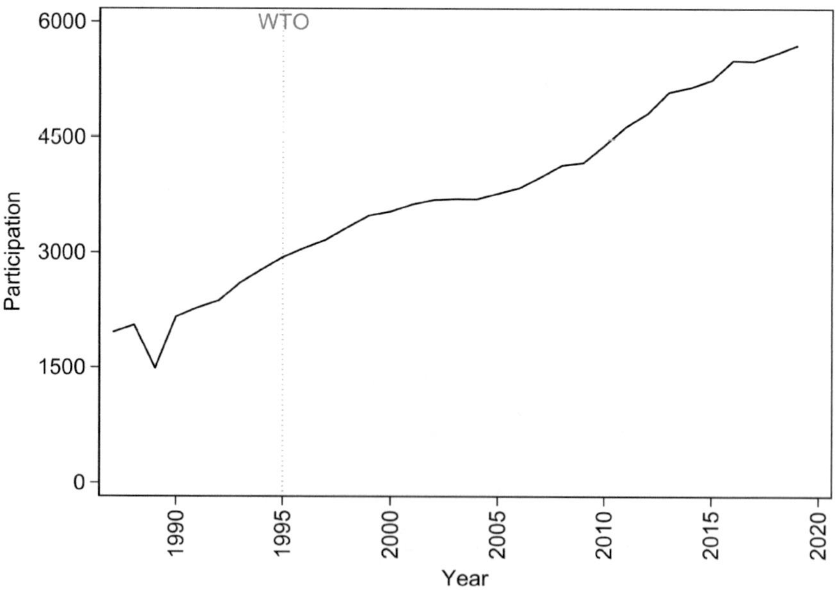

FIGURE 23 ISO member participation, 1947–2019
AUTHOR'S ILLUSTRATION

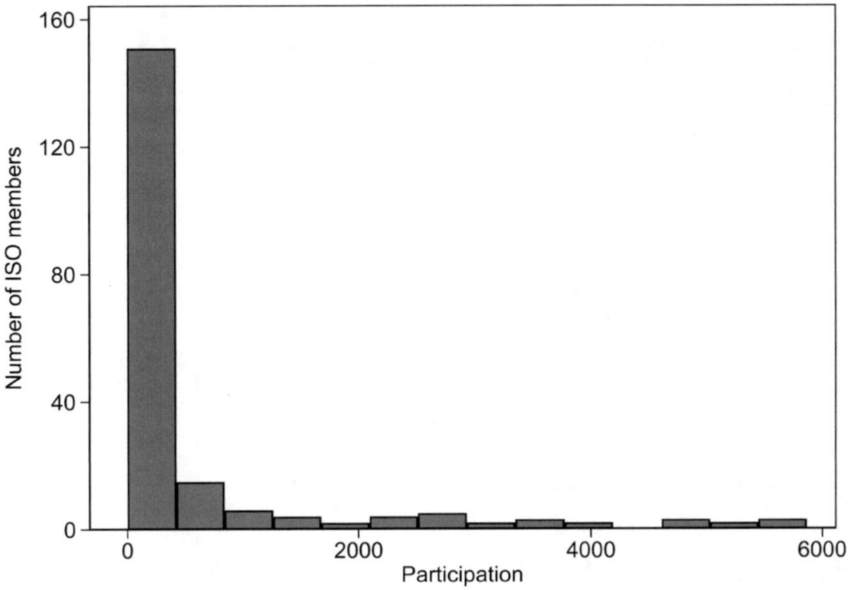

FIGURE 24 Distribution of ISO member participation, 1987–2019
AUTHOR'S ILLUSTRATION

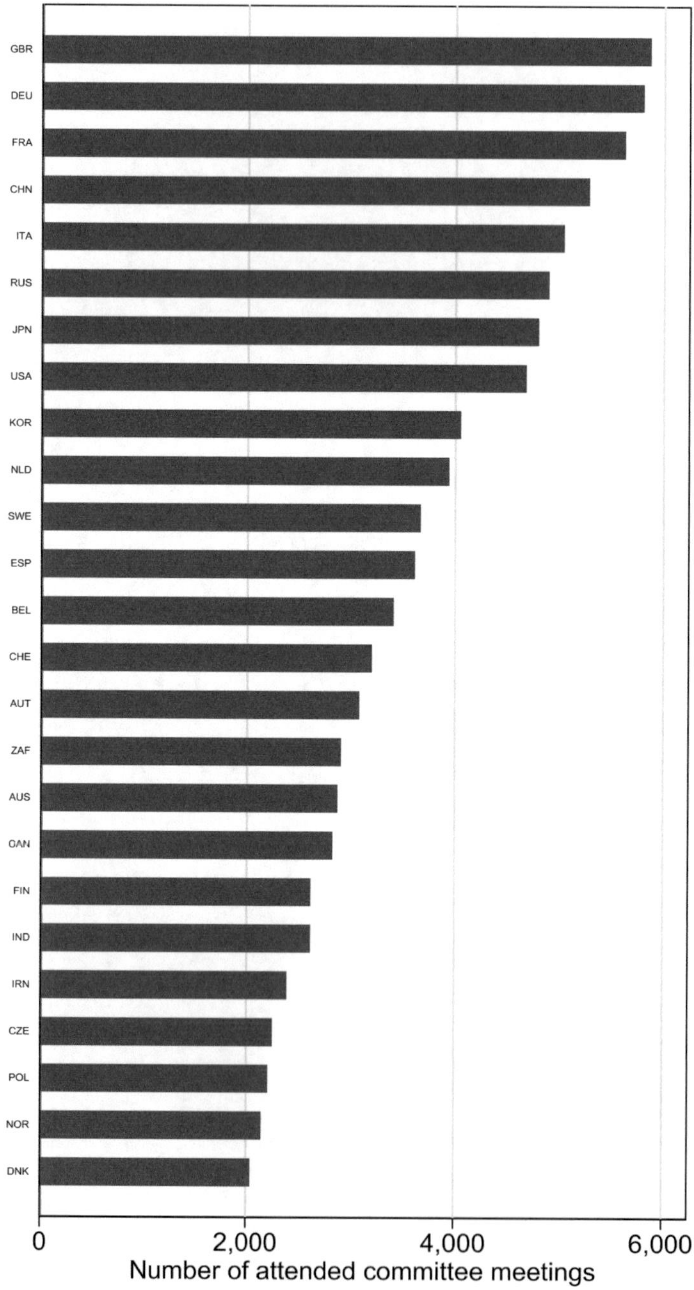

FIGURE 25 ISO member participation (top 25), 1987–2019
AUTHOR'S ILLUSTRATION

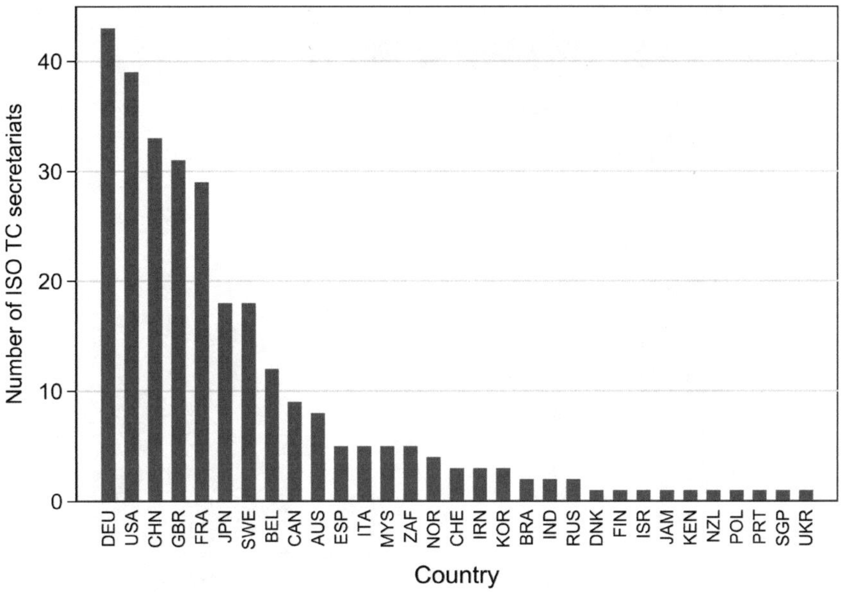

FIGURE 26 ISO technical committee secretariats, August 2020
AUTHOR'S ILLUSTRATION

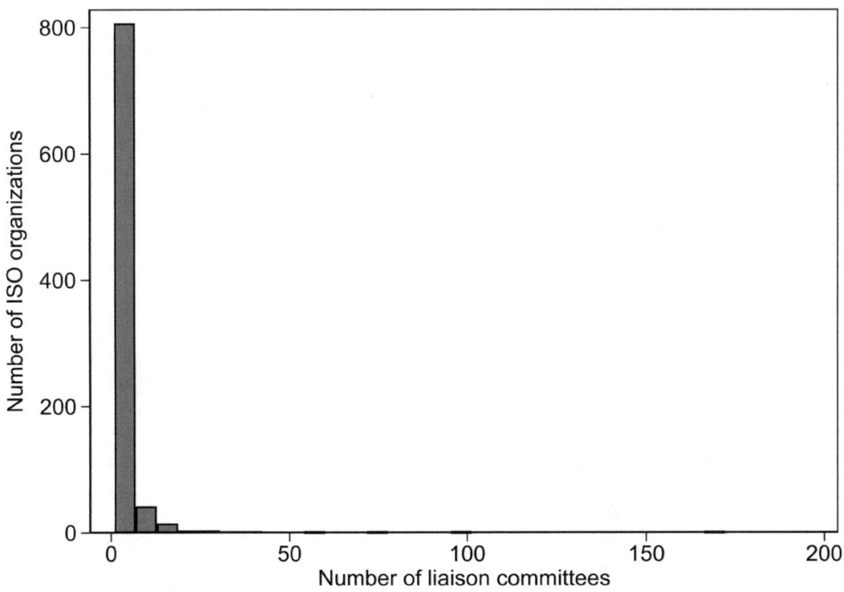

FIGURE 27 Distribution of ISO cooperation organization liaisons, July 2019
AUTHOR'S ILLUSTRATION

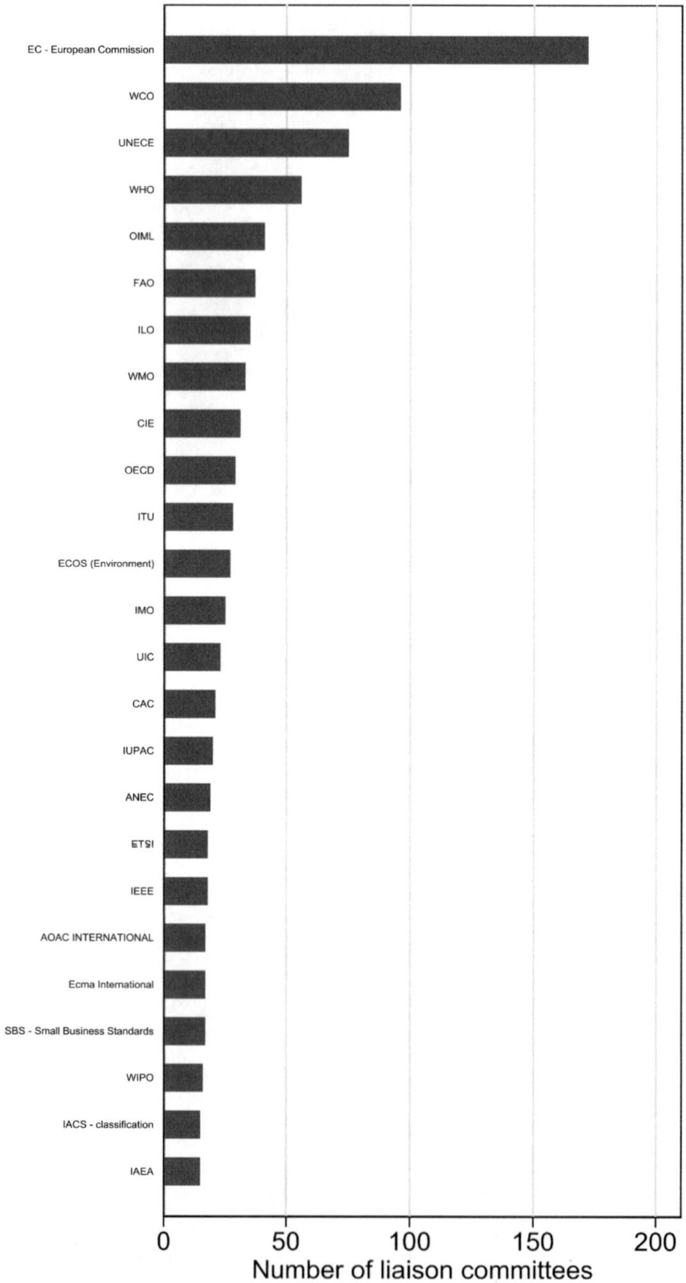

FIGURE 28 ISO cooperation organization liaisons (top 25), July 2019
AUTHOR'S ILLUSTRATION

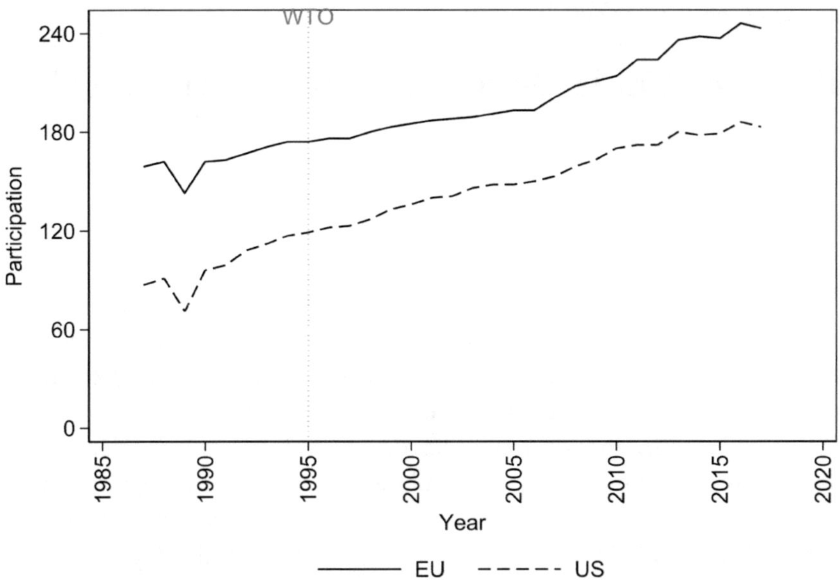

FIGURE 29 ISO participation, EU vs US
AUTHOR'S ILLUSTRATION

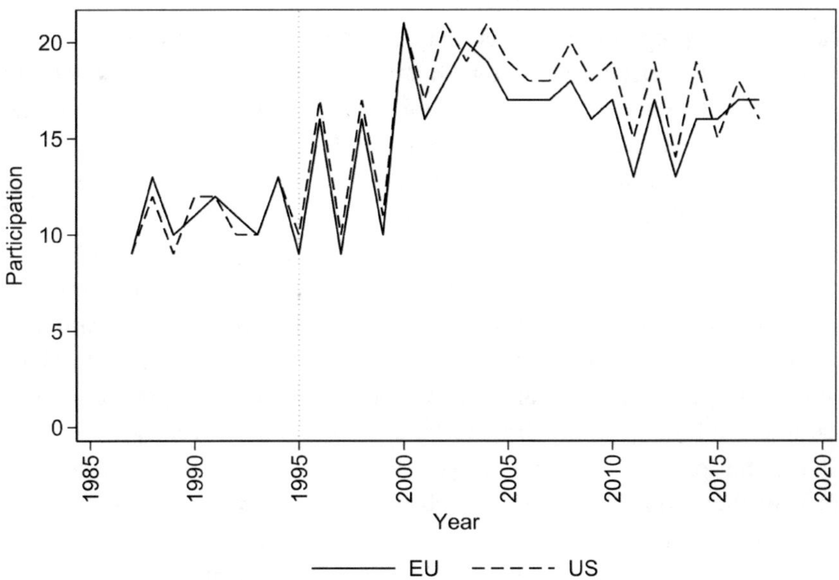

FIGURE 30 Codex participation, EU vs US
AUTHOR'S ILLUSTRATION

CHAPTER 4

Multilateral Trade Agreements and International Standardization

This Chapter explores the linkage between the multilateral trade policy regime and the international standardization regime, and posits that the institutional design of multilateral trade agreements affects countries' participation in international standardization organizations. The institutional design of multilateral trade agreements is the independent variable of interest, and countries' participation in international standardization organizations is the dependent variable of interest. Empirically, the multilateral trade policy regime is represented by the World Trade Organization's (WTO) Agreement on Technical Barriers to Trade (TBT Agreement) and the Agreement on the Application of Sanitary and Phytosanitary Measures (SPS Agreement). The international standardization regime is empirically represented by the two international standardization organizations Codex Alimentarius (Codex) and the International Organization for Standardization (ISO).

The principal proposition of this Chapter is the following. In a world characterized by international regulatory heterogeneity, firms face considerable adjustment costs when exporting to other countries. International standards can help to reduce these costs and allow compliant firms to reap benefits associated with better comparability, lower transaction costs, and economies of scale. However, international standards can also function as strategic tools and competitive devices for industrial promotion with which actors can exploit the presence of asymmetric information and organizational differences. Indeed, since technological innovation usually precedes standardization, different previously existing standards compete for becoming the international standard to which harmonization will take place. This may result in adjustment costs and conflicts of interest of the distributional consequences of those costs. As a result, internationally active firms as well as governments which represent the interests of their domestic firms, have strong incentives to actively influences international standard-setting processes in order to shape the design of standards in their economic and political interests. This incentive is even stronger if certain international standards are likely to become the basis for future regulations. Indeed, while compliance with international standards is *de jure* voluntary, compliance may become *de facto* legally binding if the international standards are incorporated into laws and regulations. In short, the legalization of international standards is expected to increase actors' incentives to participate in the relevant international standardization organizations even further.

To explore this argument further, this Chapter focuses on the WTO's TBT and SPS Agreements, and their respective relationship with the international standardization organizations ISO and Codex. The TBT Agreement aims to ensure that technical regulations, standards, and conformity assessment procedures are non-discriminatory and do not create unnecessary obstacles to trade. The SPS Agreement covers all measures whose purpose is to protect human, animal, and plant life or health from pests or diseases, and aims to ensure that such measures do not constitute disguised restrictions on international trade. What is common in both Agreements is that they strongly encourage WTO members to base their national TBT and SPS measures on international standards. Measures that are based on international standards benefit from the presumption of conformity with the TBT and SPS Agreements and therefore provide safe legal harbourage in WTO disputes. A key difference between the two Agreements is that the SPS Agreement explicitly endorses Codex as the relevant international organization to develop food safety-related international standards upon which national SPS measures are to be based.[1] The TBT Agreement, by contrast, is less explicit in its endorsement of a standardizing body but arguably gives a certain preference to ISO.[2]

The objective of this Chapter is to explore these differences in the institutional design of the TBT and SPS Agreements, and the consequences for countries' incentives to participate in ISO and Codex, respectively. In line with the principal argument outlined above, it is expected that the legalization of Codex standards through the SPS Agreement increases countries' political and economic stakes in Codex standards, limits countries' ability to engage in forum-shopping and/or regime shifting, and ultimately increases countries' incentives to participate more in the standard-setting processes of Codex. By

1 The International Office of Epizootics (OIE) is responsible for the development of international standards, guidelines and recommendations for animal health and zoonoses. The Secretariat of the International Plant Protection Convention (IPPC) in cooperation with regional organizations operating within the framework of the International Plant Protection Convention is responsible for the development of international standards, guidelines and recommendations for plant health. With regards to the SPS Agreement, this chapter focuses on Codex and not on the OIE and the IPPC.

2 Other relevant standard-setting organizations for the TBT Agreement include the International Electrotechnical Commission (IEC), the International Telecommunication Union (ITU), and Codex.

contrast, since ISO is not explicitly endorsed in the TBT Agreement, the positive effect of the TBT Agreement on countries' incentives to participate in ISO is expected to be more subdued.

This Chapter is organized as follows. Section 4.1 provides a brief introduction into the TBT and SPS Agreements, and their respective relationship with ISO and Codex. An overview of the existing literature on this topic is presented in Section 4.2. Section 4.3 outlines the principal hypotheses of this Chapter. The data and methodology employed to explore these hypotheses are described in Section 4.4. Section 4.5 presents the empirical results, and Section 4.6 concludes this Chapter.

4.1 Introduction

During and shortly after the end of World War II, the allied nations began to negotiate the architecture of the *post*-war international economy. At the Bretton Woods conference in 1944, the International Bank for Reconstruction and Development (IBRD), commonly known as the World Bank, and the International Monetary Fund (IMF) were established. The negotiation of an agreement on international trade proved to be more difficult but was eventually concluded in 1947 (Jansen et al., 2020).

The General Agreement on Tariffs and Trade (GATT) was signed by 23 countries in Geneva in 1947, and came into force in 1948. The members recognized "that their relations in the field of trade and economic endeavour should be conducted with a view to raising standards of living, ensuring full employment and a large and steadily growing volume of real income and effective demand, developing the full use of the resources of the world and expanding the production and exchange of goods" (GATT, 1947, p. 1).

To contribute to these objectives, the 23 members entered "into reciprocal and mutually advantageous arrangements directed to the substantial reduction of tariffs and other barriers to trade and to the elimination of discriminatory treatment in international commerce" (GATT, 1947, p. 1). The initial GATT negotiations meet the definition of "multilateral" in the sense that three or more parties were involved but do not necessarily correspond to what are understood to be multilateral trade negotiations today. Nonetheless, the GATT became "more multilateral" over time as an increasing number of parties joined in the course of the eight negotiation rounds (Figure 31).

Until the late 1960s, the GATT negotiations focused primarily on tariff concessions. With the beginning of the Tokyo Round in 1973, negotiators began

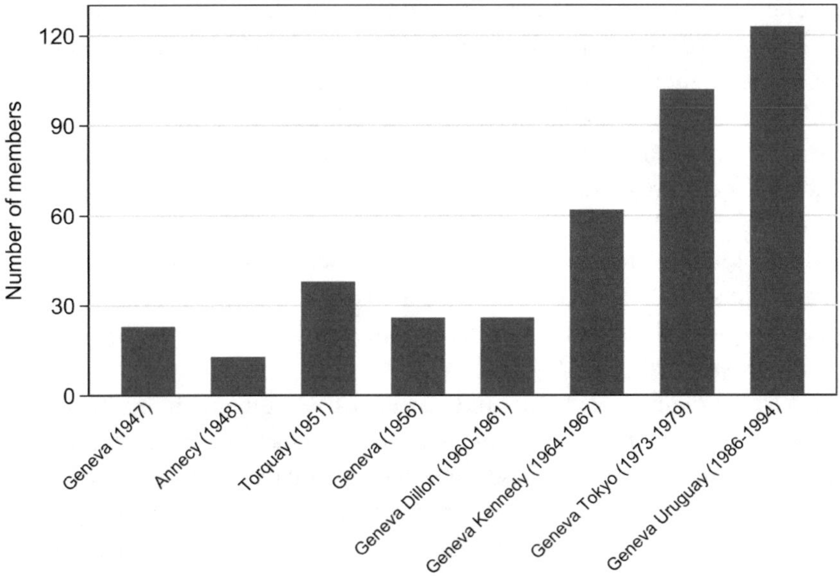

FIGURE 31 Negotiation rounds of the GATT, 1947–1994
AUTHOR'S ILLUSTRATION BASED ON WTO (2020)

to discuss non-tariff measures (NTMs)[3] NTMs are generally defined as policy measures other than ordinary customs tariffs that can potentially have an economic effect on international trade in goods, changing quantities traded, or prices or both (UNCTAD, 2019). Amongst other Agreements, or so-called "Codes", the Tokyo Round resulted in the Agreement of Technical Barriers to Trade, the Arrangement regarding Bovine Meat, and the International Dairy Arrangement. The former Agreement presented a blueprint for the Uruguay Round TBT Agreement, the latter two Arrangements cover products that would later fall under the Uruguay Round SPS Agreement.

Between 1986 and 1994, the GATT members negotiated a wide range of topics in the Uruguay Round, which resulted in the Marrakesh Declaration, and the creation of the World Trade Organization (WTO) as the successor of the

3 See Aisbett and Silberberger (2021) for a study on the relationship between tariff liberalization and the notification of sanitary and phytosanitary measures to the World Trade Organization, Cadot et al. (2015) for a study on the effect of NTM harmonization on international trade flows, Santeramo and Lamonaca (2022) for a study on the effects of trade agreements' sanitary and phytosanitary measures on international trade ows, and Ghodsi and Stehrer (2022) for a study on the relationship between NTMs and the quality of imported products.

GATT. The establishment of the WTO is widely regarded as the beginning of a new phase in the institutionalization and legalization of international trade policy (Abbott, 1997, 2000; Abbott and Snidal, 2000; Goldstein and Martin, 2000; Ansell and Vogel, 2006; Shaffer and Pollack, 2013).

With the creation of the WTO, the multilateral trading system extended into several new areas, notably trade in services and intellectual property. The Marrakesh Declaration also concluded the long-standing negotiations on agriculture, textiles, trade-related investment measures, anti-dumping, rules of origin, subsidies and countervailing measures, and safeguards. The two Uruguay Agreements that are of particular interest in this Chapter are the TBT and SPS Agreements.

The TBT Agreement extends and clarifies the Agreement on Technical Barriers to Trade reached in the Tokyo Round. It seeks to ensure that technical negotiations and standards, as well as testing and certification procedures, do not create unnecessary obstacles to trade. However, the TBT Agreement also recognizes that WTO members have the right to establish protection, at levels they consider appropriate, for example for human, animal, or plant life or health, or the environment, and should not be prevented from taking measures necessary to ensure those levels of protection are met. The TBT Agreement therefore encourages WTO members to use international standards where these are appropriate, but it does not require them to change their levels of protection as a result of standardization. The TBT Agreement, in comparison to the Tokyo Round Standards Code, also covers processing and production methods related to the characteristics of the product itself. The coverage of conformity assessment procedures is enlarged and the disciplines made more precise. Notification provisions applying to local government and non-governmental bodies are elaborated in more detail than in the Tokyo Round Agreement. A Code of Good Practice for the Preparation, Adoption and Application of Standards by standardizing bodies, which is open to acceptance by private sector bodies as well as the public sector, is included as an annex to the TBT Agreement. (WTO, 2020b)

The SPS Agreement concerns the application of sanitary and phytosanitary measures — in other words food safety, animal, and plant health regulations. The SPS Agreement recognizes that WTO members have the right to take sanitary and phytosanitary measures but that they should be applied only to the extent necessary to protect human, animal or plant life or health and should not arbitrarily or unjustifiably discriminate between members where identical or similar conditions prevail. In order to harmonize sanitary and phytosanitary measures on as wide a basis as possible, WTO members are encouraged to base their measures on international standards, guidelines and recommendations where they exist. However, WTO members may maintain or introduce measures which result in higher standards if there is scientific justification or as a consequence of consistent risk decisions based on an appropriate risk assessment. The SPS Agreement spells out procedures and criteria for the assessment of risk and the determination of appropriate levels of sanitary or phytosanitary protection. It is expected that WTO members would accept the sanitary and phytosanitary measures of others as equivalent if the exporting country demonstrates to the importing country that its measures achieve the importing country's appropriate level of health protection. (WTO, 2020a)

There is a large body of legal literature that analyses and compares the TBT and SPS Agreements (Pauwelyn, 2006; Marceau and Trachtman, 2014; Delimatsis, 2015c) and, in particular, the role of international standards in both Agreements (Schroder, 2009, 2011; Wouters and Geraets, 2012; Villarreal, 2018). The following Sections briefly outline the historical context, the design, and the consequences of the TBT and SPS Agreements as they are discussed in the existing literature.

4.2 Literature and Research Gap

4.2.1 *The WTO SPS Agreement and Codex*

4.2.1.1 Context

The SPS Agreement has been described as "the biggest single step in the history of the globalization of food standards" (Braithwaite and Drahos, 2000, p. 403), "so significant that [it] will not only change the rules of the game, [it] will revolutionize the game itself" (Thiermann, 1997, p. 2). Much of this characterization is due to the Agreement's role in the highly politicized GATT/WTO dispute settlement cases on growth hormone-treated beef between the European Union (EU) on one side, and the United States (US) and Canada on the other side (Naiki, 2009). Some observers even argue that the SPS Agreement itself was initiated by the US as a response to the advancing integration of the EU (Trachtman, 2003) and out of frustration with the GATT's inability to address US concerns about the EU's ban of growth hormone-treated beef introduced in 1989 (Braithwaite and Drahos, 2000).

Nonetheless, during the early stages of the GATT Uruguay Round the SPS negotiations were actually regarded as a "sleeper issue" (Davis, 2003, p. 328) in which many actors, including the EU, lost interest early on (Büthe, 2008). Indeed, many countries focused their efforts on the more intense agricultural negotiations, which were expected to lead to significant cuts in agricultural tariffs, quotas, and subsidies (Stanton, 1997, 2004; Croome, 1999; Jansen, 2012a,b).

The SPS Agreement was envisaged to protect and extend the degree of trade liberalization that was achieved by the agriculture negotiations by making sure that governments would not use other means, such as SPS measures, to restrict import competition (Stanton, 1997; Thiermann, 1997; Roberts, 1998; Marceau and Trachtman, 2014). Furthermore, the SPS Agreement was supposed to provide more legal clarity and enforcement on a number of disputes brought under the GATT, in which countries were accused of introducing protectionist SPS measures in response to consumer and other pressures (Croome, 1999; Jansen, 2012a,b). In particular the case of the EC Animal Hormones Directive (85/649/EEC; GD/175) between the then-European Economic Community (EEC) and the US is argued to have been an important impetus for the SPS negotiations (Braithwaite and Drahos, 2000).

4.2.1.2 Actors and Interests

The Uruguay Round SPS negotiations took place in the Working Group on Sanitary and Phytosanitary Regulations and Barriers, which was a subcommittee of the Agricultural Negotiation Group. While the formal meetings were open to all GATT members, the “inner core” group of countries included Australia, Canada, the Nordic countries led by Finland, the EU, and the US. Argentina, Japan and New Zealand were part of the larger core but, overall, less involved in the negotiations. (Braithwaite and Drahos, 2000; Skogstad, 2001; Büthe, 2008, 2009) Another important actor was the so-called Cairns Group, formed in 1986 to promote agricultural trade liberalization (Veggeland and Borgen, 2005), and informally represented by Australia (Büthe, 2009). By some accounts, the Cairns Group wrote around 40% of the SPS Agreement (Braithwaite and Drahos, 2000).

The negotiators agreed early on the scope of the SPS Agreement and that it should cover food safety, animal health protection, and plant protection (Stanton, 1997). Of course, however, there were also more controversially debated topics. For the US it was a priority that SPS measures are scientifically justified and that countries recognize other countries’ standards if these provide substantially equivalent levels of safety (Croome, 1999). More broadly, the US wanted an obligatory and enforceable SPS Agreement to finally address issues such as the previously mentioned GATT dispute on animal hormones (Skogstad, 2001; Braithwaite and Drahos, 2000). The EU attempted to include animal welfare, environmental concerns linked to agricultural production, and consumer concerns in the SPS Agreement (Stanton, 1997). Furthermore, the EU was in favour of consultation and notification arrangements similar to those under the Tokyo Round Standards Code as well as countries’ ability to apply SPS measures more stringent than those agreed internationally

(Croome, 1999). The EU and the US agreed that SPS measures should be based on "sound science" but disagreed on the legitimacy of the criteria to justify SPS measures, the adoption of the precautionary principle, and the party with the burden of proving the legitimacy of a certain SPS measure in the absence of an internationally agreed standard (Skogstad, 2001). The latter item was also a priority of the Cairns Group (Jansen, 2012b).

While there was broad agreement that SPS measures should be based on internationally agreed standards, it was clear that the WTO did not have the expertise to develop these standards itself (Büthe, 2008). The debate quickly focused on four potential international standardization organizations: Codex, ISO, the United Nations Economic Commission for Europe (UNECE), and the Organisation for Economic Co-operation and Development (OECD). The EU sought to endorse the UNECE and/or the OECD. While this position was not opposed by the inner core, developing countries were strongly against either of the organizations to be referenced in the SPS Agreement (Büthe, 2009).

The decision between ISO and Codex was more complex. ISO enjoyed the support of the European and Nordic countries as well as by some members of the Cairns Group and developing countries. The European and Nordic countries had been active and influential members of ISO for decades (See Chapter 3). ISO was also regarded as a legitimate choice because it was already noted as an international standardization organization in the Tokyo Round Standards Code. (Büthe, 2009) The US, by contrast, was in favour of explicitly endorsing Codex in the SPS Agreement (Drezner, 2007; Büthe, 2009). The choice of Codex was supported by one of its parent organizations — the Food and Agriculture Organization of the United Nations (FAO) (See Chapter 3) — which was actively involved in the agriculture and SPS negotiations (Büthe, 2009; Margulis, 2018). The FAO managed to generate support among developing countries by linking Codex to FAO development and technical assistance. Furthermore, Codex representatives actively sought to de-legitimate ISO as an alternative choice by arguing that, as a non-governmental organization, it is dominated by private interests (Büthe, 2009). Ultimately, it was the active lobbying of the FAO and Codex as well as EU (US) negotiators' insufficient (detailed) knowledge of the Codex procedures that are argued to have paved the way for the explicit reference to Codex (Büthe, 2009).[4] Indeed, as discussed in further detail below, the US was well aware that, in the absence of consensus, Codex standards such as on growth hormone-treated beef could be adopted

4 To some degree, this process may also be regarded as an example of what Margulis (2021) calls *intervention*.

with a simple majority in Codex whereas ISO requires large super-majorities (Büthe, 2009) (See Chapter 3).

This historical account lends support to both a rational choice institutionalism and historical institutionalism view of the world. On the one hand, path dependency and institutional context appear to have shaped actors' preferences. The US' preferences on the institutional design of the SPS Agreement, for instance, were clearly influenced by previous events such as the EU ban on hormone-treated meat. On the other hand, this historical account suggests that the US did indeed attempt to influence the institutional design of the SPS Agreement in a rational way to further their own goals. Finally, the EU's insufficient understanding of Codex's procedures, and the associated consequences, speaks to the concept of bounded rationality. As will become clearer in the next Sections, the WTO SPS Agreement certainly presented a critical juncture that, to a certain extent, locked-in actors to Codex standards and that led to unintended consequences — in particular for the EU.

An advanced draft of the SPS Agreement was completed and circulated among the Uruguay Round countries by the end of 1990 (Croome, 1999; Büthe, 2008). By the late 1980s, Codex members already knew that the international standardization organization would be referenced in the SPS Agreement (Victor, 2004). Indeed, even prior to the conclusion of the Uruguay Round, legal scholars already published on Codex's new role within the WTO system (Rosman, 1993).

4.2.1.3 Design

The SPS Agreement can be regarded as an Agreement with a relatively high degree of legalization as it is characterized by obligation, precision, and delegation (Abbott et al., 2000). Obligation means that states or other actors are legally bound by a rule or commitment. Precision refers to rules that unambiguously define the conduct they require, authorize, or proscribe. Delegation means that third parties have been granted authority to implement, interpret, and apply the rules; to resolve disputes; and possible make further rules. (Abbott et al., 2000)

With regard to obligation, Article 3.1 of the SPS Agreement states that "[t]o harmonize sanitary and phytosanitary measures on as wide a basis as possible, [WTO] Members **shall** base their sanitary or phytosanitary measures on international standards, guidelines or recommendations, where they exist, except as otherwise provided for in this Agreement [...]" (emphasis added). With regard to precision and delegation, Annex A.3.3 adds that "for food safety, the standards, guidelines and recommendations [are to be] established by the **Codex Alimentarius Commission** [...]" (emphasis added). The International Office of

Epizootics (OIE) and the International Plant Protection Convention (IPPC) are referenced to set the standards relating to animal health and zoonoses, and to plant health, respectively. Among the three organizations mentioned in the SPS Agreement, Codex is argued to be the one most affected by the explicit endorsement by the WTO (Stewart and Johanson, 1998; Braithwaite and Drahos, 2000; Alemanno, 2007).

4.2.1.4 Consequences

In the political science and international relations literature, the SPS Agreement is understood as a case of delegation (Bradley and Kelley, 2008; Büthe, 2008, 2009, 2015), orchestration (Abbott et al., 2015; Elsig, 2015), regulatory outsourcing (Delimatsis, 2015b), and/or a regulatory border shift (Dupont and Elsig, 2017). The legalization (Abbott et al., 2000) of Codex is widely argued to have altered the legal authority of Codex standards (Ansell and Vogel, 2006; Livermore, 2006; Avant et al., 2010; Prakash and Potoski, 2010), and upgraded them from *de jure* voluntary standards to *de facto* legally binding standards (Veggeland and Borgen, 2005; Arcuri, 2015; Delimatsis, 2015a) with hard law characteristics (Abbott and Snidal, 2000; Büthe, 2008; Shaffer and Pollack, 2013).[5] As one observer notes, "[i]t is uncontested that the WTO has contributed to the transformation of Codex from a rather obscure standard-setting institution into a powerful global regulatory agency in the field of food safety" (Arcuri, 2015, p. 79).

For the purposes of the SPS Agreement, a standard is considered as adopted by all Codex members as soon as it has been approved by the Codex Alimentarius Commission (CAC) (See Chapter 3). In contrast, prior to the SPS Agreement countries had to formally accept standards. (Victor, 2004) As a result of the SPS Agreement and its explicit reference to Codex, Codex standards are now considered as *the* benchmark for international food standards (Dawson, 1995, 1997; Braithwaite and Drahos, 2000; Boutrif, 2003; Poli, 2004; Post, 2005, 2006; Smythe, 2009; Pernet, 2015). The presumption of conformance with the SPS Agreement also means that Codex standards are considered as a safe harbourage in WTO disputes (Garrett et al., 1998; Horton, 2001).

The legalization of Codex by the WTO is not only argued to have affected its standards but also transformed the organization itself (Arcuri, 2015). The SPS Agreement is claimed, for instance, to have established a more science-based regime of risk analysis in Codex (Winickoff and Bushey, 2009). At the same time, however, the Codex negotiations are argued to have shifted focus from health

5 Fontanelli (2011) presents one of the few studies, if not the only study, that questions this literature consensus.

to trade considerations (Lee, 2005; Lin, 2011). Previous research also points out that, as a consequence of the SPS Agreement, Codex has moved from a logic of appropriateness to a logic of consequences (Veggeland and Borgen, 2005), and from technical-scientific collaboration to political-strategic behaviour (Büthe and Harris, 2011). Indeed, in the literature the SPS Agreement is widely argued to have led to a politicization of Codex (Braithwaite and Drahos, 2000; Victor, 2004; Veggeland and Borgen, 2005; Büthe, 2008, 2009, 2015; Smythe, 2009; Clapp and Fuchs, 2009; Fuchs and Kalfagianni, 2010). While claims that Codex standard-setting processes have become "trade battlegrounds and forums for deregulation" (Silverglade, 2000, p. 521) are the exception, existing research does associate *post*-1995 Codex with regulatory protectionism (Sykes, 1999), regulatory capture (Victor, 2000; Roberts et al., 2004), regulatory capitalism (Levi-Faur, 2005), and regulatory globalization (Demortain, 2015).

Since the SPS Agreement strongly encourages WTO members to base their national measures on the international standards developed by Codex, the Agreement has certainly increased actors' economic and political stakes (Stewart and Johanson, 1998; Smythe, 2009; Pollack and Shaffer, 2009; Büthe and Harris, 2011; Büthe, 2008, 2009, 2015). As a consequence, it has become harder for countries to agree on Codex standards (Braithwaite and Drahos, 2000; Victor, 2000; Sklair, 2002; Livermore, 2006; Alemanno, 2007; Smythe, 2009; Clapp and Fuchs, 2009; Fuchs and Kalfagianni, 2010). The 14 year long negotiations to find mutually acceptable guidelines on labelling genetically modified food (Smythe, 2009) or the 17 year long development of a Framework for Risk Analysis (Demortain, 2012) present examples that illustrate the increased difficulty to find consensus. One infamous case that illustrates the consequences of the SPS Agreement and its explicit reference to Codex is the so-called Beef Hormone Controversy between the EU and the US. The controversy received considerable attention in the literature (Vogel, 1995; Stewart and Johanson, 1998; Rountree, 1999; Mavroidis, 2003; Johnson, 2015; Veggeland, 2015; Veggeland and Sørbye, 2015). The Box below adds to this literature by outlining the detailed timeline in which events unfolded.[6]

Box: Beef Hormone Controversy

Due to increasing consumer pressures, notably from the European Consumer Organisation (BEUC), the European Commission enacted a ban on the production and importation of meat derived from animals treated with growth-promoting hormones in 1981 (European Council,

6 Details on how countries voted can be found in Chapter 3.

1981). Supported by the European Parliament (European Parliament, 1987), the ban went into effect in 1989.

For major meat exporters such as Argentina, Australia, and Brazil, the ban was of limited importance because they did not use growth-promoting hormones in their meat production. By contrast, 90% of US meat exports to the EU relied on growth-promoting hormones. (Vogel, 1995)

The US unsuccessfully attempted to resolve the issue under the GATT (EC Animal Hormones Directive; 85/649/EEC; GD/175). Simultaneously, the topic was already debated intensely during the first meeting of the Codex Committee on Residues of Veterinary Drugs in Foods (CCRVDF) in Washington, DC in October 1986. The EU reiterated its concern about growth-promoting hormones in beef also during the 17th CAC in 1987 and the 19th CAC in 1991 in Rome. It was around that time that the US pushed in the GATT Uruguay Round to include Codex as the relevant standard-setting body for food safety in the SPS Agreement.

The SPS Agreement came into force on 1 January 1995. Only six months after, during the 21st CAC meeting in July 1995 in Rome, the US was determined to resolve the issue. The CAC was split into two groups regarding the adoption of "Draft Maximum Residue Limits (MRLs) for 5 Growth Hormones at Step 8" (See Chapter 3 for details on the 8-step process). One group of countries, including the US, was in favour of adopting the MRLs without further delay. The other group of countries, including many European countries, was in favour of adjourning the debate.

As no consensus was achieved, a vote on the adjournment was held in which 28 countries, including many European countries, voted in favour of adjournment, 31 countries, including the US, voted against adjournment, and five countries abstained.

The majority of countries voted to proceed by the use of a secret ballot, as was requested by the US. As a result of the secret ballot, the CAC adopted the Draft MRL with 33 votes in favour, 29 votes opposed, and seven abstentions. The representative of the EU commented "that it was regrettable that this important and far-reaching decision was made by a secret ballot which was contradictory to the [Codex Alimentarius] Commission's decision to increase transparency" (Codex, 1995, p. 9). He further noted that the vote "cast[s] doubts on the validity and value of Codex work and standards and that consequences would be grave including the European Community's rethinking of participation in Codex work" (Codex, 1995, p. 9).

In the same CAC meeting, the EU did manage to adjourn the adoption of the "Draft MRLs for Bovine Somatotropins at Step 8" by calling a vote in which 33 countries, including many European countries, were in favour of adjournment, 31 countries, including the US, against adjournment, and six countries abstained.

Only half a year later, on 26 January 1996, the US requested consultations with the EU at the WTO. Canada, which had joined as a third party along with Australia, New Zealand and Norway, requested consultations with the EU on 26 July 1997. The US and Canada argued that their exports of meat produced with growth-promoting hormones were in line with the relevant Codex standards, adopted less than a year before during the 21st meeting of the CAC, and that the EU's importation ban therefore violates the SPS Agreement. The WTO ruled against the EU and authorized the imposition of retaliatory duties worth an annual US$ 116.8 million for the US and C$ 11.3 million for Canada.

4.2.2 *The WTO TBT Agreement and ISO*

4.2.2.1 Context

The Negotiation Group 8 was the formal forum for the negotiation of the 'new' TBT Agreement on the basis of the TBT Agreement reached in the Tokyo Round. Most of the discussions, however, took place in the TBT Committee which then informed to the Negotiation Group 8. Prominent topics included labelling requirements, voluntary measures, and process and production methods. Most of these topics had been discussed for many years. The discussions on the definitions of the terms "standard" and "standardizing body", for instance, date back to the 1960s. (WTO, 1995; Kim, 2018)

4.2.2.2 Actors and Interests

The most active countries in the negotiation of the TBT Agreement included Canada, the EU, Japan, the Nordic countries led by Finland, and the US. India, Mexico, and New Zealand also played active roles on certain topics. Similar to Codex representatives' active role in the SPS negotiations, it is interesting to note that ISO representatives were actively involved in the TBT negotiations. Indeed, after years of negotiations on the term "standard", it was an ISO representative that proposed a definition in June 1990 that is close to the one found in the finalized TBT Agreement. (WTO, 1995; Croome, 1999) Interestingly, however, the negotiators never agreed on a definition of the term "standardizing body", primarily due to different views of the EU and the US (Naiki, 2009).

4.2.2.3 Design

These transatlantic differences are also argued to be the principal reason as to why ISO is not explicitly named as a standardizing body in the TBT Agreement (Mattli, 2001a; Abbott, 2003; Naiki, 2009; Elsig, 2015). Indeed, while there were also concerns by developing countries on ISO, it was mainly the disagreement between the EU and the US that prevented an explicit endorsement. That said, ISO is the only[7] organization mentioned in the TBT Agreement and it is mentioned 16 times. In comparison, Codex is mentioned four times in the SPS Agreement. In the literature, there is consensus that ISO is regarded as one, if not *the*, relevant standardizing body for TBT-related international standards. (Bernstein and Hannah, 2008; Büthe, 2010; Büthe, 2010; Büthe and Mattli, 2010b,a; Jansen, 2012a,b; Delimatsis, 2015c,b; Elsig, 2015; Lindahl, 2015; Mavroidis and Wolfe, 2017)

With regards to legalization, the TBT Agreement is similar to the SPS Agreement in terms of obligation. Indeed, Article 2.4 states that "[w]here technical regulations are required and relevant international standards exist or their completion is imminent, [WTO] Members **shall** use them, or the relevant parts of them, as a basis for their technical regulations except when such international standards or relevant parts would be an ineffective or inappropriate means for the fulfilment of the legitimate objectives pursued, for instance because of fundamental climatic or geographical factors or fundamental technological problems." (emphasis added). However, the TBT Agreement does neither define the term "international standard" (precision) nor who the "standardizing bodies" are that develop these standards (delegation).[8]

4.2.2.4 Consequences

Potentially due to the lack of an explicit reference in the TBT Agreement, there is only a relatively small body of research on the effect of the TBT Agreement on ISO. While some observers (Büthe and Mattli, 2010a; Delimatsis, 2015b, 2018) point out that ISO has become more prominent since the TBT Agreement, little empirical evidence exists on the linkage between the WTO and ISO.

7 ISO is mentioned together with the IEC. On the history and relationship between ISO and IEC, see Chapter 3.

8 To clarify some of these issues, in 2000 the TBT Committee published a "Decision of the Committee on principles for the development of international standards, guides and recommendations with relation to Articles 2, 5 and Annex 3 of the Agreement". The Decision states that international standards are to be developed according to the six principles of transparency, openness, impartiality and consensus, effectiveness and relevance, coherence, and to address the concerns of developing countries.

4.2.3 *Research Gap*

The existing literature provides interesting insights into the context, the actors, and the interests that shaped the institutional design of the TBT and SPS Agreements. Similarly, the literature offers insightful anecdotal evidence on the consequences of the TBT and SPS Agreements for ISO and Codex, respectively.

The objective of this Chapter is to contribute to the literature in different ways. First, while the existing literature analyses the TBT and SPS Agreements separately, this Chapter provides an overview of the historical context for both Agreements in a comparative manner. Second, this Chapter adds novel and more detailed empirical insights into the consequences of the TBT and SPS Agreements for ISO and Codex. Indeed, the large majority of the discussed literature on the consequences of the TBT and SPS Agreements is based on qualitative evidence from case studies and interviews.[9] This Chapter, by contrast, exploits two original datasets collected for this book and analyses these using a number of empirical methodologies.

4.3 Hypotheses

The principal proposition of this Chapter, and its link to the subsequent Chapter 5, is outlined in detail in Chapter 2. To briefly reiterate, this Chapter focuses on the linkage between the multilateral trade policy regime and the international standardization regime. The institutional design of multilateral trade agreements is the independent variable of interest, and countries' participation in international standardization organizations is the dependent variable of interest. Empirically, the multilateral trade policy regime is represented by the WTO's TBT and SPS Agreements. The international standardization regime is empirically represented by Codex and ISO. (Figure 32, bold arrow)

In a nutshell, the principal proposition of this Chapter is as follows. The multilateral WTO SPS Agreement, which entered into force in 1995, strongly

9 Two notable exceptions are presented by Veggeland and Borgen (2005) and Lim and Prakash (2018). Veggeland and Borgen (2005) provide a descriptive analysis of countries' participation in the Codex Alimentarius Commission and the Codex Committee on General Principles (CCGP) for the years between 1985 and 2003. For these two committees, the authors find an increase in countries' participation that correlates with the entry into force of the SPS Agreement. Lim and Prakash (2018) provide the first systematic study of countries' membership in ISO. The authors' focus, however, is not to explore the extent to which the WTO affects countries' ISO membership but rather the extent to which countries substitute between WTO and ISO membership.

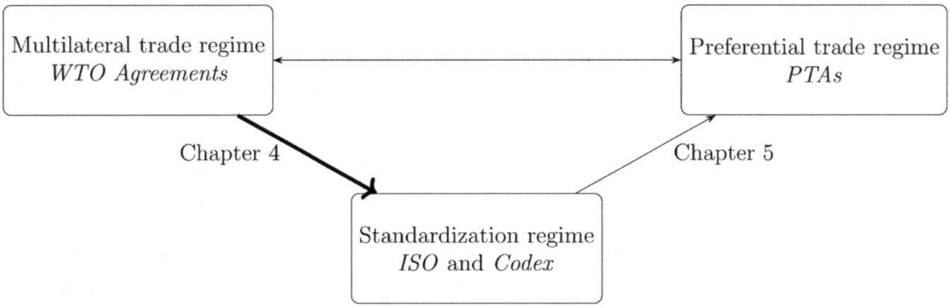

FIGURE 32 Schematic overview of international regime linkages
AUTHOR'S ILLUSTRATION

encourages WTO members to base their national SPS-related measures on international standards. The SPS Agreement also explicitly endorses the Codex Alimentarius as *the* organization to develop the international standards upon which national food safety measures shall be based. By contrast, the WTO TBT Agreement, which also entered into force in 1995, does not explicitly endorse any organization as the relevant standard-setter for TBT-related international standards. This has two implications. First, while the TBT Agreement leaves room for countries to engage in forum-shopping and/or regime-shifting, this is not, or at least less so, the case for the SPS Agreement. Second, while the SPS Agreement essentially upgrades Codex standards from being *de jure* voluntary to being *de facto* legally binding, or from a soft(er) to a hard(er) law system, this is not the case for the TBT Agreement. Even though ISO is generally regarded as *the* TBT-related international standardization organization, its standards are not explicitly endorsed by the TBT Agreement and therefore remain voluntary. In line with this argument, it is therefore expected that the SPS Agreement significantly increases actors' incentives to actively participate in the standard-setting processes of Codex. The TBT Agreement, by contrast, is expected to have less of an effect on actors' incentives to participate in the standard-setting processes of ISO. To empirically explore this argument, the following Hypotheses are put forward.

> **H1:** *The participation of countries in international standardization organizations increases with countries' accession to the WTO.*

As outlined in detail in Chapter 2, international standards play an important role in global trade, for internationally active firms, and for governments. Indeed, in a world in which rules and regulations differ between countries and markets, internationally active firms face different adjustment costs related to finding relevant information on country-specific rules and regulations, adapting production processes to specific country-specific rules and regulations, and demonstrating conformity with country-specific rules and regulations (Karttunen, 2020). International standards can help to reduce these adjustment costs and allow compliant firms to reap benefits associated with better compatibility, lower transactions costs, and economies of scale (Heires, 2008).

However, international standards can also function as strategic tools (de Vries, 2006; Delimatsis, 2015b; Larouche and van Overwalle, 2015; Chu, 2020) and competitive devices (Heires, 2008) for industrial promotion (Victor, 2000) with which actors can exploit the presence of asymmetric information and organizational differences (Delimatsis, 2015c; Mavroidis and Wolfe, 2017). Indeed, since technological innovation usually precedes standardization and different previously existing standards compete for becoming the international standard to which harmonization will take place. This may result in adjustment costs and conflicts of interest of the distributional consequences of those costs. (Krasner, 1991; Braithwaite and Drahos, 2000; Mattli and Büthe, 2003; Heires, 2008; Büthe, 2010; Blind, 2015; Delimatsis, 2015c; Mattli and Seddon, 2015; Berman, 2017)

As a result, internationally active firms as well as governments which represent the interests of their domestic industries, have strong incentives to actively influence international standard-setting processes in order to shape standards in their economic and political interests. Arguably, the most effective and efficient way in which firms and governments can influence the design of standards is to actively participate in international standard-setting processes. (Hüller and Maier, 2006; Büthe and Mattli, 2010b; Weiler, 2012; Schroeder et al., 2012; Bailer and Weiler, 2015; Halliday et al., 2013; Bailer, 2017; Berman, 2017; Onderco, 2019)

In the context of **H1**, it is argued that countries increase their participation in ISO and Codex with their accession to the WTO. The logic is as follows. With the accession to the WTO, WTO members accept all GATT/WTO Agreements, including the TBT and SPS Agreement. Both Agreements strongly encourage WTO members to base their national TBT- and SPS-related measures on international standards. This increased obligation, one of the components of legalization (Abbott et al., 2000), upgrades international standards from being *de jure* voluntary to being *de facto* legally binding (Veggeland and Borgen, 2005; Ansell and Vogel, 2006; Livermore, 2006; Avant et al., 2010; Prakash and Potoski, 2010; Arcuri, 2015), or from a soft(er) to a hard(er) law system (Abbott and Snidal, 2000; Büthe, 2008; Shaffer and Pollack, 2013).

As a consequence of this increased legalization, actors' economic and political stakes in international standards increase (Stewart and Johanson, 1998;

Smythe, 2009; Pollack and Shaffer, 2009; Büthe and Harris, 2011; Büthe, 2008, 2009, 2015) and potential distributional conflicts become more significant (Braithwaite and Drahos, 2000; Victor, 2000; Sklair, 2002; Livermore, 2006; Alemanno, 2007; Smythe, 2009; Clapp and Fuchs, 2009; Fuchs and Kalfagianni, 2010). To protect their political and economic interests and to shape international standards in their interests, countries increase their participation in international standardization organizations.

However, the extent to which the TBT and SPS Agreements increase countries' incentives to participate in ISO and Codex varies with the institutional design of the two Agreements.

> **H2:** *The more legalized the international standardization organization, the stronger the positive relationship between countries' WTO membership and their participation in the international standardization organization.*

While both, the TBT and SPS Agreement are similar in terms of the obligation component of legalization, they differ significantly with regards to the delegation component of legalization (Abbott et al., 2000). More specifically, the SPS Agreement explicitly endorses Codex as the relevant international organization to develop the food safety-related international standards upon which WTO members shall base their national measures. While ISO is widely regarded as the counterpart for TBT-related international standards (Bernstein and Hannah, 2008; Büthe, 2010; Büthe, 2010; Büthe and Mattli, 2010b,a; Jansen, 2012a,b; Delimatsis, 2015c,b; Elsig, 2015; Mavroidis and Wolfe, 2017), there is no explicit endorsement of the organization in the TBT Agreement.

In other words, the TBT Agreement leaves countries room for forum-shopping and/or regime-shifting, while this is not, or at least less so, the case for the SPS Agreement. As a result of this difference in institutional design, the effect of the SPS Agreement on countries' participation is expected to be more significant than the effect of the TBT Agreement on countries' participation in ISO (H2). The empirical analysis outlined in the next section provides supportive evidence of this Chapter's principal argument and the two Hypotheses.

4.4 Data and Methodology

4.4.1 *Dependent Variable and Methodology*

The principle dependent variables capture countries' participation in ISO and Codex. In the case of Codex, *Participation* is the number of standard-setting committee meetings in which a country participates per year. A second

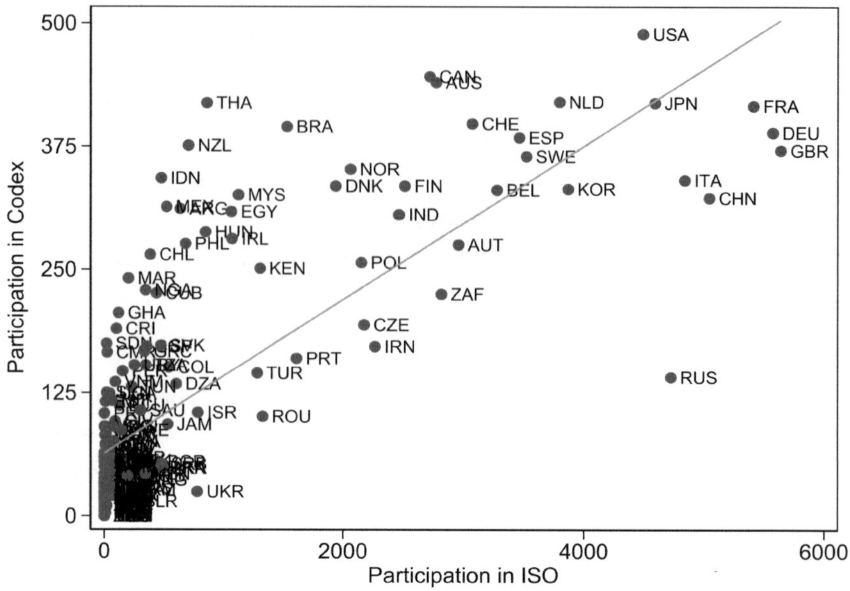

FIGURE 33 Countries' participation in ISO and Codex, 1987–2019
AUTHOR'S ILLUSTRATION

dependent variable, *Participants*, captures the number of delegates that a country sends to participate in the standard-setting committees in a given year. Due to data availability limitations, the empirical analysis on ISO only includes *Participation*, which is equal to the number of standard-setting committees a country is a member of in a given year.

The empirical analysis is based on a panel dataset which includes 187 countries and covers the years between 1987 and 2019. As indicated in Chapter 3, countries' participation in ISO and Codex is severely positively skewed, meaning that only very few countries have a very high *Participation*. Since *Participation*, and in the case of Codex also *Participants*, are over-dispersed count variables, the empirical analysis relies on a number of Poisson regressions as well as negative binomial regressions. To check the robustness of the results, the regressions are also re-run as ordinary least squares regressions. Furthermore, a panel event study is conducted. All regressions include year-fixed effects, regional-fixed effects, and a general time trend. The reported robust standard errors are clustered at the country level.

Before discussing the independent and control variables, it is interesting to compare countries' *Participation* in ISO and Codex. Perhaps unsurprisingly, countries' participation in the two international standardization organizations is strongly positively correlated (r=0.78, Figure 33). Over the period between

1987 and 2019, seven countries (France, Germany, the UK, China, Italy, Japan, and the US) were particularly well represented in both organizations. Thailand and Russia present two interesting extremes. Thailand has been among the most active countries in Codex but only participated little in ISO. In contrast, Russia has been among the most active countries in ISO but participated much less in the standard-setting processes of Codex.

4.4.2 *Independent Variable*

The independent variable of interest is a binary variable that indicates countries' membership in the WTO in a given year. *WTO membership* is equal to one once a country joined the WTO, and equal to zero otherwise (Table 7, Annex). The empirical set-up is comparable to other recent contributions with related research questions (Kim et al., 2019).

4.4.3 *Control Variables*

The empirical analysis includes a number of control variables to account for differences in countries' economic and political characteristics. *GDP* and *GDP per capita* capture a country's log-transformed gross domestic product and gross domestic product per capita, respectively. To control for countries' integration in the global economy, the empirical analysis controls for their exports and imports. Since Codex standards are primarily concerned with food products, the analysis controls for countries' *Food exports* and *Food imports*, which correspond to the share of food exports and food imports in total exports and total imports, respectively. ISO standards cover a broader range of products, which is why the analysis controls for countries' total *Exports* and *Imports* as a share of GDP. The data on countries' economic characteristics is collected from the World Bank's Open Database (World Bank, 2020).

To control for differences in countries' political regimes, their *Polity* score is included in the analysis. The data on *Polity*, which ranges between -10 (hereditary monarchy) and +10 (consolidated democracy), is collected from the Center for Systemic Peace (2020). Table 5 (Annex) and Table 6 (Annex) present the summary statistics for datasets on Codex and ISO, respectively.

4.5 Empirical Analysis

4.5.1 *The WTO SPS Agreement and Codex*

As a first step in the analysis, a panel event study is conducted. This relatively recently developed methodology (Clarke and Schythe, 2020) is a generalized extension of a difference-in-differences or two-way fixed effect regression

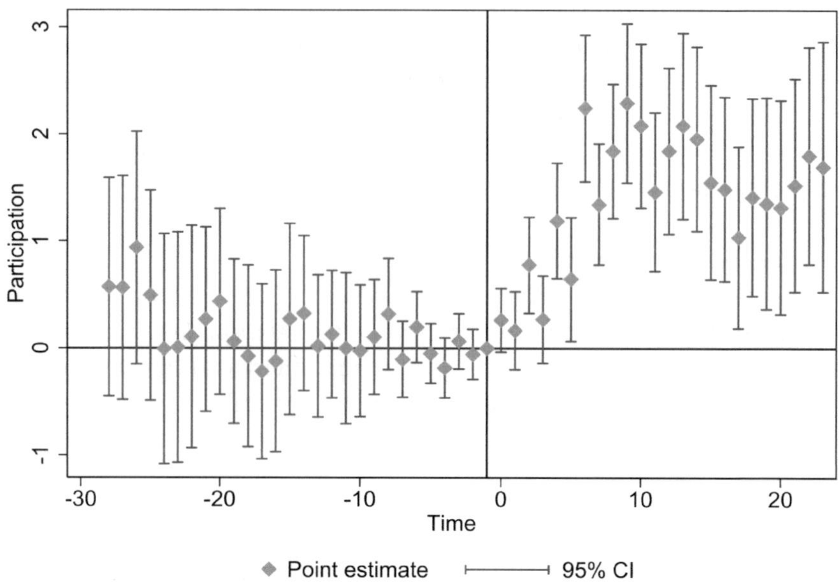

FIGURE 34 Codex: Results from a panel event study
AUTHOR'S ILLUSTRATION

which allows for dynamic lags and leads to the event of interest to be estimated. In the present analysis, the event of interest is countries' accession to the WTO and, relatedly, their obligations under the SPS Agreement. While many countries become members of the WTO in 1995, others joined only later (Table 7, Annex). The empirical methodology is therefore akin to a staggered (Athey and Imbens, 2018) or stacked (Liyang Sun and Sarah Abraham, 2020) difference-in-differences approach. The estimation is based on a panel data ordinary least square regression (OLS) which controls for *GDP*, *GDP per capita*, *Food exports*, *Food imports*, and *Polity* (Table 8, Annex). As is generally standard in event studies, the reference period is set as −1: the period immediately preceding the event of interest (Clarke and Schythe, 2020).

The panel event study indicates a positive and statistically significant association between countries' WTO accession and their participation in the Codex standard-setting committees (Figure 34). While this association appears to be a lagged by a few years, the coefficient remains statistically significant from the seventh lagged year onwards. The statistically not significant *pre*-event coefficients indicate that the parallel trend assumption holds.

To investigate the relationship between countries' WTO membership and their participation in Codex further, the empirical analysis relies on results from a number of Poisson, negative binomial (NBREG), and OLS regressions for both dependent variables *Participation* and *Participants* (Table 3). For the

TABLE 3 Codex: Results from regression analyses

	(1)	(2)	(3)	(4)	(5)	(6)
VARIABLES	Participation	Participants	Participation	Participants	Participation	Participants
WTO membership	0.160	0.247**	0.181***	0.429***	1.040***	4.251***
	(0.225)	(0.118)	(0.0569)	(0.0602)	(0.216)	(1.186)
GDP	0.475	2.151**	0.546***	0.363***	1.163***	5.562***
	(0.422)	(0.960)	(0.0312)	(0.0185)	(0.114)	(0.751)
GDP per capita	−0.115	−1.135	−0.108**	0.0313	0.00923	1.794
	(0.458)	(0.935)	(0.0437)	(0.0304)	(0.230)	(1.861)
Food exports (% of exports)	−0.00151	−0.00292	−0.00118	−0.00169*	−0.00459	−0.0120
	(0.00363)	(0.00288)	(0.000973)	(0.00101)	(0.00299)	(0.0129)
Food imports (% of imports)	−0.00262	−0.0120	−0.00502	−0.00847**	0.0157	0.0967
	(0.00601)	(0.0101)	(0.00318)	(0.00342)	(0.0144)	(0.0706)
Polity	0.0170	0.0166*	0.0164***	0.0256***	0.0271	0.170*
	(0.0114)	(0.00889)	(0.00305)	(0.00356)	(0.0193)	(0.0967)
Constant					−59.99***	74.00
					(16.81)	(101.6)
Observations	5,797	5,797	5,797	5,797	5,797	5,797
Time	Yes	Yes	Yes	Yes	Yes	Yes
Region	Yes	Yes	Yes	Yes	Yes	Yes
Model	Poisson	Poisson	NBREG	NBREG	OLS	OLS

Robust standard errors clustered at the country level in parentheses.
*p<.05; **p<.01; ***p<.001

Poisson and NBREG results, average marginal effects are reported, while standard coefficients are reported for the OLS regressions. With the exception of the Poisson results for *Participation*, all regressions confirm a positive and statistically significant association between countries' WTO membership and their participation in Codex. The average marginal effects of the Poisson and NBREG regressions are similar in sign, size, and statistical significance. The results also indicate that countries' participation in Codex is positively and statistically significantly associated with their *GDP*.

4.5.2 *The* WTO TBT *Agreement and* ISO

The panel event study on countries' WTO accession and their participation in ISO standard-setting committees confirms the previous positive and statistically significant results (Figure 35). The underlying panel OLS regression controls for *GDP*, *GDP per capita*, *Exports*, *Imports*, and *Polity* (Table 9, Annex). The statistically not significant *pre*-event coefficients indicate that the parallel trend assumption holds. In contrast to Codex, there appears to be less of a time lag. The OLS coefficient remains positive, statistically significant, and gradually becomes larger over time.

In contrast to the results on Codex, however, the ISO results from Poisson and NBREG regressions are less consistent (Table 4). Indeed, the average marginal effects differ considerably in their sign, size, and statistical significance. While the average marginal effect of *WTO membership* is positive and statistically not significant in the Poisson regression, the NBREG indicates a negative and statistically significant association. Overall, the empirical results differ considerably by choice of regression model — not only with regards to the dependent variable but also the control variables.

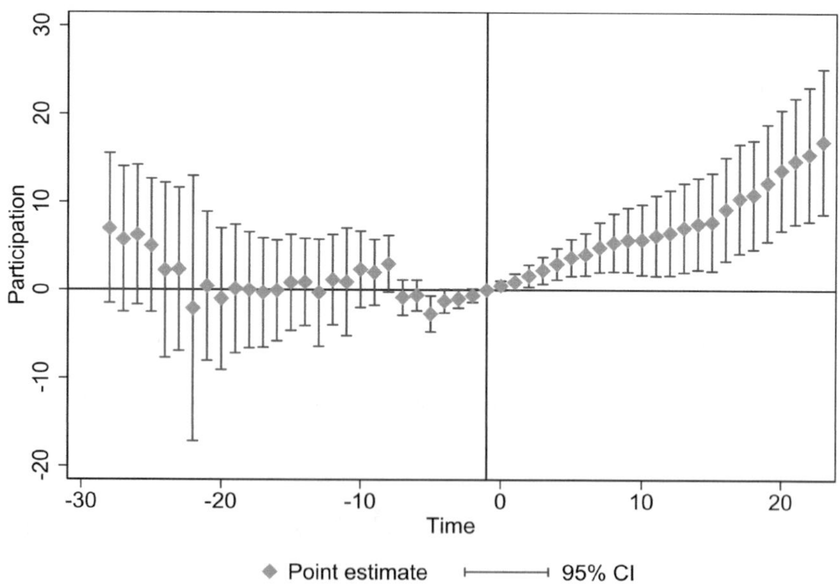

FIGURE 35 ISO: Results from a panel event study
AUTHOR'S ILLUSTRATION

TABLE 4 ISO: Results from regression analyses

	(1)	(2)	(3)
VARIABLES	Participation	Participation	Participation
WTO membership	0.0163	−0.0940**	4.028***
	(0.0639)	(0.0473)	(1.376)
GDP	1.439**	0.626***	−0.164
	(0.658)	(0.0271)	(1.736)
GDP per capita	−1.328*	0.0934*	3.840
	(0.747)	(0.0535)	(2.644)
Exports (% of GDP)	0.00309	0.00685***	0.0327
	(0.00320)	(0.00154)	(0.0383)
Imports (% of GDP)	−0.00182	−0.00617***	0.0243
	(0.00450)	(0.00183)	(0.0289)
Polity	0.0225***	0.0428***	−0.396***
	(0.00683)	(0.00306)	(0.131)
Observations	5,642	5,642	5,642
Time	Yes	Yes	Yes
Region	Yes	Yes	Yes
Model	Poisson	NBREG	OLS

Robust standard errors clustered at the country level in parentheses.
*p<.05; **p<.01; ***p<.001

4.5.3 *Comparison*

The empirical analysis of Codex and ISO provides supportive evidence for this Chapter's principal argument. In support of **H1**, the panel event studies for both Codex and ISO indicate a positive and statistically significant association between countries' accession to the WTO (and, relatedly, their commitments under the SPS and TBT Agreements) and countries' participation in the respective international standardization organization. With regard to **H2**, the empirical results are also supportive. The average marginal effects of *WTO membership* are smaller in the ISO regressions than in the Codex regressions, particularly when considering the variables' summary statistics. More importantly, the average marginal effects for ISO appear to be less robust and actually vary in sign and statistical significance by regression type. For Codex, the average marginal effects calculated in the Poisson and negative binomial regressions are similar in sign, size, and statistical significance.

4.6 Interim Conclusion

This Chapter explores the linkage between the multilateral trade policy regime and the international standardization regime, and posits that the institutional design of multilateral trade agreements affects countries' participation in international standardization organizations. More precisely, it is argued that the WTO TBT and SPS Agreements increased countries' political and economic stakes in international standards, limited countries' ability to engage in forum-shopping and/or regime-shifting, and ultimately increased countries' incentives to participate more in the standard-setting processes of ISO and Codex. Due to differences in the institutional design of the two WTO Agreements, this positive relationship is expected to be stronger between the SPS Agreement and Codex than between the TBT Agreement and ISO.

The empirical analysis of the Chapter provides supportive evidence for this argument. Based on panel event studies as well as a set of Poisson regressions, negative binomial regressions, and ordinary least square regressions, the Chapter finds a positive and statistically significant relationship between countries' obligations under the TBT and SPS Agreements, and their participation in the international standard-setting processes of ISO and Codex, respectively. This relationship is found to be stronger and statistically more robust for the SPS Agreement and Codex than for the TBT Agreement and ISO.

While there exists a small body of research on the linkage between the institutional design of multilateral trade agreements and the work of international standardization organizations, these contributions rely primarily on case studies and qualitative evidence. Furthermore, the majority of this literature focuses either on the link between the TBT Agreement and ISO or on the link between the SPS Agreement and Codex. This Chapter contributes to this literature by providing a comparative, historical account on the context, actors, and interests that led to the institutional design differences between the SPS Agreement and the TBT Agreement. Furthermore, this Chapter contributes to the existing literature by analysing two original datasets on countries' participation in ISO and Codex. The Chapter therefore provides valuable insights into the, so far under-researched, linkage between the multilateral trade policy regime and the international standardization regime.

Of course, there are a number of caveats. On the side of the independent variable it might be argued that a binary indicator of countries' *WTO membership* only partly allows to capture the institutional design (differences) of the

SPS and TBT Agreements. Furthermore, while the empirical analysis includes a number of control variables and fixed effects, it might be argued that countries' accession to the WTO has a number of consequences that go beyond their obligations under the TBT and SPS Agreement and that therefore could also have an impact on their participation in international standardization organizations. Future research might attempt to create a more nuanced independent variable to capture the institutional design differences between the TBT and SPS Agreement, and apply more sophisticated empirical methods, such as instrumental variable approaches, to better address potential issues related to omitted variables. On the side of the dependent variable, future research might investigate variables that go beyond counties' participation and/or that are affected by changes in participation. Some ongoing research (Cheng and Klotz, 2023), for instance, explores whether the increased participation of countries in Codex, as a consequence of the SPS Agreement, results in deadlocked and prolonged standard-setting processes. Notwithstanding these caveats, this Chapter provides relevant insights that may inform future multilateral trade policies. There is, for instance, an increasing pressure for the WTO to negotiate an Agreement on e-commerce. As there is a multitude of relevant international standardization organizations active in this area (See Chapter 6), the question of whether or not to explicitly endorse one of them in a future e-commerce Agreement is already being discussed in Geneva. This Chapter outlines some of the potential consequences of such institutional design choices.

4.7 Appendices

TABLE 5 Codex: Summary statistics

Variable	Mean	Std. Dev.	Min.	Max.
WTO membership	0.602	0.49	0	1
Participation	3.633	4.544	0	21
Participants	11.148	23.204	0	259
GDP	23.866	2.376	16.881	30.517
GDP per capita	8.387	1.484	5.108	11.626
Polity	2.419	5.945	−10	10
Food exports (% of exports)	26.269	27.9	0	354.553
Food imports (% of imports)	15.509	8.535	0.474	62.416
N	5797			

TABLE 6 ISO: Summary statistics

Variable	Mean	Std. Dev.	Min.	Max.
WTO membership	0.605	0.489	0	1
Participation	19.748	40.964	0	230
GDP	23.919	2.371	17.285	30.517
GDP per capita	8.377	1.483	5.108	11.626
Exports (% of GDP)	40.202	29.168	0.005	228.994
Imports (% of GDP)	46.402	28.495	0	236.391
Polity	2.443	5.987	−10	10
N	5642			

TABLE 7 Countries and WTO membership

Country	WTO	Country	WTO	Country	WTO
Antigua & Barbuda	1995	Mauritius	1995	Kyrgyzstan	1998
Argentina	1995	Mexico	1995	Estonia	1999
Australia	1995	Morocco	1995	Latvia	1999
Austria	1995	Mozambique	1995	Albania	2000
Bahrain	1995	Myanmar (Burma)	1995	Croatia	2000
Bangladesh	1995	Namibia	1995	Georgia	2000
Barbados	1995	Netherlands	1995	Jordan	2000
Belgium	1995	New Zealand	1995	Oman	2000
Belize	1995	Nicaragua	1995	China	2001
Bolivia	1995	Nigeria	1995	Lithuania	2001
Botswana	1995	Norway	1995	Moldova	2001
Brazil	1995	Pakistan	1995	Armenia	2003
Brunei	1995	Paraguay	1995	Macedonia	2003
Bulgaria	1995	Peru	1995	Cambodia	2004
Burkina Faso	1995	Philippines	1995	Nepal	2004
Burundi	1995	Poland	1995	Saudi Arabia	2005
Cameroon	1995	Portugal	1995	Tonga	2007
Canada	1995	Romania	1995	Vietnam	2007
Central African Republic	1995	Senegal	1995	Cape Verde	2008
Chile	1995	Sierra Leone	1995	Ukraine	2008

TABLE 7 Countries and WTO membership (*cont.*)

Country	WTO	Country	WTO	Country	WTO
Colombia	1995	Singapore	1995	Montenegro	2012
Costa Rica	1995	Slovakia	1995	Russia	2012
Cuba	1995	Slovenia	1995	Samoa	2012
Cyprus	1995	South Africa	1995	Vanuatu	2012
Czechia	1995	South Korea	1995	Laos	2013
Côte d'Ivoire	1995	Spain	1995	Tajikistan	2013
Denmark	1995	Sri Lanka	1995	Yemen	2014
Djibouti	1995	St. Lucia	1995	Kazakhstan	2015
Dominica	1995	St. Vincent & Grenadines	1995	Seychelles	2015
Dominican Republic	1995	Suriname	1995	Afghanistan	2016
Egypt	1995	Swaziland	1995	Liberia	2016
El Salvador	1995	Sweden	1995	Algeria	.
Finland	1995	Switzerland	1995	Andorra	.
France	1995	Tanzania	1995	Azerbaijan	.
Gabon	1995	Thailand	1995	Bahamas	.
Germany	1995	Togo	1995	Belarus	.
Ghana	1995	Trinidad & Tobago	1995	Bhutan	.
Greece	1995	Tunisia	1995	Bosnia & Herzegovina	.
Guatemala	1995	Turkey	1995	Comoros	.
Guinea	1995	Uganda	1995	Equatorial Guinea	.
Guinea-Bissau	1995	United Kingdom	1995	Eritrea	.
Guyana	1995	United States	1995	Ethiopia	.
Honduras	1995	Uruguay	1995	Faroe Islands	.
Hong Kong SAR China	1995	Venezuela	1995	Iran	.
Hungary	1995	Zambia	1995	Iraq	.
Iceland	1995	Zimbabwe	1995	Kiribati	.
India	1995	Angola	1996	Lebanon	.
Indonesia	1995	Benin	1996	Libya	.
Ireland	1995	Chad	1996	Micronesia (Federated States of)	.

TABLE 7 Countries and WTO membership (*cont.*)

Country	WTO	Country	WTO	Country	WTO
Israel	1995	Ecuador	1996	Palau	.
Italy	1995	Fiji	1996	Palestinian Territories	.
Jamaica	1995	Gambia	1996	Serbia	.
Japan	1995	Grenada	1996	Sudan	.
Kenya	1995	Haiti	1996	São Tomé & Príncipe	.
Kuwait	1995	Niger	1996	Turkmenistan	.
Lesotho	1995	Papua New Guinea	1996	Tuvalu	.
Luxembourg	1995	Qatar	1996	Uzbekistan	.
Macau SAR China	1995	Rwanda	1996		
Madagascar	1995	Solomon Islands	1996		
Malawi	1995	St. Kitts & Nevis	1996		
Malaysia	1995	United Arab Emirates	1996		
Maldives	1995	Congo – Brazzaville	1997		
Mali	1995	Congo – Kinshasa	1997		
Malta	1995	Mongolia	1997		
Mauritania	1995	Panama	1997		

TABLE 8 Codex: Panel event study

	(1)
VARIABLES	**Participation**
GDP	0.956*
	(0.543)
GDP per capita	−0.0304
	(0.548)
Food exports (% of exports)	−0.00766**
	(0.00347)
Food imports (% of imports)	0.0112
	(0.0141)
Polity	0.0215
	(0.0205)
Constant	−35.28
	(36.24)
Observations	5,797
	0.346
Time	Yes
Region	Yes
Model	OLS

Robust standard errors clustered at the country level in parentheses.
*p<.05; **p<.01; ***p<.001

TABLE 9 ISO: Panel event study

	(1)
VARIABLES	**Participation**
GDP	-18.80***
	(4.507)
GDP per capita	20.40***
	(5.510)
Exports (% of GDP)	0.0321
	(0.0359)
Imports (% of GDP)	0.0138
	(0.0271)
Polity	-0.265**
	(0.123)
Constant	-622.6**
	(281.5)
Observations	5,642
	0.317
Time	Yes
Region	Yes
Model	OLS

Robust standard errors clustered at the country level in parentheses.
*p<.05; **p<.01; ***p<.001

CHAPTER 5

International Standardization and Preferential Trade Agreements

This Chapter explores the linkage between the international standardization regime and the preferential trade policy regime, and posits that countries' participation in international standardization organizations affects the institutional design of preferential trade agreements (PTAs). Countries' participation in international standardization organizations is the independent variable of interest and the institutional design of PTAs is the dependent variable of interest. Empirically, the international standardization regime is represented by the two international standardization organizations Codex Alimentarius (Codex) and the International Organization for Standardization (ISO). The preferential trade regime is empirically represented by the Technical Barriers to Trade (TBT) and Sanitary and Phytosanitary (SPS) chapters of 200 PTAs signed between the World Trade Organization's (WTO) establishment in 1995, and 2016.

The principal proposition of this Chapter is the following. In a world characterized by international regulatory heterogeneity, firms face considerable adjustment costs when exporting to other countries. To facilitate international trade and the competitiveness of their domestic exporting firms, governments have strong incentives to sign PTAs in which they commit to cooperation based on international standards. However, due to economic and political considerations, governments may have different views on exactly which international standards cooperation is to based. In a game theoretical sense, governments fight a "Battle of Sexes" in which they have an incentive to coordinate but due to distributional conflicts disagree on the outcome of coordination. From an economic point of view, governments have strong incentives to commit to cooperation based on international standards which are designed in their domestic firms' interest and with which their domestic firms can comply at a low adjustment cost. From a political point of view, governments have strong incentives to commit to cooperation based on international standards which are aligned with their own regulatory philosophy. In short, governments have an incentive to commit to cooperation based on international standards which are designed in their economic and political interests. Arguably, active participation in relevant international standardization organizations is the most effective and efficient way to influence the design of standards in one's interest. The principal argument is, therefore, that the more PTA members have participated in relevant international standardization organizations, the more they have been able to shape the design of standards in their political and economic interests, and the more likely they are to refer to international standards as a basis for cooperation in their PTAs.

To explore this argument, this Chapter focuses on the linkage between countries' participation in ISO and Codex, and the institutional design of the TBT and SPS chapters of countries' PTAs. The expectation is that countries' participation in the standard-setting processes of ISO and Codex increases the probability that they have been able to shape the design of ISO and Codex standards in their political and economic interests which, consequently, increases the probability that countries refer to international standards as a basis for cooperation in the area of TBT and SPS, respectively. This relationship, however, is expected to be stronger for Codex and SPS than for ISO and TBT. Since, as outlined in detail in Chapter 4, the WTO SPS Agreement explicitly endorses Codex as *the* relevant international standardization organization in the area of food safety, countries' participation in Codex is expected to have a significant impact on the institutional design of the SPS chapters of the PTAs countries sign. By contrast, since the WTO TBT Agreement does not explicitly and exclusively endorse ISO as the relevant international standardization organization in the area of TBT, the impact of countries' participation in ISO is expected to have a more subdued effect on the institutional design of the TBT chapters of the PTAs countries sign.

This Chapter is organized as follows. Section 5.2 provides an overview of the existing literature on the institutional design of PTAs and, in particular, the institutional design of TBT and SPS chapters in PTAs. The principal hypotheses of this Chapter are outlined in 5.3. Section 5.4 describes the data and methodology employed to explore these hypotheses. The results of the empirical analysis are discussed in Section 5.5. Section concludes this Chapter.

5.1 Introduction

Preferential trade agreements have mushroomed over the last three decades (Figure 36).[1] As of September 2023, 360 PTAs are notified to the WTO and in force. Since 2016, each WTO member has at least one PTA in force. The total number of PTAs, also including PTAs not notified to the WTO, exceeds 700 (Design of Trade Agreements (DESTA) dataset, version 2.0, Dür et al. (2014)).

1 For a recent and comprehensive overview of this development and a glimpse of the potential future of PTAs, see Dadush and Prost (2023).

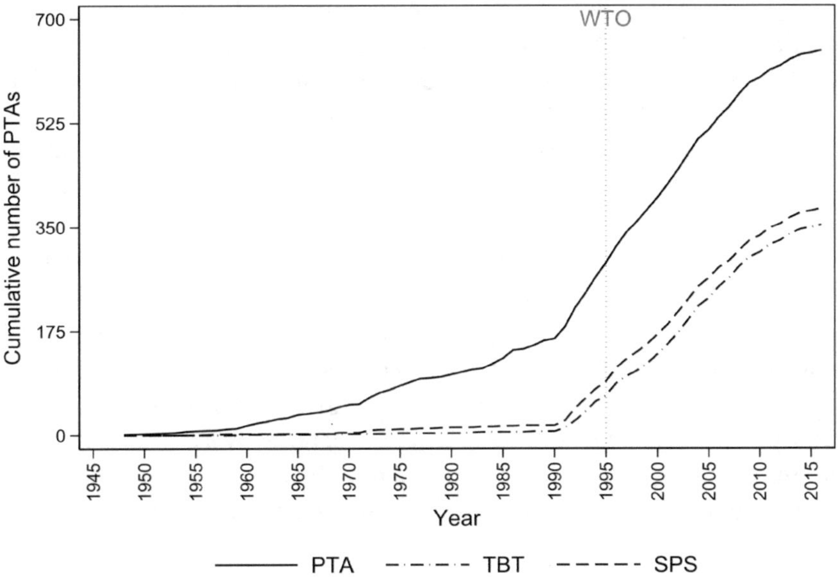

FIGURE 36 TBT and SPS in PTAs
AUTHOR'S ILLUSTRATION BASED ON THE DESIGN OF TRADE AGREEMENTS DATABASE (DESTA) (DÜR ET AL., 2014)

These PTAs differ significantly in their purpose, design, and effects (Dür and Elsig, 2015). Indeed, countries sign PTAs for a number of domestic and international economic (Baier and Bergstrand, 2004) and political (Manger, 2009) reasons.[2] Over time, however, the political science and international relations literature has increasingly moved from investigating the determinants of PTA signature to analyzing the determinants of PTAs' institutional design. This development was facilitated by the publication of detailed datasets including the DESTA dataset (Dür et al., 2014), the Text of Trade Agreements (ToTA) dataset (Alschner et al., 2018), and the World Bank's Deep Trade Agreements datasets (Hofmann et al., 2019; Mattoo et al., 2020). While these sources cover a range of different issue areas, other recent contributions focus on specific topics such as the environment (Morin et al., 2018), labour rights (Raess and

2 For a comprehensive literature overview, see Baccini (2019). For a more specific study on how China uses trade agreements to lock in domestic reform, see Eckhardt and Wang (2021). Mansfield and Pevehouse (2022) explore how nationalism and populism impact countries' interest and willingness to enter PTAs. Oswald and Eckhardt (2023) focus on China and India and argue that domestic politics trumps international politics.

Sari, 2018; Carrère et al., 2022),[3] e-commerce (Burri and Polanco, 2020), intellectual property rights (Morin and Surbeck, 2020), and various other non-trade issues (Lechner, 2016; Milewicz et al., 2018). In a nutshell, this literature finds that PTAs not only differ in the scope of issue areas covered but also in their legal depth (Dür et al., 2014; Hofmann et al., 2019), flexibility (Rosendorff and Milner, 2001; Baccini et al., 2015a), and enforcement (Allee and Elsig, 2014).

As discussed in Chapter 2, there is a clear link and a dialectical relationship between the multilateral trade policy regime and the preferential trade policy regime. Indeed, the WTO is ubiquitous in many of the PTAs signed since the WTO establishment in 1995 (Allee et al., 2017b). Around 85% of the PTAs signed since 1995 include a reference to the WTO and even replicate sizeable parts of the relevant WTO Agreements (Allee et al., 2017b). In some areas, such as TBT and SPS, PTA partners may agree on deeper cooperation (WTO plus, WTO+). In other areas, such as competition and human rights, PTA partners may agree on cooperation that goes beyond the WTO mandate altogether (WTO extra, WTO-X) (Horn et al., 2010).

There are also considerable institutional design spillovers within the preferential trade regime (See Chapter 2). More precisely, PTA negotiators not only replicate from WTO Agreements but also from other PTAs. Whether it is to increase negotiation and drafting efficiency or to diffuse one's preferred language and priorities, PTA negotiators rely heavily on their own country's as well as other countries' previous PTAs (Allee and Lugg, 2016; Allee et al., 2017a; Allee and Elsig, 2019; Peacock et al., 2019).

The institutional design templates of the European Union (EU) and the United States (US), for instance, differ significantly from one another — not least with regards to standardization in TBT and SPS. Both templates have successfully diffused through the network of PTAs as third countries replicate sizeable parts of EU and US PTAs (Horn et al., 2010, 2011; WTO, 2011; Lester and Barbee, 2013; Egan and Pelkmans, 2015; Baccini et al., 2015b; Elsig and Klotz, 2019; Klotz and Appleton, 2024). The predecessor of the Comprehensive and Progressive Agreement for Trans-Pacific Partnership (CPTPP), the Trans-Pacific Partnership (TPP), presents an illustrative example. On average, nearly 45% of the text of US PTAs from 1995 to 2015 can be found in verbatim in the TPP (Allee and Lugg, 2016). While the EU also has a certain template, it appears less consistent. For instance, on average only seven percent of the Canada-EU Comprehensive Economic and Trade Agreement (CETA) language is replicated

3 See Lavenex and Jurje (2021) for a specific study on trade agreements and labour mobility in China and India.

directly from any of their previous PTAs, and relatively more text was actually taken from Canadian PTAs (Allee et al., 2017a).

5.2 Literature and Research Gap

The institutional design of TBT and SPS chapters in PTA follows the general pattern outlined above. Three-quarters of the PTAs that include TBT and/or SPS provisions signed since 1995, for instance, include a reference to the WTO. On average, around eleven percent of these TBT and SPS chapters are replicated in verbatim from the respective WTO Agreements. (Allee et al., 2017b) The median textual overlap between the TBT and SPS chapters of different PTAs is around 70% (Allee and Elsig, 2019).

The importance of TBT and SPS templates becomes particularly evident when considering the relatively recent mega-regional PTAS CETA and TPP. On average, 16% of previous Canadian and EU TBT chapters were replicated in the CETA TBT chapter. The PTA between and Canada and Jordan (2009) was particularly important — more than 50% of its TBT chapter made its way into CETA. Similarly, around 17% of the SPS chapter of the PTA between Canada and Colombia (2008) was replicated in CETA. (Elsig and Klotz, 2019; Klotz and Appleton, 2024)

An analysis of the TBT and SPS chapters of TPP draws a similar picture. Around 35% of the US-Bahrain (2004) TBT chapter and 28% of the US-Australia (2005) SPS chapter were duplicated in TPP. Even though the US resigned from the TPP in 2017, the PTA's TBT and SPS chapters appear to have been remarkably influential for the institutional design of the United States-Mexico-Canada Agreement (USMCA) signed in 2018. A respective 37% and 65% of TPP's TBT and SPS chapter were duplicated in the USMCA. (Elsig and Klotz, 2019; Klotz and Appleton, 2024)

5.2.1 *The Design of SPS Chapters*

The literature on the institutional design of SPS chapters includes both, detailed case studies and large-N studies. The case studies often focus on specific countries or regions such as the EU (Rudloff and Simons, 2004), Canada (Puig and Dalke, 2016), or Asia (Kleimann, 2014) as well as cross-regional comparisons such as, for instance, between North American and European PTAs (von Lampe and Jeong, 2013).

One of the first large-N studies (Fulponi et al., 2011) analyses 51 PTAs signed between 1992 and 2009. Of these PTAs, more than 80% include SPS provisions on harmonization, equivalence, regionalization, risk assessment, transparency, and technical cooperation and joint committees. Around 20% of these PTAs went beyond WTO rules (WTO+) on harmonization, equivalence, regionalization and risk assessment. Almost 50% of the PTAs went beyond WTO rules on transparency. Later studies (Lejárraga, 2013, 2014) increase the sample size of PTAs considerably and analyse 124 PTAs signed between 2000 and 2012 with a particular focus on transparency measures (Lejárraga, 2013) and the legal enforceability of SPS provisions (Lejárraga, 2014). In line with the discussion outlined in Chapter 2, these studies point towards a close relationship between the multilateral trade policy regime and the preferential trade policy regime. More precisely, these studies indicate a close relationship between countries' work in the WTO, here specifically in the SPS Committee, and the institutional design of their SPS chapters in PTAs. The two most recent studies (Jackson and Vitikala, 2016; Stone and Casalini, 2020) cover almost the full list of WTO-notified PTAs and present a detailed mapping of SPS-related institutional design features.

5.2.2 *The Design of TBT Chapters*

Similarly to the literature on SPS measures in PTAs, the literature on the governance of TBT-related issues in PTAs includes regional case studies on, for instance, African PTAs (Meyer et al., 2010), Asian PTAs (Kleimann, 2014), and Canadian PTAs (Puig and Dalke, 2016) as well as large-N studies.

Early large-N studies (Lesser, 2007; Piermartini and Budetta, 2009) find that the extent of TBT liberalization and the approach used to remove TBT-related trade barriers is particularly influenced by the PTA members' level of development, the degree of integration the PTA seeks to achieve, and the involvement of the EU and the US in the PTA. More recent studies (Molina and Khoroshavina, 2015, 2018; Espitia et al., 2020) largely confirm these early findings and, in particular, the importance of the transatlantic divide as a determinant for institutional design.

5.2.3 *The Transatlantic Divide in the Design of TBT and SPS Chapters*

As the previous discussion indicates, there is a remarkable difference between the EU and the US approach when it comes to the institutional design of TBT and SPS chapters in PTAs (Lesser, 2007; Heydon and Woolcock, 2009; Piermartini and Budetta, 2009; Stoler, 2011; Ti-Ting, 2012; Molina and Khoroshavina, 2015, 2018; Espitia et al., 2020; Melillo, 2022). Broadly speaking, the literature suggests that the EU favours the harmonization towards EU regulations, standards and conformity assessment procedures when it signs PTAs with geographically close partner countries, and towards international standards when in PTAs with geographically more distant partner countries.

The US, by contrast, is found to put more emphasis on equivalence, mutual recognition, and transparency. A second difference between the EU and the US approach is the explicit reference to particular international standards and standardization organizations (Heydon and Woolcock, 2009; Stoler, 2011; WTO, 2011a,b; Wijkström and McDaniels, 2013). By contrast, the US emphazises in its PTAs that any standard that is developed in line with the "Six Principles" of transparency, openness, impartiality and consensus, effectiveness and relevance, coherence, and a development dimension are to be considered as international standards (McDaniels et al., 2018).

The inclusion of specific TBT and SPS provisions in PTAs follows a certain hub-and-spoke nature (Horn et al., 2010, 2011; WTO, 2011). The type of transparency provisions favoured by the US, for instance, are also commonly included in other North American, East Asian, South-Central American, and Oceanian PTAs but are much less commonly featured in EU and African PTAs (WTO, 2011; Lejárraga, 2013, 2014).

To what extent the EU and the US diffuse their templates through negotiated, concerted integration, or rather through unilateral, hegemonic integration is difficult to assess (Baldwin, 2000; Maur and Shepherd, 2011). Chile might present an illustrative example though. The country negotiated simultaneously with the EU and the US, and signed the respective PTAs in 2002 and 2003. In its Chile Strategy Paper 2007–2013 (European Commission, 2007, p. 35), "[t]he EU observed with concern a marked tendency for the Chilean standardisation process to incorporate solely a reference to the US standards, particularly when no agreed international standards exist. The immediate effect of such behaviour is to divert trade to imports of non-EU origin or to give rise to additional costs to adapt products made in the EU. The EU will focus on increased cooperation and pay political attention to the promotion of international standards, or in their absence, to double recognition of both US and EU norms. Such an approach should be followed, in particular, for new technologies where the EU local value added is still prominent."

The divergence between the EU and US approach to TBT and SPS integration appears deep enough to also present a major impediment to their bilateral trade negotiations. Indeed, TBT and SPS issues were contentious topics in the, now stalled, negotiations on the Transatlantic Trade and Investment Partnership (TTIP) agreement. (Congressional Research Service, 2014; Egan and Pelkmans, 2015; Veggeland and Sørbye, 2015; European Commission, 2016; Matthews, 2016; Young, 2016)

TBT and SPS-related concerns have also been raised repeatedly in the annually published National Trade Estimate Report on Foreign Trade Barriers of the Office of the United States Trade Representative (USTR). In its 2020 edition, for example, the Report identifies a long list of TBT-related concerns including transparency and notification, European standardization and conformity assessment procedures; chemicals; renewable fuels; sustainability criteria; energy efficiency regulations; transport fuel quality; agriculture quality schemes; wine traditional terms; distilled spirits aging requirements and the certification of animal welfare. SPS-related concerns include hormones and beta agonists; antimicrobials; agricultural biotechnology; pathogen reduction treatments; certification requirements; somatic cell count; animal byproducts; live cattle; agricultural chemicals and pesticide MRLs. Interestingly, the Report also explicitly laments that "[t]he EU's approach to standards-related measures, including its conformity assessment framework, and its efforts to encourage governments around the world to adopt its approach, including European regional standards, creates a challenging environment for U.S. exporters." (USTR, 2020, p. 178)

To summarize, there is consensus in the literature that the EU and the US PTAs follow, and diffuse to their PTA partners, distinctly different approaches in terms of TBT and SPS-related institutional design. There is also consensus that this divergence is primarily driven by the institutional difference in their national standardization systems outlined in detail in Chapter 3.

5.2.4 *Research Gap*

The previously outlined literature provides interesting insights into the design and the evolution of TBT and SPS chapters in PTAs. Not only have TBT and SPS chapters become more common in PTAs over the past decades, they have also become more detailed and more heterogeneous. While many of the discussed contributions provide descriptive mappings of the institutional design differences, others go one step further and investigate the potential determinants behind these differences. This latter body of research finds that countries' level of economic development as well as the geographic distance between PTA members present important factors for the institutional design of TBT and SPS chapters.

These studies also suggest that the different EU and US templates are not only present in the respective PTAs the EU and the US sign but also influence the design of PTAs signed among third countries. This transatlantic divide is argued to be a consequence of different regulatory philosophies and standardization systems. While the US advocates for the importance of scientific risk assessment, the EU tends to emphasize the importance of the precautionary principle and a "multiple approach" in which standards are also assessed from a health, technological, economic, and administrative point of view (Arcuri, 2015). Furthermore, partly due to differences in their national economic structures (Tate, 2003; Winn, 2009), the US standardization system is often described as atomistic and market-oriented, while the EU system is centralized and hierarchical (Abbott, 2003; Mattli and Büthe, 2003; Heires, 2008; Büthe and Mattli, 2011). As a consequence, the EU and the US differ with regards to their institutional complementarity with international standardization systems. As discussed in detail in Chapter 3, for instance, the ISO system is institutionally more complementary to the EU system (Büthe and Mattli, 2011), which provides the EU with a first-mover advantage (Mattli, 2001b,a).

The existing literature therefore acknowledges the link between standardization and the design of TBT and SPS chapters in PTAs. It can be argued, however, that the literature limits its attention primarily to the EU and the US and, as a consequence, fails to generalize this debate. If institutional complementarity matters for the EU's approach to designing TBT and SPS chapter, it will arguably also matter to other countries. While institutional complementarity is conceptually interesting and important, it is difficult to capture empirically. In an attempt to investigate the linkage between standardization and institutional design more broadly, this Chapter proposes to focus on countries' participation in standard-setting processes. The key assumption is that the more countries participate in a standardization organization, the more they can influence the design of standards in a way that is complementary with their domestic standards and, therefore, more aligned with their political and economic interests. This, in turn, is expected to be reflected in the way in which countries design the TBT and SPS chapters of their PTAs.

5.3 Hypotheses

The principal proposition of this Chapter, and its link to the previous Chapter 4, is outlined in detail in Chapter 2. To briefly reiterate, this Chapter focuses on the linkage between the international standardization regime and the preferential trade policy regime. Countries' participation in international standardization organizations is the independent variable of interest and the institutional design of PTAs is the dependent variable of interest. Empirically, the international standardization regime is represented by the two international standardization organizations Codex and the ISO. The preferential trade regime is empirically represented by the TBT and SPS chapters of 200 PTAs signed between the WTO establishment in 1995, and 2016. (Figure 37, bold arrow)

In a nutshell, the principal proposition of this Chapter is as follows. In a world characterized by international regulatory heterogeneity, firms face considerable adjustment costs when exporting to other countries. To facilitate

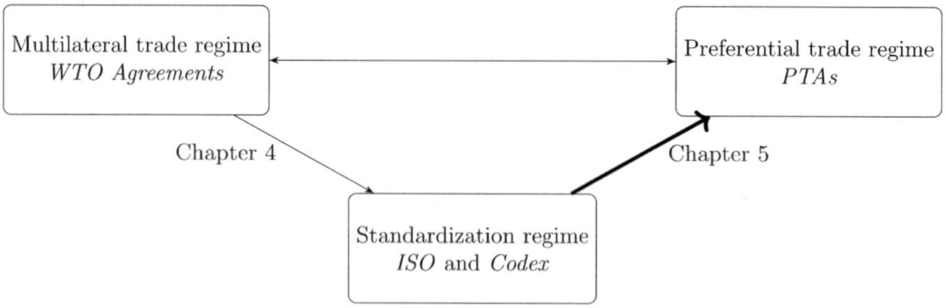

FIGURE 37 Schematic overview of international regime linkages
AUTHOR'S ILLUSTRATION

international trade and the competitiveness of their domestic exporting firms, governments have strong incentives to sign PTAs in which they commit to cooperation based on international standards. However, due to economic and political considerations, governments may have different views on exactly which international standards cooperation is to based. In a game theoretical sense, governments fight a "Battle of Sexes" in which they have an incentive to coordinate but due to distributional conflicts disagree on the outcome of coordination. From an economic point of view, governments have strong incentives to commit to cooperation based on international standards which are designed in their domestic firms' interest and with which their domestic firms can comply at a low adjustment cost. From a political point of view, governments have strong incentives to commit to cooperation based on international standards which are aligned with their own regulatory philosophy. In short, governments have an incentive to commit to cooperation based on international standards which are designed in their economic and political interests. Arguably, active participation in relevant international standardization organizations is the most effective and efficient way to influence the design of standards in one's interest. The principal argument is, therefore, that the more PTA members have participated in relevant international standardization organizations, the more they have been able to shape the design of standards in their political and economic interests, and the more likely they are to refer to international standards as a basis for cooperation in their PTAs.

To explore this argument, this Chapter focuses on the linkage between countries' participation in ISO and Codex, and the institutional design of the TBT and SPS chapters of countries' PTAs, respectively. The expectation is that countries' participation in the standard-setting processes of ISO and Codex increases the probability that they have been able to shape the design of ISO and Codex standards in their political and economic interests which, consequently, increases the probability that countries refer to international standards as a basis for cooperation in the area of TBT and SPS, respectively. This leads to the following first Hypothesis.

> **H1:** *The more countries have participated in the processes of international standardization organizations, the more likely they are to commit to cooperation based on international standards in their PTAs.*

This relationship, however, is expected to be stronger for Codex and SPS than for ISO and TBT. Since, as outlined in detail in Chapter 4, the WTO SPS Agreement explicitly endorses Codex as *the* relevant international standardization organization in the area of food safety, countries' participation in Codex is expected to have a significant impact on the institutional design of the SPS chapters of the PTAs countries sign. Indeed, the endorsement of Codex arguably locks-in countries to Codex standards and limits their ability to engage in forum-shopping and/or regime-shifting. If countries want to shape international food safety standards in their political and economic interests, Codex is *the* organization in which they would do so. By contrast, since the WTO TBT Agreement does not explicitly and exclusively endorse ISO as the relevant international standardization organization in the area of TBT. As a consequence, countries may engage in forum-shopping and/or regime-shifting to set TBT-related standards in organizations which are institutionally more aligned with their political and economic interests and in which they can influence the design of standards more efficiently. The impact of countries' participation in ISO is therefore expected to have less of an effect on the institutional design of the TBT chapters of the PTAs countries sign. This is captured in the second Hypothesis below.

> **H2:** *The more legalized the international standardization organization, the stronger the positive relationship between countries' participation in this standardization organization and the likelihood of committing to cooperation based on international standards in their PTAs.*

5.4 Data and Methodology

5.4.1 *Dependent Variable and Methodology*

The principal dependent variable captures the type of standards-based *Integration*[4] that PTA parties commit to in the TBT and SPS chapters of their

4 The term "Integration" is chosen here in line with the two publications (Espitia et al., 2020; Stone and Casalini, 2020) based on which the dependent variable is constructed.

PTAs. *Integration* is constructed as an ordinal variable that ranges between four and zero. More precisely, *Integration* equals four if the PTA parties commit to harmonizing their TBT and SPS measures on the basis of international standards. If PTA parties commit to harmonizing their TBT and SPS measures on the basis of regional standards, *Integration* equals three. *Integration* is equal to two if the PTA parties commit to harmonizing their TBT and SPS measures on specific, often national, standards. *Integration* is equal to one if the PTA parties mutually recognize each other's standards or consider them as equivalent. *Integration* is zero if the PTA parties do not commit to any type of standards-based integration. If a PTA includes multiple degrees of *Integration*, the higher degree prevails. For instance, if PTA parties commit to integration based on a specific standard and that specific standard is a regional standard, the degree of *Integration* for this PTA would be coded as equal to three.

The dependent variable *Integration* is constructed based on Stone and Casalini (2020) and Espitia et al. (2020).[5] These two sources present the most recent, most detailed, and most comprehensive data that is currently available. Focusing on SPS, the original dataset of Stone and Casalini (2020) covers 275 PTAs signed between 1971 and 2018. The dataset on TBT, collected by Espitia et al. (2020), covers 269 PTAs signed between 1960 and 2017. To facilitate the comparison of the TBT and SPS results, the empirical analysis presented below focuses on the PTAs that are included in both datasets.

In total, both datasets have 242 PTAs in common. However, since the empirical analysis presented below includes a number of WTO-related variables (TBT/SPS related disputes, specific trade concerns, and notifications), only PTAs signed since the WTO's establishment in 1995 are included. The PTAs are matched to the DESTA database (Dür et al., 2014) to obtain the country dyads of the PTAs. Ultimately, this results in a list of 200 PTAs (Table 18), and 942 PTA party dyads, to be included in the empirical analysis.

Given the ordinal scale of the dependent variable *Integration*, and in line with related literature (Allee and Elsig, 2014; Wüthrich and Elsig, 2021), the empirical analysis relies on a number of ordered probit regressions at the PTA level as well as at the PTA party dyad level. The results indicate whether the probability of a higher degree of *Integration* increases or decreases with a positive one unit change in the respective independent variable. While the sign and statistical significance of ordered probit regressions can be interpreted, the results offer limited insights into the magnitude of the coefficients. To get a sense of the magnitude of the relationship between the dependent

5 The author would like to thank both groups of authors for sharing their data, and clarifying any data related questions.

and independent variable, a number of predicted probability calculations are performed.

To assess the robustness of the empirical results, all models are re-run using ordered logit regressions and ordinary least squares regressions (Section 5.5.3). Furthermore, the dependent variable is transformed into a binary variable which equals one if the PTA has any provision on standards-based *Integration* (regardless of the type), and equal to zero otherwise. A number of probit and logit models are run to assess the relationship between this binary dependent variable, and the independent and control variables. In line with the literature, in all models the dependent variable is lagged by one year and the reported robust standard errors are clustered at the PTA level. All models also include year-fixed effects as well as regional-fixed effects.

Before presenting the independent and control variables, it is interesting to note the different distribution of standards-based *Integration* in the TBT and SPS chapters of the 200 PTAs. In the case of SPS, 113 PTAs (56.5%) do not include any provisions on standards-based SPS integration. In 15 PTAs (7.5%), the PTA parties agree to mutually recognize each other's SPS standards or consider them as equivalent. Only five PTAs (2.5%) include provisions that seek to harmonize SPS measures based on specific standards. In 15 PTAs (7.5%), the PTA parties commit to harmonize their SPS measures based on regional standards. PTA parties agree to harmonize their SPS measures based on international standards in 52 of the 200 PTAs (26%) assessed.

In the case of TBT, standards-based *Integration* is less common. In only 22 of the 200 assessed PTAs (11%), PTA parties commit to harmonize their TBT measures based on international standards. 19 PTAs (9.5%) include provisions that call for the harmonization of TBT measures based on regional standards. In three PTAs (1.5%), the PTA parties commit to harmonize their TBT measures based on specific standards. Only two PTAs (1%) include provisions that mutually recognize each other's standards or consider them as equivalent. The large majority of PTAs, 154 PTAs of the 200 PTAs assessed (77%), does not include any provisions on standards-based TBT integration.

It is interesting to note that there appears to be only a weak relationship between PTA's degree of *Integration* in TBT and degree of *Integration* in SPS (r=0.08, Figure 38). Almost half of the 200 PTAs (45.5%) have no provisions on either standards-based *Integration* in TBT or standards-based *Integration* in SPS. 42 PTAs (21%) have no provisions on standards-based *Integration* in TBT but do include a provision in which the PTA parties commit to base their SPS *Integration* on international standards. In contrast, nine PTAs (4.5%) have no provisions on standards-based *Integration* in SPS but do include a provision in which the PTA parties commit to base their TBT *Integration* on international

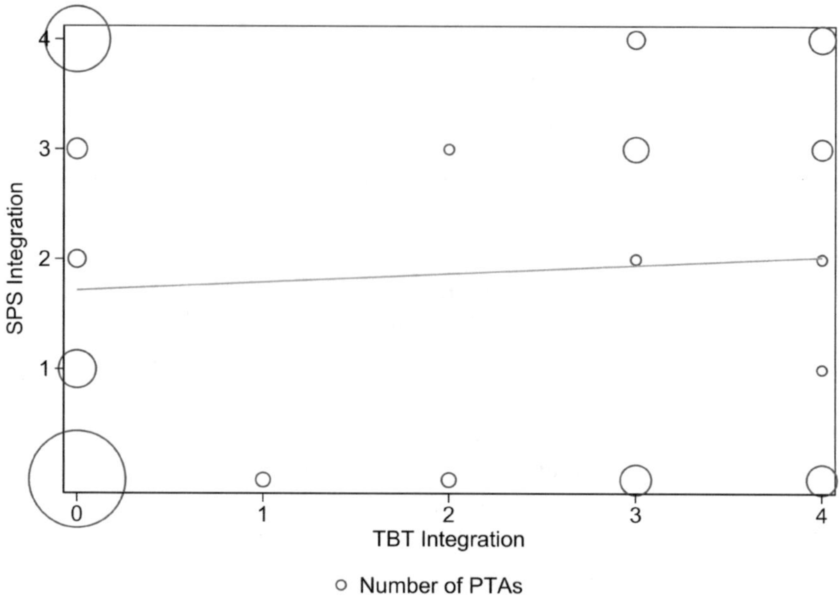

FIGURE 38 Degree of standards-based integration in TBT and SPS
AUTHOR'S CALCULATION AND ILLUSTRATION

standards. In only seven PTAS (3.5%), do PTA parties commit to basing both TBT and SPS *Integration* on international standards.[6]

5.4.2 *Independent Variables*

The principle independent variables capture countries' participation in the standard-setting processes of Codex and ISO. The data collected for Codex and ISO is described in detail in Chapter 3. The empirical analysis is conducted both at the PTA level as well as at the PTA party dyad level. As explained in more detail below, the analysis at the PTA level focuses on PTA parties' *overall* participation in the standard-setting processes of Codex and ISO. The analysis at the dyad level focuses on PTA parties' *common* participation in the standard-setting processes of Codex and ISO. Hypothetically, it might be the case that country A and country B have participated in a large number of standard-setting meetings *overall*. However, it might be the case that country A and country B have participated in a large number of different standard-setting meetings and therefore had little interaction. In contrast, it could also be

6 These seven PTA are Chile-Central America (1999), Korea-Chile (2003), El Salvador-Cuba (2011), Costa Rica Colombia (2013), Korea-Colombia (2013), EU-Ukraine (2014), and Australia-China (2015).

the case that country A and country B participated in a large number of the same, or *common*, standard-setting meetings and therefore had a lot of interaction. The motivation behind conducting the empirical analysis at the PTA and at the dyad level is to see if and how *overall* and *common* participation in standard-setting processes are related to the degree of standards-based *Integration* countries commit to in the TBT and SPS chapters of their PTAS.

In the case of Codex, four different measures of countries' participation in the standard-setting processes are created. The first measure, *Membership*, is based on a simple count of years that a country has been a member of Codex. Arguably, the longer a country has been a member of Codex, the more experience the country has gained in the standard-setting processes of the organization, and the more the country is able to shape standards in its political and economic interests. At the PTA level, *Membership* captures the average number of years that a given PTA's parties have been members of Codex. At the dyad level, *Membership* captures the number of years that two PTA parties have both been members of Codex.

A second measure, *Chair*, is related to the number of Codex standard-setting meetings a country has chaired. Arguably, the more meetings a country has chaired, the more influential the country has been in the standard-setting processes of Codex. At the PTA level, *Chair* is the average number of meetings which have been chaired by a given PTA's parties. Since, by definition, only one country holds the chair of a meeting, *Chair* is not included in the analysis at the dyad level.

A third measure, *Participation*, captures the number of Codex standard-setting committee meetings in which a country has participated. Arguably, the more meetings a country has participated in, the more standards the country has been able to influence in line with its political and economic interests. At the PTA level, *Participation* captures the average number of meetings a given PTA's parties have participated in. At the dyad level, *Participation* is equal to the number of meetings in which both PTA parties have participated together.

The fourth measure, *Participants*, captures the number of delegates that a country sends to participate in the Codex standard-setting committee meetings. Arguably, the more delegates a country sends, the more actively a country can influence the standard-setting processes in line with its political and economic interests. At the PTA level, *Participants* is equal to the average number of delegates that a given PTA's parties have sent to Codex meetings. At the dyad level, *Participants* is the number of delegates two PTA parties have sent to participate in the same meetings.

Due to data availability limitations, the data on countries' participation in ISO is less detailed. Similarly to the Codex data, *Membership* relates to the number of years that a country has been a member of ISO. At the PTA level,

Membership captures the average number of years that a given PTA's parties have been members of ISO. At the dyad level, *Membership* captures the number of years that two PTA parties have both been members of ISO.

The second measure, *Participation*, is related to the number of ISO standard-setting committees a country is a member of. At the PTA level, *Participation* is equal to the average number of standard-setting committees a given PTA's parties has been a member of. At the dyad level, *Participation* is equal to the number of standard-setting committees in which both PTA parties have been members at the same time.

The previously outlined variables capture countries' participation in the standard-setting processes of ISO and Codex. It can be argued, however, that not only their absolute participation but also their relative participation plays a role. Consider, for instance, a hypothetical PTA between country A and country B. It might be the case that both country A and country B participated in 100 standard-setting meetings. For this PTA, *Participation* would be equal to 100 (the average of country A and country B). Alternatively, it might be the case that country A participated in 190 standard-setting meetings and country B participated in ten standard-setting meetings. Again, *Participation* would be equal to 100 (the average of country A and country B). The empirical analysis includes measures of *asymmetry*, calculated using the approach of Kim and Hofmann (2018), for the respective independent variables to control for this.

5.4.3 *Control Variables*

The empirical analysis outlined Section 5.5.1 and Section 5.5.2 accounts for a number of control variables commonly identified in the literature.

One factor that may affect the institutional design of PTAs is related to countries' previous interactions in WTO dispute settlement cases (Wüthrich and Elsig, 2021). To control for this, the empirical analysis accounts for *WTO SPS disputes* and *WTO TBT disputes*. Data on *WTO SPS disputes* and *WTO TBT disputes* was kindly shared by Wüthrich and Elsig (2021) and complemented with information available from the WTO's website (WTO, 2020a). At the PTA level, *WTO SPS disputes* and *WTO TBT disputes* capture the average number of SPS or TBT-related dispute settlement cases in which a given PTA's parties have been involved in as complainant, respondent, or third party since the establishment of the WTO in 1995. At the dyad level, *WTO SPS disputes* and *WTO TBT disputes* capture the number of SPS or TBT-related dispute settlement cases in which a PTA party dyad has been involved as complainant, respondent, or third party since 1995.

Another body of literature (Wijkström and McDaniels, 2013; Lejárraga, 2013, 2014; McDaniels and Karttunen, 2016; McDaniels et al., 2018) points out that PTA parties' interaction in the WTO through specific trade concerns (STCs) and

WTO committees may affect the design of their PTAs.[7] To account for this, the empirical analysis controls for SPS and TBT-related STCs (*WTO SPS STC* and *WTO TBT STC*). The data on *WTO SPS STC* and *WTO TBT STC* is collected from the WTO's SPS and TBT Information Management System (WTO, 2020b). At the PTA level, *WTO SPS STC* and *WTO TBT STC* capture the average number of SPS- or TBT-related STCs in which a given PTA's parties have been involved in as a complainant or respondent since the establishment of the WTO in 1995. At the dyad level, *WTO SPS STC* and *WTO TBT STC* capture the number of SPS- or TBT-related STCs in which a PTA party dyad has been involved in as complainant and respondent since 1995. To control for a third type of PTA parties' interaction in the WTO, the empirical analysis controls for SPS- and TBT-related notifications (*WTO SPS notifications* and *WTO TBT notifications*). This data is also collected from the WTO's SPS and TBT Information Management System (WTO, 2020b). At the PTA level, *WTO SPS notifications* and *WTO TBT notifications* capture the average number of SPS- or TBT-related notifications submitted to the WTO by a given PTA's parties since the establishment of the WTO in 1995. At the dyad level, *WTO SPS notifications* and *WTO TBT notifications* capture the number of SPS- or TBT-related notifications submitted to the WTO by a PTA party dyad since 1995.

The design of PTAs is also argued to be affected by countries' embeddedness in the global economy (Piermartini and Budetta, 2009). To control for this, the empirical analysis on the design of SPS chapters includes *Food exports* and *Food imports*, both collected from the World Bank's Open Database (World Bank, 2020). At the PTA level, *Food exports* and *Food imports* capture the average annual food exports (% of merchandise exports) and food imports (% of merchandise imports) of a given PTA's parties. At the dyadic level, *Food exports* and *Food imports* capture the average annual food exports and food imports of a PTA party dyad. The analysis on the design of TBT chapters includes *Exports* and *Imports*, both also collected from the World Bank's Open Data (World Bank, 2020). At the PTA level, *Exports* and *Imports* capture the average annual exports of goods and services (% of GDP) and imports of goods and services (% of GDP) of a given PTA's parties. At the dyadic level, *Exports* and *Imports* capture the average annual exports and imports of a PTA dyad.

Another economic indicator that is commonly argued to affect the design of PTAs is the gross domestic product (*GDP*) (Baier and Bergstrand, 2004). Data on *GDP* is collected from the World Bank's Open Database (World Bank, 2020). At the PTA level, *GDP* captures the average annual log-transformed GDP (in constant 2010 USD) of a given PTA's parties. At the dyadic level, *GDP* captures the

7 For a recent study on the importance of specific trade concerns and WTO Committees, see Posada et al. (2022).

average annual GDP of a PTA party dyad. *GDP* is also used to proxy for PTA parties' economic power asymmetries — another factor that is commonly argued to have a potential effect on PTA design (Smith, 2000; Baier and Bergstrand, 2004; Lewis, 2011; Baccini et al., 2015a; Kim and Hofmann, 2018; Cartwright, 2019). *GDP asymmetry* is calculated using the methodology employed by Kim and Hofmann (2018). At the PTA level, *GDP asymmetry* captures the economic power asymmetry among all parties of a given PTA. At the dyadic level, *GDP asymmetry* captures the economic power asymmetry between a given PTA party dyad.

As discussed in detail above, PTA templates in general, and in particular with regards to SPS and TBT, differ significantly between the EU and the US (Lesser, 2007; Piermartini and Budetta, 2009; Heydon and Woolcock, 2009; Horn et al., 2010, 2011; Stoler, 2011; WTO, 2011; Ti-Ting, 2012; Baccini et al., 2015b; Egan and Pelkmans, 2015; Molina and Khoroshavina, 2015; Veggeland and Sørbye, 2015; Elsig and Klotz, 2019; Espitia et al., 2020; Klotz and Appleton, 2024). To account for this, binary indicators for the *EU* and *US* are included in the empirical analysis. The variables are equal to one if either actor is a PTA party, and equal to zero otherwise. To control for the potential effect of the number of PTA parties on PTA design, the number of *PTA parties* is also included in the empirical analysis.[8]

To control for countries' legal capacity in trade negotiations, the empirical analysis also accounts for countries' *WTO mission* size. This data was kindly shared by Wüthrich and Elsig (2021). At the PTA level, *WTO mission* captures the average number of staff PTA parties have at their WTO mission in Geneva. At the dyad level, *WTO mission* is equal to the average number of WTO mission staff of the two PTA parties.

The two last control variables commonly used in the literature capture countries' political regimes (Baccini et al., 2015a) and the geographic distance between them (Baier and Bergstrand, 2004; Lesser, 2007; Piermartini and Budetta, 2009; Ti-Ting, 2012). Data on political regimes (*Polity*) is collected from the Center for Systemic Peace (2020). At the PTA level, *Polity* captures the average annual score of a PTA's parties, ranging between −10 (hereditary monarchy) to +10 (consolidated democracy). At the dyad level, *Polity* captures the average annual score of a country dyad. Data on the geographic *Distance* is collected from the GEODIST dataset (CEPII, 2020). At the PTA level, *Distance* captures the log-transformed average geographic distance in kilometres between the PTA parties. At the dyad level, captures the log-transformed geographic distance in kilometres between the dyad countries.

8 The EU is counted as one party.

The summary statistics for the analysis of Codex and standards-based SPS integration at the PTA level (Table 19) and at the dyad level (Table 20) as well as the analysis of ISO and standards-based TBT integration at the PTA level (Table 21) and at the dyad level (Table 22) are presented in the Appendix (Section 5.7).

5.5 Empirical Analysis

This Section presents the results of the empirical analysis. Before reporting and discussing these results, a visual examination of the relationship between the principal dependent and independent variables provides preliminary descriptive insights. Interestingly, the relationship between countries' participation in the standard-setting processes of Codex appears to be negatively related to the type of standards-based integration they commit to in the SPS chapters of their PTAs (Figure 39). In contrast, there appears to be a positive relationship between countries' participation in the standard-setting processes of ISO and the type of standards-based integration they commit to in the TBT chapters of their PTAs (Figure 40).

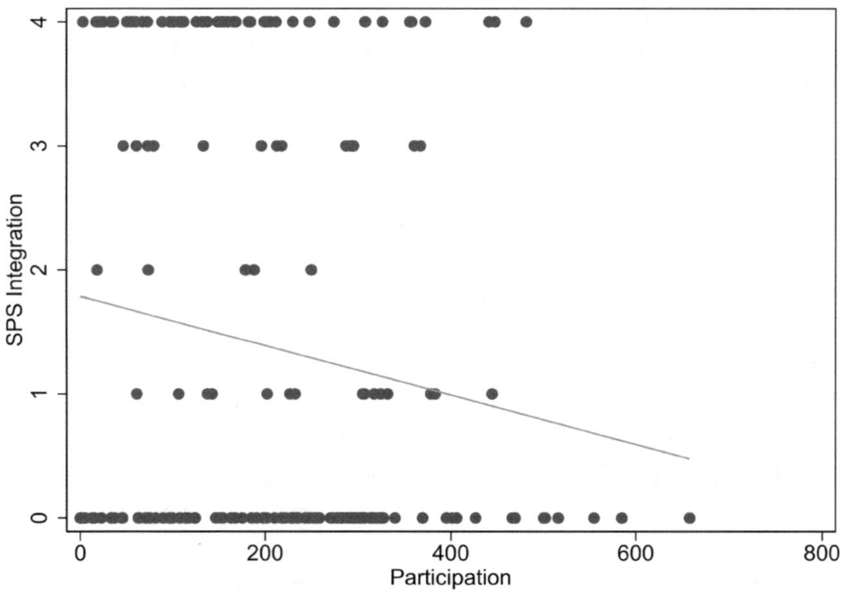

FIGURE 39 Participation in Codex standard-setting and degree of standards-based SPS integration in PTAs
AUTHOR'S CALCULATION AND ILLUSTRATION

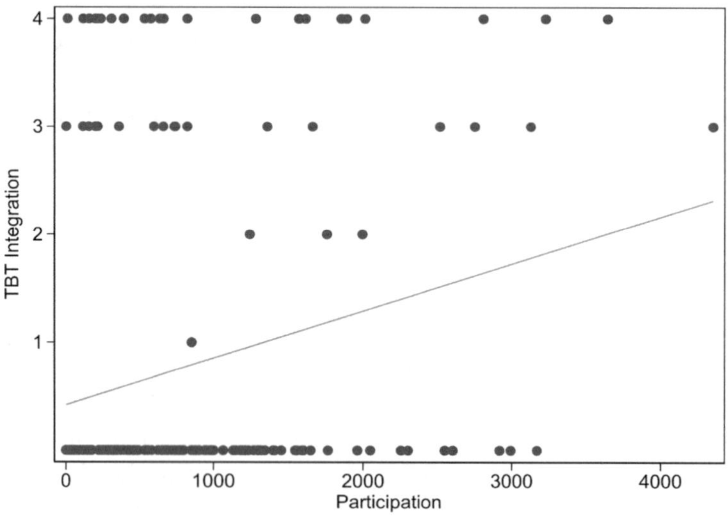

FIGURE 40 Participation in ISO standard-setting and degree of standards-based TBT integration in PTAs
AUTHOR'S CALCULATION AND ILLUSTRATION

5.5.1 *Codex and SPS Chapters*

The empirical results from a set ordered probit (OProbit) regressions at the PTA level indicate a negative and statistically significant association between standards-based SPS *Integration* and the four different variables on countries' participation in the standard-setting processes of Codex (Table 10). The relationship between *Chair* and *Participation*, and the type of *Integration* remains statistically significant even when controlling for the years of *Membership* as well as the respective *asymmetries*. The statistical significance of the relationship between *Participants* and *Integration* is lower and actually becomes statistically not significant once the model controls for years of *Membership* and *Participants asymmetry*.

The statistical significance of this relationship does hold, however, in the analysis conducted at the dyad level (Table 11). Overall, the analysis at the dyad level confirms the findings on the principal independent variables of the analysis conducted at the PTA level. With regards to the control variables, a number of differences can be observed. While the direction and statistical significance of *Food imports*, for instance, holds at the PTA and at the dyad level, this is not the case for *WTO SPS STC*. The coefficient of the *EU* being a PTA party looses in statistical significance in the dyad level analysis and actually changes sign from positive to negative. The negative sign and statistical significance of the coefficient on the *US* being a PTA party is stable across the PTA level and dyad level analyses.

TABLE 10 SPS: Results from ordered probit regression on standards-based integration at the PTA level

	(1)	(2)	(3)	(4)	(5)	(6)	(7)	(8)	(9)	(10)
VARIABLES	Membership	Chair	Chair	Chair	Participation	Participation	Participation	Participants	Participants	Participants
Membership	−0.0518***			−0.0539***			−0.0378**			−0.0506***
	(0.0149)			(0.0150)			(0.0171)			(0.0156)
Chair		−0.0595***	−0.0586***	−0.0609***						
		(0.0169)	(0.0169)	(0.0170)						
Chair asymmetry			−0.00325 (0.00502)	−0.00160 (0.00492)						
Participation					−0.00711***	−0.00708***	−0.00561**			
					(0.00208)	(0.00211)	(0.00222)			
Participation asymmetry						0.00135 (0.00421)	−0.00103 (0.00465)			
Participants								−0.000717*	−0.000715*	−0.000632
								(0.000406)	(0.000409)	(0.000416)
Participants asymmetry									0.000560 (0.00466)	−0.00177 (0.00493)
WTO SPS disputes	0.0960 (0.0838)	0.0473 (0.0819)	0.0509 (0.0826)	0.0795 (0.0865)	0.159* (0.0936)	0.158* (0.0938)	0.165* (0.0934)	0.0473 (0.0816)	0.0475 (0.0815)	0.0818 (0.0856)
WTO SPS STC	0.0350* (0.0210)	0.0586** (0.0245)	0.0580** (0.0245)	0.0601** (0.0254)	0.0463** (0.0223)	0.0469** (0.0224)	0.0437** (0.0222)	0.0605** (0.0268)	0.0608** (0.0270)	0.0562** (0.0272)

TABLE 10 SPS: Results from ordered probit regression on standards-based integration at the PTA level (*cont.*)

	(1)	(2)	(3)	(4)	(5)	(6)	(7)	(8)	(9)	(10)
VARIABLES	Membership	Chair	Chair	Chair	Participation	Participation	Participation	Participants	Participants	Participants
WTO SPS	-0.00181	-0.00122	-0.00112	-0.00178	-0.00187	-0.00187	-0.00222	-0.00139	-0.00140	-0.00194
notifications	(0.00140)	(0.00137)	(0.00139)	(0.00148)	(0.00153)	(0.00154)	(0.00152)	(0.00133)	(0.00133)	(0.00135)
Food exports	0.0211*	0.0130	0.0138	0.0186*	0.0189*	0.0186*	0.0224**	0.0142	0.0140	0.0198*
	(0.0113)	(0.0111)	(0.0110)	(0.0109)	(0.0111)	(0.0111)	(0.0111)	(0.0111)	(0.0112)	(0.0112)
Food imports	-0.139***	-0.134***	-0.129***	-0.124**	-0.123**	-0.123**	-0.124**	-0.126**	-0.126**	-0.122**
	(0.0485)	(0.0490)	(0.0497)	(0.0496)	(0.0493)	(0.0496)	(0.0496)	(0.0499)	(0.0499)	(0.0500)
GDP	-0.170	-0.371***	-0.342***	-0.151	-0.0165	-0.0119	0.0479	-0.312***	-0.313**	-0.125
	(0.130)	(0.122)	(0.129)	(0.138)	(0.155)	(0.155)	(0.154)	(0.121)	(0.121)	(0.133)
GDP	0.00128	0.00416	0.00377	-0.00347	-0.000568	-0.00104	-0.00343	0.00508	0.00487	-0.000768
asymmetry	(0.00497)	(0.00468)	(0.00471)	(0.00512)	(0.00532)	(0.00536)	(0.00540)	(0.00494)	(0.00516)	(0.00524)
EU	1.836**	3.356***	3.501***	3.353***	1.400	1.406	1.400	2.565**	2.544**	2.422**
	(0.906)	(1.205)	(1.200)	(1.299)	(0.936)	(0.937)	(0.945)	(1.021)	(1.034)	(1.106)
US	-2.808***	-0.855	-0.868	-1.027	-2.985***	-3.041***	-2.957***	-2.111**	-2.139**	-2.203**
	(0.957)	(0.941)	(0.948)	(0.982)	(0.939)	(0.964)	(0.952)	(0.939)	(0.988)	(1.004)
PTA parties	-0.0223	0.0311	0.0287	-0.0166	0.00104	0.00307	-0.0268	0.0222	0.0229	-0.0222
	(0.0577)	(0.0643)	(0.0640)	(0.0641)	(0.0590)	(0.0595)	(0.0615)	(0.0600)	(0.0603)	(0.0617)
WTO mission	-0.0479	0.0261	0.0244	0.0225	-0.0538*	-0.0553*	-0.0526*	0.0204	0.0197	0.0112
	(0.0303)	(0.0329)	(0.0325)	(0.0355)	(0.0303)	(0.0305)	(0.0311)	(0.0430)	(0.0440)	(0.0476)
Polity	-0.0703*	-0.0532	-0.0497	-0.0367	-0.0276	-0.0277	-0.0303	-0.0628	-0.0626	-0.0531
	(0.0401)	(0.0410)	(0.0406)	(0.0420)	(0.0458)	(0.0457)	(0.0469)	(0.0426)	(0.0427)	(0.0448)

TABLE 10 SPS: Results from ordered probit regression on standards-based integration at the PTA level (*cont.*)

	(1)	(2)	(3)	(4)	(5)	(6)	(7)	(8)	(9)	(10)
VARIABLES	Membership	Chair	Chair	Chair	Participation	Participation	Participation	Participants	Participants	Participants
Distance	0.467***	0.228*	0.239*	0.383**	0.339***	0.343***	0.427***	0.272**	0.272**	0.416***
	(0.144)	(0.136)	(0.136)	(0.161)	(0.126)	(0.128)	(0.139)	(0.134)	(0.134)	(0.159)
Observations	200	200	200	200	200	200	200	200	200	200
Time	Yes	Yes	Yes	Yes	Yes	Yes	Yes	Yes	Yes	Yes
Region	Yes	Yes	Yes	Yes	Yes	Yes	Yes	Yes	Yes	Yes
Model	Oprobit	Oprobit	Oprobit	Oprobit	Oprobit	Oprobit	Oprobit	Oprobit	Oprobit	OProbit

Robust standard errors clustered at the PTA level in parentheses.

*p<.05; **p<.01; ***p<.001

TABLE 11 SPS: Results from ordered probit regressions on standards-based integration at the dyad level

	(1)	(2)	(3)	(4)	(5)	(6)	(7)
VARIABLES	Membership	Participation	Participation	Participation	Participants	Participants	Participants
Membership	−0.0191***			−0.0245***		−0.0207***	
	(0.00695)			(0.00796)		(0.00724)	
Participation		−0.00187**	−0.00238**	−0.00193**			
		(0.000891)	(0.00100)	(0.000932)			
Participation asymmetry			−0.00557	−0.0142**			
			(0.00509)	(0.00687)			
Participants					−0.000111**	−0.000126**	−9.40e−05*
					(4.75e−05)	(4.99e−05)	(4.93e−05)
Participants asymmetry						−0.00527	−0.0103*
						(0.00462)	(0.00561)
WTO SPS disputes	0.111	0.168	0.178*	0.178*	0.149	0.145	0.149
	(0.100)	(0.106)	(0.106)	(0.108)	(0.0967)	(0.0965)	(0.0979)
WTO SPS STC	−0.0622	−0.0495	−0.0475	−0.0631	−0.0396	−0.0353	−0.0521
	(0.0702)	(0.0732)	(0.0732)	(0.0698)	(0.0748)	(0.0741)	(0.0698)
WTO SPS notifications	4.44e−05	7.77e−05	8.55e−05	8.41e−05	9.46e−05	0.000108	0.000111
	(0.000117)	(0.000131)	(0.000136)	(0.000136)	(0.000115)	(0.000116)	(0.000118)

TABLE 11 SPS: Results from ordered probit regressions on standards-based integration at the dyad level (*cont.*)

	(1)	(2)	(3)	(4)	(5)	(6)	(7)
VARIABLES	Membership	Participation	Participation	Participation	Participants	Participants	Participants
Food exports	0.0103*	0.0105**	0.0108**	0.0113**	0.0101**	0.0102**	0.0103**
	(0.00528)	(0.00510)	(0.00509)	(0.00523)	(0.00501)	(0.00499)	(0.00519)
Food imports	−0.0703***	−0.0691***	−0.0684***	−0.0704***	−0.0703***	−0.0695***	−0.0717***
	(0.0257)	(0.0239)	(0.0240)	(0.0255)	(0.0248)	(0.0250)	(0.0265)
GDP	0.0582	0.0355	0.0377	0.0918	0.00627	0.00297	0.0564
	(0.0859)	(0.0834)	(0.0858)	(0.0891)	(0.0801)	(0.0837)	(0.0904)
GDP asymmetry	0.000701	0.00240	0.00436	0.00311	0.00344	0.00637	0.00473
	(0.00401)	(0.00417)	(0.00499)	(0.00535)	(0.00392)	(0.00548)	(0.00588)
EU	−0.995	−1.122*	−1.157*	−1.121*	−1.226*	−1.214*	−1.134*
	(0.645)	(0.652)	(0.654)	(0.655)	(0.660)	(0.662)	(0.665)
US	−3.061***	−2.969***	−2.958***	−3.108***	−2.875***	−2.824***	−2.957***
	(0.965)	(0.939)	(0.939)	(0.966)	(0.950)	(0.948)	(0.967)
PTA parties	0.175***	0.174***	0.173***	0.170***	0.168***	0.165***	0.164***
	(0.0464)	(0.0463)	(0.0463)	(0.0470)	(0.0467)	(0.0465)	(0.0470)
WTO mission	0.0281***	0.0300***	0.0310***	0.0308***	0.0393***	0.0408***	0.0379***
	(0.0103)	(0.0106)	(0.0108)	(0.0107)	(0.0127)	(0.0130)	(0.0133)

TABLE 11 SPS: Results from ordered probit regressions on standards-based integration at the dyad level (*cont.*)

	(1)	(2)	(3)	(4)	(5)	(6)	(7)
VARIABLES	**Membership**	**Participation**	**Participation**	**Participation**	**Participants**	**Participants**	**Participants**
Polity	0.00499	−0.00171	−0.000816	0.0157	−0.00879	−0.0104	0.00530
	(0.0266)	(0.0272)	(0.0272)	(0.0284)	(0.0258)	(0.0258)	(0.0267)
Distance	0.231***	0.164*	0.156*	0.213**	0.105	0.0965	0.165
	(0.0882)	(0.0942)	(0.0932)	(0.0898)	(0.115)	(0.116)	(0.112)
Observations	942	942	942	942	942	942	942
Time	Yes	Yes	Yes	Yes	Yes	Yes	Yes
Region	Yes	Yes	Yes	Yes	Yes	Yes	Yes
Model	Oprobit	Oprobit	Oprobit	Oprobit	Oprobit	Oprobit	OProbit

Robust standard errors clustered at the PTA level in parentheses.
*p<.05; **p<.01; ***p<.001

To provide a comprehensive overview on the magnitude, the predicted probabilities are calculated for the four independent variables at their first, second, and third quartile as well as the 95th percentile, holding all other variables in the model at their means. The predicted probabilities are calculated based on the regressions which control for *Membership* and the respective *asymmetries* (Column 1, 4, 7 and 10 of Table 12, and column 1, 3 and 7 of Table 13). The predicted probabilities indicate that the more countries' participate in the standard-setting processes of Codex, the less likely they are to commit to a higher degree of standards-based *Integration* in their PTAs. It is interesting to note that in particular the probability of *Integration* based on international standards drops with higher participation in the standard-setting processes of Codex.

TABLE 12 Predicted probabilities on SPS integration at the PTA level

Independent variable	Percentile	Integration				
		0	1	2	3	4
Membership	25	0.67	0.10	0.03	0.08	0.12
	50	0.82	0.07	0.02	0.05	0.15
	75	0.88	0.05	0.01	0.03	0.03
	95	0.93	0.03	0.01	0.02	0.01
Chair	25	0.26	0.12	0.04	0.14	0.44
	50	0.35	0.13	0.04	0.14	0.35
	75	0.70	0.10	0.03	0.08	0.10
	95	1.00	0.00	0.00	0.00	0.00
Participation	25	0.52	0.12	0.04	0.11	0.20
	50	0.76	0.09	0.02	0.06	0.07
	75	0.90	0.05	0.01	0.02	0.02
	95	0.98	0.01	0.00	0.00	0.00
Participants	25	0.40	0.12	0.04	0.13	0.31
	50	0.53	0.12	0.04	0.11	0.20
	75	0.72	0.10	0.03	0.07	0.09
	95	1.00	0.00	0.00	0.00	0.00

TABLE 13 Predicted probabilities on SPS integration at the dyad level

Independent variable	Percentile	Integration				
		0	1	2	3	4
Membership	25	0.48	0.20	0.01	0.23	0.08
	50	0.60	0.18	0.01	0.17	0.04
	75	0.69	0.15	0.01	0.12	0.02
	95	0.75	0.13	0.01	0.09	0.02
Participation	25	0.57	0.19	0.01	0.19	0.05
	50	0.57	0.18	0.01	0.18	0.05
	75	0.60	0.18	0.01	0.17	0.04
	95	0.73	0.14	0.01	0.10	0.02
Participants	25	0.58	0.18	0.01	0.18	0.04
	50	0.59	0.18	0.01	0.18	0.04
	75	0.60	0.18	0.01	0.17	0.04
	95	0.60	0.16	0.01	0.13	0.02

5.5.2 *ISO and TBT Chapters*

The empirical results from the ordered probit regressions, at the PTA level (Table 14) and at the dyad level (Table 15), indicate a positive and statistically significant association between countries' years of *Membership* in ISO and the probability of committing to a higher degree of standards-based *Integration* in the TBT chapters of their PTAs. There is, however, no evidence of a statistically significant relationship between countries' *Participation* in ISO standard-setting processes and the degree of standards-based TBT *Integration* in their PTAs. The results further indicate a positive and statistically significant relationship between the EU being a PTA party and the probability of a higher degree of *Integration*. In contrast, the US being a member of a PTA is negatively and statistically significantly associated with the degree of standards-based *Integration*.

The calculated predicted probabilities (Table 16 and Table 17) reflect the observations above. As in the previous section, the predicted probabilities are calculated for the four independent variables at their first, second and third quartile as well as the 95th percentile, holding all other variables in the model at their means. The predicted probabilities are calculated based on the regressions which control for Membership and the respective asymmetries (Column 1 and 10 of Table 14 and Table 15). The predicted probabilities indicate that while a longer *Membership* in ISO is related to a slightly increased probability of a higher degree of *Integration*, this is not the case for *Participation*.

TABLE 14 TBT: Results from ordered probit regressions on standards-based integration at the PTA level

	(1)	(2)	(3)	(4)
VARIABLES	Membership	Participation	Participation	Participation
Membership	0.0513***			0.0570**
	(0.0185)			(0.0227)
Participation		−0.000407	9.77e−05	0.000562
		(0.000471)	(0.000555)	(0.000616)
Participation asymmetry			0.0160**	0.0176**
			(0.00689)	(0.00714)
WTO TBT disputes	−0.0899	−0.0452	−0.0591	−0.126
	(0.0743)	(0.0728)	(0.0727)	(0.0782)
WTO TBT STC	−0.0187*	−0.0152	−0.0156	−0.0180
	(0.0112)	(0.0106)	(0.0108)	(0.0112)
WTO TBT notifications	0.00427	0.00374	0.00368	0.00409
	(0.00262)	(0.00262)	(0.00263)	(0.00272)
Exports	0.0107***	0.00891***	0.00836***	0.0103***
	(0.00342)	(0.00309)	(0.00323)	(0.00361)
Imports	−0.00838	−0.00882	−0.0133	−0.0132
	(0.00917)	(0.00923)	(0.00981)	(0.00979)
GDP	−0.0417	0.325*	0.222	−0.102
	(0.214)	(0.190)	(0.247)	(0.306)
GDP asymmetry	−0.00532	−0.0155***	−0.0253***	−0.0157**
	(0.00519)	(0.00483)	(0.00586)	(0.00665)
EU	1.966**	1.477	1.731*	2.203**
	(0.919)	(0.915)	(0.964)	(1.068)
US	−5.271***	−5.538***	−5.623***	−5.368***
	(0.979)	(0.861)	(0.829)	(1.025)
PTA parties	0.0941	0.0260	0.0696	0.151*
	(0.0722)	(0.0677)	(0.0703)	(0.0811)
WTO mission	−0.0901**	−0.0747**	−0.0714*	−0.0896**
	(0.0378)	(0.0374)	(0.0398)	(0.0451)
Polity	−0.0110	−0.0325	−0.0116	0.0174
	(0.0539)	(0.0525)	(0.0513)	(0.0558)
Distance	−0.202	−0.137	−0.0911	−0.167
	(0.138)	(0.136)	(0.145)	(0.151)

TABLE 14 TBT: Results from ordered probit regressions on standards-based integration at the PTA level (*cont.*)

	(1)	(2)	(3)	(4)
VARIABLES	Membership	Participation	Participation	Participation
Observations	200	200	200	200
Time	Yes	Yes	Yes	Yes
Region	Yes	Yes	Yes	Yes
Model	OProbit	OProbit	OProbit	OProbit

Robust standard errors clustered at the PTA level in parentheses.
*p<.05; **p<.01; ***p<.001

TABLE 15 TBT: Results from ordered probit regressions on standards-based integration at the dyad level

	(1)	(2)	(3)	(4)
VARIABLES	Membership	Participation	Participation	Participation
Membership	0.0408***			0.0416***
	(0.0109)			(0.0117)
Participation		0.000327	0.000414	8.81e−05
		(0.000396)	(0.000385)	(0.000443)
Participation asymmetry			0.00373	0.00493*
			(0.00257)	(0.00272)
WTO TBT disputes	−0.929***	−0.939***	−0.943***	−0.936***
	(0.336)	(0.262)	(0.262)	(0.338)
WTO TBT STC	−0.217*	−0.173**	−0.175**	−0.218*
	(0.126)	(0.0843)	(0.0846)	(0.119)
WTO TBT notifications	−0.000437**	−0.000274	−0.000262	−0.000427*
	(0.000214)	(0.000207)	(0.000208)	(0.000233)
Exports	0.00509**	0.00240	0.00236	0.00509**
	(0.00218)	(0.00207)	(0.00206)	(0.00217)
Imports	−0.00654	−0.00375	−0.00431	−0.00729
	(0.00495)	(0.00500)	(0.00496)	(0.00499)

TABLE 15 TBT: Results from ordered probit regressions on standards-based integration at the dyad level (*cont.*)

	(1)	(2)	(3)	(4)
VARIABLES	**Membership**	**Participation**	**Participation**	**Participation**
GDP	−0.197***	−0.0251	−0.0403	−0.219***
	(0.0692)	(0.0649)	(0.0657)	(0.0788)
GDP asymmetry	0.00559	−0.00949***	−0.0100***	0.00518
	(0.00520)	(0.00359)	(0.00378)	(0.00526)
EU	3.842***	3.480***	3.519***	3.898***
	(0.823)	(0.691)	(0.691)	(0.817)
US	−7.818***	−8.217***	−8.212***	−7.784***
	(0.939)	(0.927)	(0.919)	(0.925)
PTA parties	0.0593	0.0316	0.0309	0.0590
	(0.0581)	(0.0580)	(0.0581)	(0.0582)
WTO mission	−0.0719***	−0.0501*	−0.0501*	−0.0720***
	(0.0249)	(0.0264)	(0.0263)	(0.0266)
Polity	−0.00331	0.00150	−0.00204	−0.00847
	(0.0369)	(0.0349)	(0.0357)	(0.0375)
Distance	−0.0737	−0.00975	−0.00295	−0.0690
	(0.0628)	(0.0857)	(0.0838)	(0.0820)
Observations	942	942	942	942
Time	Yes	Yes	Yes	Yes
Region	Yes	Yes	Yes	Yes
Model	OProbit	OProbit	Oprobit	OProbit

Robust standard errors clustered at the PTA level in parentheses.
*p<.05; **p<.01; ***p<.001

TABLE 16 Predicted probabilities on TBT integration at the PTA level

Independent variable	Percentile	Integration				
		0	1	2	3	4
Membership	25	0.99	0.00	0.00	0.01	0.00
	50	0.97	0.00	0.01	0.02	0.00
	75	0.93	0.01	0.01	0.04	0.01
	95	0.85	0.02	0.02	0.08	0.02
Participation	25	0.99	0.00	0.00	0.00	0.00
	50	0.99	0.00	0.00	0.00	0.00
	75	0.97	0.00	0.01	0.01	0.00
	95	0.88	0.01	0.02	0.07	0.02

TABLE 17 Predicted probabilities on TBT integration at the dyad level

Independent variable	Percentile	Integration				
		0	1	2	3	4
Membership	25	0.71	0.12	0.01	0.15	0.01
	50	0.51	0.16	0.02	0.29	0.03
	75	0.26	0.15	0.02	0.48	0.10
	95	0.09	0.09	0.01	0.54	0.27
Participation	25	0.47	0.16	0.02	0.32	0.03
	50	0.47	0.16	0.02	0.32	0.03
	75	0.47	0.16	0.02	0.32	0.03
	95	0.46	0.16	0.02	0.33	0.03

5.5.3 *Robustness Checks*

To assess the robustness of the empirical results, a set of alternative regression models are run. The results on the relationship between countries' *Participation* in Codex and the type of standards-based *Integration* in the SPS chapters of PTAs is confirmed by a number of ordered logit regressions (Ologit, Table 23 and Table 24, Annex) and ordinary least squares regressions (OLS, Table 25 and Table 26, Annex). Additionally, a binary dependent variable is constructed which is equal to one if the PTA includes any type of standards-based *Integration*, and equal to zero otherwise. A number of probit regressions (Table 27 and Table 28, Annex) and logit regressions (Table 29 and Table 30, Annex) confirms the previously identified negative relationship between countries' *Participation* in Codex and the probability of committing to international standards-based *Integration* in the SPS chapters of their PTAs.

The empirical results are also found to be robust for the relationship between countries' *Participation* in ISO and the type of standards-based *Integration* in the TBT chapters of PTAs. Indeed, ordered logit regressions (OLogit, Table 31 and Table 32, Annex) as well as OLS regressions (Table 33 and Table 34, Annex) confirm that there is no statistically significant relationship between countries' *Participation* in ISO and the type of standards-based *Integration* chosen in the TBT chapters of PTAs. A number of probit (Table 35 and Table 36, Annex) and logit (Table 37 and Table 38, Annex) regressions on a binary dependent variable for the presence of any type standards-based *Integration* in the TBT chapters of PTAs also confirm the previous observations.

5.5.4 *Comparison*

The results of the empirical analysis are striking and only partly aligned with the expectations of **H1** and **H2**. Indeed, the expectation was that countries' participation in the standard-setting process of ISO and Codex increases the probability that they are able to shape the design of ISO and Codex standards in their political and economic interests, and that countries would therefore be more likely to base their TBT and SPS cooperation in PTAs on international standards.

In the case of Codex, the empirical results indicate the opposite. Countries which have been participating a lot in Codex standard-setting processes are found to be less likely to refer to international standards in the SPS chapter of their PTAs. In the case of ISO, countries' participation in the standard-setting processes appears to be positively associated with the probability of referring to international standards in the TBT chapters of their PTAs. However, this positive association is not statistically robust.

These findings are surprising and call for further inquiry. One explanation for these findings is that there is only limited coordination between the participants of ISO and Codex on the one hand, and PTA trade negotiators on the other hand. In the European Commission, for instance, the Directorate-General (DG) TRADE is in charge of PTA negotiations, while DG SANTE works on SPS-related topics, and the DG for Internal Market, Industry, Entrepreneurship and SMEs (DG GROW) is responsible for TBT-related topics. To what extent the DG SANTE and DG GROW are involved in PTA negotiations may be explored by future research.[9]

A second explanation is related to the nature of TBT and SPS standards and the problems they are supposed to address. Indeed, one dimension according to which standards may be distinguished is whether they address technological/ physical externalities or regulatory externalities. A second dimension according to which standards may be distinguished is whether they address network externalities or traditional externalities. This results in a two-by-two matrix in which standards may be designed to address technological interconnectivity (technological/physical externalities and network externalities), physical externalities (technological/physical externalities and traditional externalities), transactional interconnectivity (regulatory externalities and network externalities), and policy externalities (regulatory externalities and traditional externalities) (Abbott and Snidal, 2001). It can be argued that ISO standards, in general, are more focused on addressing network externalities and facilitating technological and transactional interconnectivity. By contrast, Codex standards are related to health topics and can therefore be argued to address rather traditional externalities such as physical externalities and policy externalities. Importantly, network externalities may be solved in simple Coordination games where actors prefer to adopt the same standard. Alternatively, network externalities may be solved in a more complex Coordination game, such as the "Battle of Sexes", where actors do have a preference to adopt one standard but due to distributional conflicts may disagree which standard this should be. By contrast, in the case of traditional externalities, actors may rather play a Prisoners Dilemma game in which they have incentives to set their own standards rather than coordinate. (Abbott and Snidal, 2001) This line of argument may help to explain why countries seem to be hesitant to base their SPS-related cooperation on international standards — even though they have been actively involved the setting these standards.

A third explanation may be that countries are hesitant to base their SPS-related cooperation on international standards because of previous, negative experiences. As discussed in detail in Chapter 3 and Chapter 4, the EU, for instance, lost the WTO dispute settlement cases of *EC-Hormones* and *EC-Sardines* because it did not comply with the related Codex standards. Even though the EU and its member states had been active participants in the

9 Elsig and Dupont (2012) provide a useful framework to think about the way in which the European Commission manages trade negotiation processes and uses its position in strategic ways to pursue its interests.

development of the standards relevant to the EC-*Hormones* and EC-*Sardines* disputes, the standards were decided on against the EU's reservations and by a narrow margin (See Chapter 3 and 4).

5.6 Interim Conclusion

This Chapter explores the linkage between the international standardization regime and the preferential trade policy regime, and posits that countries' participation in international standardization organizations affects the institutional design of preferential trade agreements. More precisely, it is argued that the more PTA members have participated in relevant international standardization organizations, the more they have been able to shape the design of standards in their political and economic interests, and the more likely they are to refer to international standards as a basis for cooperation in their PTAs. In the specific context of ISO and Codex it is argued that countries' participation in the standard-setting processes of ISO and Codex increases the probability that they have been able to shape the design of ISO and Codex standards in their political and economic interests which, consequently, increases the probability that countries refer to international standards as a basis for cooperation in the area of TBT and SPS, respectively. This relationship, however, is expected to be stronger for Codex and SPS than for ISO and TBT. Indeed, while Codex is explicitly endorsed by the WTO SPS Agreement, the WTO TBT Agreement does not include such endorsement for ISO. As a consequence, countries are arguably locked-in to Codex standards, whereas they have the ability to engage in forum-shopping and/or regime-shifting in the area of TBT-related standards. The relationship between countries' participation in Codex and the institutional design of SPS chapters in PTAs is therefore expected to be more pronounced than in the case of countries' participation in ISO and the institutional design of TBT chapters in PTAs.

The results of the empirical analysis are only partly in line with this expectation. The relationship between countries' participation in ISO and the probability that they refer to international standards as a basis for cooperation in the TBT chapters of their PTAs appears indeed to be positive. However, this relationship is found not be statistically robust. The relationship between countries' participation in the standard-setting processes of Codex is statistically significant but, in contrast to the expectation, is negative. One potential explanation for these findings is that there is only limited coordination between participants in international standard-setting on the one hand, and negotiators of preferential trade agreements on the other hand. A second potential explanation is related to the nature of ISO and Codex standards. It can be argued that TBT-related standards are primarily designed to facilitate interconnectivity and that countries therefore have strong incentives to base their cooperation on international standards. SPS-related standards, by contrast, are directly related to health topics and arguably politically more sensitive. Countries may therefore be more reluctant to commit to internationally agreed standards. A third potential explanation is related to countries' prior experiences with WTO dispute settlement cases related to international standards. Countries which lost such disputes because they were found not to be compliant with certain international standards may be reluctant to emphasize the importance of such standards in future PTAs.

One caveat of this Chapter, which future research is encouraged to address, is related to the independent variable of *Participation*. As previously discussed, participation may only capture influence to a certain extent. While it is unlikely that countries are able to influence the design of international standards without participating, there might still be other important factors that drive influence such as, for instance, expertise. Future research may take a closer look at who the participants in standard-settings are, from which ministries they come, which industries they present, how senior they are, and what scientific expertise they possess. A second caveat is related to the dependent variable of PTAs' institutional design. Here, the empirical approach of constructing an ordinal variable to capture standards-based *Integration* may be challenged. That said, the results from a binary variable approach are in line with those of the ordinal variable approach. Still, future research may attempt to create a more fine-grained dependent variable that captures PTAs' approach to standards-based *Integration*.

Notwithstanding these caveats, this Chapter provides a valuable first attempt to capture the linkage between the work of international standardization organizations and the institutional design of PTAs. While the existing literature hints at this relationship, most contributions are limited to case studies and qualitative assessments primarily focused on the standardization systems of the EU and the US. As standardization in other sectors, such as in information and communication technology (ICT), becomes increasingly politicized (See Chapter 6), future research may focus on the linkage between countries' participation in ICT standardization organizations and the institutional design of related PTA chapters, such as on e-commerce and/or digital trade.

5.7 Appendices

TABLE 18 List of PTAs

Year	PTA	Year	PTA
1995	Armenia – Turkmenistan	2006	US – Colombia
1995	EU – Israel	2006	US – Oman
1995	EU – Tunisia	2006	US – Peru
1995	EU – Turkey	2007	Brunei Darussalam – Japan
1995	Georgia – Armenia	2007	Chile – Japan
1995	Georgia – Ukraine	2007	East African Community (EAC) – Accession of Burundi
1995	Kyrgyz Republic – Kazakhstan	2007	East African Community (EAC) – Accession of Rwanda
1995	Kyrgyz Republic – Moldova	2007	EFTA – Eqypt
1995	Kyrgyz Republic – Ukraine	2007	El Salvador – Honduras – Chinese Taipei
1995	Russian Federation – Belarus – Kazakhstan	2007	EU – Eastern and Southern Africa States Interim EPA
1995	Ukraine – Azerbaijan	2007	EU – Montenegro
1996	Canada – Chile	2007	Japan – Indonesia
1996	Canada – Israel	2007	Japan – Thailand
1996	EU – Morocco	2007	Korea – US
1996	Georgia – Turkmenistan	2007	Mauritius – Pakistan
1996	Kyrgyz Republic – Uzbekistan	2007	Pakistan – Malaysia
1996	Turkey – Israel	2007	Turkey – Georgia
1997	EFTA – Morocco	2007	US – Panama
1997	EU – Jordan	2008	ASEAN – Japan
1997	EU – Palestinian Authority	2008	Australia – Chile
1998	Dominican Republic – Central America	2008	Canada – Colombia
1998	EFTA – Palestinian Authority	2008	Canada – Peru
1998	India – Sri Lanka	2008	China – New Zealand
1998	Peru – Chile	2008	China – Singapore
1999	Armenia – Kazakhstan	2008	EFTA – Canada
1999	Chile – Central America	2008	EFTA – Colombia
1999	East African Community (EAC)	2008	EU – Bosnia and Herzegovina
1999	EU – South Africa	2008	EU – CARIFORUM
1999	Turkey – Macedonia	2008	EU – Serbia

TABLE 18 List of PTAs (*cont.*)

Year	PTA	Year	PTA
2000	EFTA – Macedonia	2008	Gulf Cooperation Council (GCC) – Singapore
2000	EFTA – Mexico	2008	Japan – Viet Nam
2000	EU – Mexico	2008	Peru – Singapore
2000	Israel – Mexico	2008	South Asian FTA (SAFTA) – Accession of Afghanistan
2000	New Zealand – Singapore	2008	Turkey – Montenegro
2000	Russian Federation – Serbia	2009	ASEAN – Australia – New Zealand
2001	Canada – Costa Rica	2009	ASEAN – India
2001	EFTA – Jordan	2009	Canada – Jordan
2001	EU – Egypt	2009	Canada – Panama
2001	Pacific Island Countries Trade Agreement (PICTA)	2009	EFTA – Albania
2001	Ukraine – Macedonia	2009	EFTA – Serbia
2001	Ukraine – Tajikistan	2009	EU – Cameroon
2002	EFTA – Singapore	2009	EU – Papua New Guinea – Fiji
2002	EU – Algeria	2009	Japan – Switzerland
2002	EU – Chile	2009	Korea – India
2002	Japan – Singapore	2009	New Zealand – Malaysia
2002	Pakistan – Sri Lanka	2009	Peru – China
2002	Panama – Central America	2009	Turkey – Chile
2002	Southern African Customs Union (SACU)	2009	Turkey – Jordan
2002	Turkey – Bosnia and Herzegovina	2009	Turkey – Serbia
2003	China – Hong Kong, China	2010	Chile – Malaysia
2003	China – Macao, China	2010	China – Costa Rica
2003	EC (25) Enlargement	2010	Costa Rica – Singapore
2003	EFTA – Chile	2010	EFTA – Peru
2003	India – Afghanistan	2010	EFTA – Ukraine
2003	Korea – Chile	2010	EU – Korea
2003	Panama – Chinese Taipei	2010	Hong Kong, China – New Zealand
2003	Singapore – Australia	2011	Chile – Viet Nam
2003	Ukraine – Moldova	2011	Commonwealth of Independent States (CIS)
2003	US – Chile	2011	Costa Rica – Peru
2003	US – Singapore	2011	EFTA – Hong Kong, China

TABLE 18 List of PTAs (*cont.*)

Year	PTA	Year	PTA
2004	Agadir Agreement	2011	EFTA – Montenegro
2004	ASEAN – China	2011	El Salvador – Cuba
2004	Dominican Republic – Central America	2011	EU (28) Enlargement
2004	EFTA – Lebanon	2011	India – Japan
2004	EFTA – Tunisia	2011	India – Malaysia
2004	Japan – Mexico	2011	Japan – Peru
2004	Jordan – Singapore	2011	Mexico – Central America
2004	MERCOSUR – India	2011	Panama – Peru
2004	Mexico – Uruguay	2011	Peru – Korea
2004	South Asian FTA (SAFTA)	2011	Peru – Mexico
2004	Turkey – Morocco	2011	Turkey – Mauritius
2004	Turkey – Palestinian Authority	2011	Ukraine – Montenegro
2004	Turkey – Syria	2012	EU – Central America
2004	Turkey – Tunisia	2012	EU – Colombia and Peru
2004	US – Australia	2012	Hong Kong, China – Chile
2004	US – Bahrain	2012	Korea – Turkey
2004	US – Morocco	2012	Malaysia – Australia
2005	Chile – China	2012	Pacific Alliance
2005	EC (27) Enlargement	2013	Canada – Honduras
2005	EFTA – Korea	2013	Costa Rica – Colombia
2005	Egypt – Turkey	2013	EFTA – Bosnia and Herzegovina
2005	Guatemala – Chinese Taipei	2013	EFTA – Central America
2005	India – Singapore	2013	Iceland – China
2005	Japan – Malaysia	2013	Korea – Colombia
2005	Korea – Singapore	2013	New Zealand – Chinese Taipei
2005	Thailand – New Zealand	2013	Singapore – Chinese Taipei
2005	Trans-Pacific Strategic Economic Partnership	2013	Switzerland – China
2006	ASEAN – Korea	2014	Canada – Korea
2006	Central European FTA (CEFTA)	2014	EU – Georgia
2006	Chile – Colombia	2014	EU – Moldova
2006	Chile – India	2014	EU – Ukraine
2006	EFTA – SACU	2014	Eurasian Economic Union (EAEU) – Accession of Armenia
2006	EU – Albania	2014	Eurasian Economic Union (EAEU) – Accession of Kyrgyz

TABLE 18 List of PTAs (*cont.*)

Year	PTA	Year	PTA
2006	Japan – Philippines	2014	Japan – Australia
2006	Nicaragua – Chinese Taipei	2014	Korea – Australia
2006	Pakistan – China	2015	Australia – China
2006	Panama – Chile	2015	China – Korea
2006	Panama – Singapore	2015	Japan – Mongolia
2006	Turkey – Albania	2015	Korea – New Zealand
2006	US – Colombia	2015	Korea – Viet Nam
2006	US – Oman	2016	Trans-Pacific Partnership

TABLE 19 Summary statistics: Codex and SPS integration (PTA level)

Variable	Mean	Std. Dev.	Min.	Max.
Integration	1.39	1.759	0	4
Membership	31.552	12.37	0	51
Chair	22.769	41.25	0	252
Chair asymmetry	38.237	37.364	0	100
Participation	199.911	137.573	0	658
Participation asymmetry	32.738	31.4	0	100
Participants	1710.94	2924.359	0	19291
Participants asymmetry	46.262	36.585	0	100
WTO SPS disputes	4.017	4.369	0	25
WTO SPS STC	17.109	25.782	0	173
WTO SPS notifications	176.806	232.227	0	1164.5
Food exports	17.968	14.156	0.288	80.505
Food imports	9.91	4.539	3.125	33.61
GDP	26.959	1.961	19.976	30.462
GDP asymmetry	60.205	34.256	0	100
EU	0.14	0.348	0	1
US	0.06	0.238	0	1
PTA parties	3.17	2.666	1	21
WTO mission	13.813	19.337	0	125
Polity	5.372	3.982	−6.286	10
Distance	8.184	1.339	0.693	9.856
N	200			

TABLE 20 Summary statistics: Codex and SPS integration (dyad level)

Variable	Mean	Std. Dev.	Min.	Max.
Integration	1.445	1.702	0	4
Membership	22.275	15.905	0	53
Participation	47.987	93.399	0	658
Participation asymmetry	70.895	17.903	50	100
Participants	597.454	2176.284	0	38582
Participants asymmetry	75.333	18.826	50	100
WTO SPS disputes	0.077	0.5	0	8
WTO SPS STC	0.098	0.537	0	9
WTO SPS notifications	233.11	599.001	0	5774
Food exports	25.015	19.642	0	89.73
Food imports	12.159	5.967	0	36.89
GDP	25.319	2.704	0	30.462
GDP asymmetry	77.489	17.872	50	100
EU	0.193	0.395	0	1
US	0.087	0.282	0	1
PTA parties	7.983	4.445	1	21
WTO mission	9.234	16.152	0	125
Polity	3.798	4.252	−8	10
Distance	7.785	1.181	0	9.856
N	942			

TABLE 21 Summary statistics: ISO and TBT integration (PTA level)

Variable	Mean	Std. Dev.	Min.	Max.
Integration	0.765	1.453	0	4
Membership	32.232	13.713	0	54
Participation	795.33	820.071	0	4349
Participation asymmetry	58.326	34.871	0	99.921
WTO TBT disputes	5.002	5.767	0	31
WTO TBT STC	30.672	57.279	0	404
WTO TBT notifications	145.016	173.48	0	959
Exports	118.634	230.894	12.191	1613.026
Imports	46.572	23.054	14.558	172.493

TABLE 21 Summary statistics: ISO and TBT integration (PTA level) (*cont.*)

Variable	Mean	Std. Dev.	Min.	Max.
GDP	26.937	1.97	19.976	30.462
GDP asymmetry	60.083	33.323	0	100
EU	0.14	0.348	0	1
US	0.06	0.238	0	1
PTA parties	3.18	2.418	1	15
WTO mission	13.769	19.354	0	125
Polity	5.2	3.877	−6.286	10
Distance	8.191	1.337	0.693	9.856
N	200			

TABLE 22 Summary statistics: ISO and TBT integration (dyad level)

Variable	Mean	Std. Dev.	Min.	Max.
Integration	1.642	1.805	0	4
Membership	18.902	16.766	0	56
Participation	85.485	334.479	0	4349
Participation asymmetry	81.602	21.386	50	100
WTO TBT disputes	0.087	0.605	0	6
WTO TBT STC	0.252	1.26	0	19
WTO TBT notifications	264.017	594.232	0	3361
Exports	90.862	195.108	0	1613.026
Imports	44.796	24.285	0	145.994
GDP	25.319	2.704	0	30.462
GDP asymmetry	77.489	17.872	50	100
EU	0.193	0.395	0	1
US	0.087	0.282	0	1
PTA parties	7.238	3.749	1	15
WTO mission	9.234	16.152	0	125
Polity	3.798	4.252	−8	10
Distance	7.787	1.179	0	9.856
N	942			

TABLE 23 SPS: Results from ordered logit regressions on standards-based integration at the PTA level

	(1)	(2)	(3)	(4)	(5)	(6)	(7)	(8)	(9)	(10)
VARIABLES	Membership	Chair	Chair	Chair	Participation	Participation	Participation	Participants	Participants	Participants
Membership	−0.0806*** (0.0281)			−0.0848*** (0.0287)			−0.0583* (0.0333)			−0.0798*** (0.0299)
Chair		−0.102*** (0.0367)	−0.101*** (0.0365)	−0.106*** (0.0370)						
Chair asymmetry			−0.00659 (0.00986)	−0.00453 (0.00961)						
Participation					−0.0116*** (0.00428)	−0.0115*** (0.00435)	−0.00907** (0.00459)			
Participation asymmetry						0.00218 (0.00827)	−0.00222 (0.00965)			
Participants								−0.00119 (0.000895)	−0.00118 (0.000898)	−0.00101 (0.000893)
Participants asymmetry									0.000395 (0.00961)	−0.00506 (0.0109)
WTO SPS disputes	0.172 (0.169)	0.0945 (0.176)	0.106 (0.182)	0.141 (0.192)	0.294 (0.199)	0.290 (0.201)	0.297 (0.207)	0.0956 (0.168)	0.0952 (0.171)	0.157 (0.188)

TABLE 23 SPS: Results from ordered logit regressions on standards-based integration at the PTA level (*cont.*)

	(1)	(2)	(3)	(4)	(5)	(6)	(7)	(8)	(9)	(10)
VARIABLES	Membership	Chair	Chair	Chair	Participation	Participation	Participation	Participants	Participants	Participants
WTO SPS STC	0.0636	0.108	0.105	0.111*	0.0756	0.0766	0.0735	0.105	0.105	0.0949
	(0.0435)	(0.0678)	(0.0668)	(0.0668)	(0.0528)	(0.0527)	(0.0506)	(0.0693)	(0.0709)	(0.0643)
WTO SPS notifications	−0.00354	−0.00294	−0.00267	−0.00355	−0.00378	−0.00378	−0.00423	−0.00295	−0.00296	−0.00366
	(0.00273)	(0.00290)	(0.00292)	(0.00320)	(0.00317)	(0.00318)	(0.00311)	(0.00256)	(0.00257)	(0.00267)
Food exports	0.0375*	0.0212	0.0227	0.0289	0.0313	0.0307	0.0369*	0.0256	0.0254	0.0352
	(0.0213)	(0.0226)	(0.0221)	(0.0219)	(0.0209)	(0.0210)	(0.0207)	(0.0219)	(0.0220)	(0.0217)
Food imports	−0.250**	−0.236**	−0.226**	−0.219*	−0.223**	−0.224**	−0.227**	−0.227**	−0.227**	−0.221**
	(0.105)	(0.111)	(0.112)	(0.116)	(0.108)	(0.109)	(0.110)	(0.108)	(0.108)	(0.110)
GDP	−0.301	−0.651**	−0.591**	−0.287	−0.0642	−0.0549	0.0273	−0.531**	−0.531**	−0.234
	(0.239)	(0.272)	(0.283)	(0.298)	(0.298)	(0.299)	(0.294)	(0.238)	(0.238)	(0.251)
GDP asymmetry	0.00407	0.00694	0.00617	−0.00452	−0.000621	−0.00132	−0.00411	0.00852	0.00838	0.00113
	(0.00970)	(0.00950)	(0.00961)	(0.0106)	(0.0107)	(0.0108)	(0.0108)	(0.00976)	(0.0100)	(0.0101)
EU	3.091*	5.736*	6.008**	5.816*	2.306	2.312	2.408	4.187**	4.173**	4.040**
	(1.666)	(3.025)	(2.962)	(3.038)	(1.803)	(1.806)	(1.801)	(2.077)	(2.108)	(2.056)
US	−4.883***	−1.336	−1.361	−1.721	−4.843***	−4.934***	−4.908***	−3.583**	−3.605*	−3.793*
	(1.878)	(1.741)	(1.753)	(1.849)	(1.824)	(1.871)	(1.889)	(1.764)	(1.875)	(1.985)
PTA parties	−0.0270	0.0631	0.0609	−0.00722	0.0147	0.0183	−0.0343	0.0468	0.0473	−0.0275
	(0.109)	(0.155)	(0.151)	(0.138)	(0.117)	(0.118)	(0.120)	(0.129)	(0.131)	(0.122)

TABLE 23 SPS: Results from ordered logit regressions on standards-based integration at the PTA level (*cont.*)

	(1)	(2)	(3)	(4)	(5)	(6)	(7)	(8)	(9)	(10)
VARIABLES	Membership	Chair	Chair	Chair	Participation	Participation	Participation	Participants	Participants	Participants
WTO mission	−0.0850	0.0399	0.0384	0.0352	−0.0852	−0.0875	−0.0877	0.0320	0.0314	0.0133
	(0.0587)	(0.0682)	(0.0665)	(0.0744)	(0.0626)	(0.0628)	(0.0633)	(0.0851)	(0.0878)	(0.0989)
Polity	−0.138	−0.0989	−0.0964	−0.0653	−0.0632	−0.0622	−0.0677	−0.117	−0.116	−0.104
	(0.0850)	(0.0869)	(0.0880)	(0.0932)	(0.0984)	(0.0984)	(0.102)	(0.0965)	(0.0985)	(0.106)
Distance	0.772***	0.413	0.427	0.622**	0.584**	0.592**	0.700**	0.490*	0.490*	0.678**
	(0.286)	(0.295)	(0.292)	(0.316)	(0.254)	(0.261)	(0.274)	(0.280)	(0.281)	(0.314)
Observations	200	200	200	200	200	200	200	200	200	200
Time	Yes	Yes	Yes	Yes	Yes	Yes	Yes	Yes	Yes	Yes
Region	Yes	Yes	Yes	Yes	Yes	Yes	Yes	Yes	Yes	Yes
Model	OLogit	OLogit	OLogit	OLogit	OLogit	OLogit	OLogit	OLogit	OLogit	OLogit

Robust standard errors clustered at the PTA level in parentheses.
*p<.05; **p<.01; ***p<.001

TABLE 24 SPS: Results from ordered logit regressions on standards-based integration at the dyad level

	(1)	(2)	(3)	(4)	(5)	(6)	(7)
VARIABLES	Membership	Participation	Participation	Participation	Participants	Participants	Participants
Membership	−0.0293**			−0.0400**			−0.0349**
	(0.0139)			(0.0160)			(0.0144)
Participation		−0.00157	−0.00219	−0.00163			
		(0.00137)	(0.00155)	(0.00151)			
Participation asymmetry			−0.00764	−0.0221			
			(0.00955)	(0.0136)			
Participants					−0.000124	−0.000147	−0.000105
					(9.45e−05)	(9.73e−05)	(0.000102)
Participants asymmetry						−0.00983	−0.0188*
						(0.00823)	(0.0105)
WTO SPS disputes	0.182	0.207	0.220	0.231	0.197	0.186	0.203
	(0.178)	(0.172)	(0.173)	(0.185)	(0.146)	(0.142)	(0.156)
WTO SPS STC	−0.128	−0.101	−0.0981	−0.131	−0.0918	−0.0860	−0.120
	(0.132)	(0.133)	(0.132)	(0.129)	(0.137)	(0.135)	(0.132)
WTO SPS notifications	2.00e−05	3.10e−05	3.75e−05	4.33e−05	7.43e−05	0.000102	0.000114
	(0.000153)	(0.000164)	(0.000171)	(0.000172)	(0.000165)	(0.000168)	(0.000170)

TABLE 24 SPS: Results from ordered logit regressions on standards-based integration at the dyad level (*cont.*)

	(1)	(2)	(3)	(4)	(5)	(6)	(7)
VARIABLES	Membership	Participation	Participation	Participation	Participants	Participants	Participants
Food exports	0.0161	0.0170	0.0177	0.0181	0.0164	0.0167	0.0167
	(0.0115)	(0.0116)	(0.0118)	(0.0118)	(0.0110)	(0.0112)	(0.0113)
Food imports	-0.135**	-0.128**	-0.125**	-0.130**	-0.130**	-0.129**	-0.135**
	(0.0611)	(0.0604)	(0.0610)	(0.0608)	(0.0602)	(0.0614)	(0.0622)
GDP	0.0133	-0.0188	-0.0136	0.0498	-0.0499	-0.0582	0.00980
	(0.201)	(0.207)	(0.213)	(0.213)	(0.200)	(0.208)	(0.211)
GDP asymmetry	0.00871	0.0119	0.0146	0.0146	0.0124	0.0182*	0.0176
	(0.00681)	(0.00766)	(0.00900)	(0.00956)	(0.00760)	(0.0101)	(0.0109)
EU	-0.651	-0.591	-0.651	-0.871	-0.801	-0.759	-0.858
	(1.648)	(1.690)	(1.713)	(1.687)	(1.688)	(1.717)	(1.669)
US	-7.062***	-6.771***	-6.754***	-7.128***	-6.659***	-6.552***	-6.867***
	(2.420)	(2.382)	(2.382)	(2.441)	(2.399)	(2.401)	(2.448)
PTA parties	0.421***	0.418***	0.417***	0.419***	0.407***	0.402***	0.405***
	(0.115)	(0.114)	(0.114)	(0.117)	(0.117)	(0.116)	(0.119)
WTO mission	0.0470**	0.0455*	0.0464*	0.0505**	0.0590**	0.0612**	0.0607**
	(0.0227)	(0.0235)	(0.0241)	(0.0237)	(0.0270)	(0.0276)	(0.0279)

TABLE 24 SPS: Results from ordered logit regressions on standards-based integration at the dyad level (*cont.*)

	(1)	(2)	(3)	(4)	(5)	(6)	(7)
VARIABLES	Membership	Participation	Participation	Participation	Participants	Participants	Participants
Polity	0.0131	−0.00972	−0.00937	0.0254	−0.0128	−0.0169	0.0155
	(0.0603)	(0.0604)	(0.0605)	(0.0657)	(0.0566)	(0.0567)	(0.0612)
Distance	0.477***	0.397**	0.383**	0.461**	0.321	0.302	0.399*
	(0.181)	(0.195)	(0.193)	(0.187)	(0.244)	(0.244)	(0.242)
Observations	942	942	942	942	942	942	942
Time	Yes	Yes	Yes	Yes	Yes	Yes	Yes
Region	Yes	Yes	Yes	Yes	Yes	Yes	Yes
Model	OLogit	OLogit	OLogit	OLogit		OLogit	OLogit

Ologit
Robust standard errors clustered at the PTA level in parentheses.
*p<.05; **p<.01; ***p<.001

TABLE 25 SPS: Results from OLS regressions on standards-based integration at the PTA level

	(1)	(2)	(3)	(4)	(5)	(6)	(7)	(8)	(9)	(10)
VARIABLES	Membership	Chair	Chair	Chair	Participation	Participation	Participation	Participants	Participants	Participants
Membership	−0.0427**			−0.0353**			−0.0274			−0.0393**
	(0.0179)			(0.0179)			(0.0202)			(0.0190)
Chair		−0.0553***	−0.0536***	−0.0501***						
		(0.0167)	(0.0170)	(0.0168)						
Chair asymmetry			−0.00346	−0.00224						
			(0.00598)	(0.00591)						
Participation					−0.00717***	−0.00730***	−0.00619***			
					(0.00191)	(0.00197)	(0.00208)			
Participation asymmetry						−0.00208	−0.00374			
						(0.00484)	(0.00507)			
Participants								−0.000829**	−0.000829**	−0.000680*
								(0.000380)	(0.000380)	(0.000377)
Participants asymmetry									−0.00108	−0.00335
									(0.00535)	(0.00550)
WTO SPS disputes	0.0954	0.0761	0.0800	0.0947	0.170*	0.173*	0.171*	0.0707	0.0713	0.0913
	(0.0943)	(0.0961)	(0.0969)	(0.0958)	(0.0978)	(0.0985)	(0.0987)	(0.0944)	(0.0949)	(0.0947)
WTO SPS STC	0.0168	0.0387*	0.0372*	0.0296	0.0281	0.0273	0.0207	0.0511**	0.0504**	0.0365
	(0.0184)	(0.0200)	(0.0203)	(0.0203)	(0.0186)	(0.0189)	(0.0188)	(0.0231)	(0.0235)	(0.0239)

TABLE 25 SPS: Results from OLS regressions on standards-based integration at the PTA level (*cont.*)

	(1)	(2)	(3)	(4)	(5)	(6)	(7)	(8)	(9)	(10)
VARIABLES	Membership	Chair	Chair	Chair	Participation	Participation	Participation	Participants	Participants	Participants
WTO SPS notifications	−0.00119	−0.00105	−0.000957	−0.00102	−0.00144	−0.00144	−0.00141	−0.00141	−0.00141	−0.00139
	(0.00130)	(0.00129)	(0.00131)	(0.00131)	(0.00125)	(0.00125)	(0.00124)	(0.00129)	(0.00129)	(0.00127)
Food exports	0.0162	0.00921	0.00959	0.0141	0.0151	0.0156	0.0187	0.0103	0.0105	0.0162
	(0.0126)	(0.0121)	(0.0121)	(0.0121)	(0.0123)	(0.0125)	(0.0127)	(0.0122)	(0.0123)	(0.0124)
Food imports	−0.0739**	−0.0731**	−0.0701*	−0.0767**	−0.0551	−0.0552	−0.0620*	−0.0643*	−0.0642*	−0.0711*
	(0.0367)	(0.0356)	(0.0359)	(0.0366)	(0.0350)	(0.0349)	(0.0360)	(0.0357)	(0.0359)	(0.0362)
GDP	−0.0654	−0.227*	−0.199	−0.0584	0.108	0.108	0.166	−0.183	−0.181	−0.0199
	(0.147)	(0.129)	(0.136)	(0.149)	(0.151)	(0.152)	(0.160)	(0.133)	(0.135)	(0.153)
GDP asymmetry	−0.00240	−0.000251	−0.000370	−0.00525	−0.00487	−0.00417	−0.00617	0.000649	0.00110	−0.00321
	(0.00523)	(0.00492)	(0.00491)	(0.00517)	(0.00525)	(0.00534)	(0.00534)	(0.00517)	(0.00559)	(0.00547)
EU	1.473	3.162**	3.270***	2.945**	1.055	1.043	1.002	2.553**	2.584**	2.299*
	(0.953)	(1.268)	(1.245)	(1.235)	(0.961)	(0.967)	(0.971)	(1.195)	(1.194)	(1.182)
US	−2.203***	−0.447	−0.400	−0.561	−2.423***	−2.378***	−2.313***	−1.576*	−1.536*	−1.576*
	(0.789)	(0.960)	(0.956)	(0.985)	(0.776)	(0.773)	(0.767)	(0.816)	(0.817)	(0.811)
PTA parties	−0.0121	0.0209	0.0202	−0.00408	−0.00508	−0.00738	−0.0243	0.0178	0.0172	−0.0113
	(0.0709)	(0.0807)	(0.0802)	(0.0756)	(0.0733)	(0.0744)	(0.0733)	(0.0773)	(0.0778)	(0.0738)
WTO mission	−0.0232	0.0372	0.0356	0.0391	−0.0304	−0.0286	−0.0214	0.0437	0.0445	0.0416
	(0.0278)	(0.0318)	(0.0311)	(0.0314)	(0.0284)	(0.0288)	(0.0283)	(0.0398)	(0.0402)	(0.0393)

TABLE 25 SPS: Results from OLS regressions on standards-based integration at the PTA level (*cont.*)

	(1)	(2)	(3)	(4)	(5)	(6)	(7)	(8)	(9)	(10)
VARIABLES	**Membership**	**Chair**	**Chair**	**Chair**	**Participation**	**Participation**	**Participation**	**Participants**	**Participants**	**Participants**
Polity	−0.0726*	−0.0602	−0.0584	−0.0513	−0.0314	−0.0308	−0.0318	−0.0648	−0.0651	−0.0586
	(0.0433)	(0.0441)	(0.0439)	(0.0439)	(0.0474)	(0.0477)	(0.0477)	(0.0445)	(0.0451)	(0.0455)
Distance	0.321***	0.131	0.142	0.173	0.271**	0.266**	0.284**	0.195	0.196	0.242*
	(0.122)	(0.146)	(0.148)	(0.143)	(0.123)	(0.124)	(0.120)	(0.142)	(0.143)	(0.138)
									(0.00535)	(0.00550)
Constant	0.982	6.312*	5.523	2.352	−3.042	−3.022	−4.239	4.415	4.352	0.591
	(3.666)	(3.541)	(3.751)	(3.881)	(3.855)	(3.870)	(3.932)	(3.481)	(3.558)	(3.815)
Observations	200	200	200	200	200	200	200	200	200	200
	0.392	0.413	0.414	0.430	0.414	0.415	0.422	0.389	0.389	0.407
Time	Yes	Yes	Yes	Yes	Yes	Yes	Yes	Yes	Yes	Yes
Region	Yes	Yes	Yes	Yes	Yes	Yes	Yes	Yes	Yes	Yes
Model	OLS	OLS	OLS	OLS	OLS	OLS	OLS	OLS	OLS	OLS

Robust standard errors clustered at the PTA level in parentheses.
*p<.05; **p<.01; ***p<.001

TABLE 26 SPS: Results from OLS regressions on standards-based integration at the dyad level

	(1)	(2)	(3)	(4)	(5)	(6)	(7)
VARIABLES	Membership	Participation	Participation	Participation	Participants	Participants	Participants
Membership	-0.0123**			-0.0175**			-0.0151**
	(0.00603)			(0.00677)			(0.00626)
Participation		-0.00109	-0.00150	-0.00118			
		(0.000971)	(0.00104)	(0.000953)			
Participation asymmetry			-0.00492	-0.0105**			
			(0.00323)	(0.00443)			
Participants					-6.63e-05	-7.47e-05	-5.87e-05
					(5.04e-05)	(5.14e-05)	(5.01e-05)
Participants asymmetry						-0.00482	-0.00857**
						(0.00299)	(0.00367)
WTO SPS disputes	0.134	0.169	0.175	0.167	0.161	0.153	0.152
	(0.110)	(0.123)	(0.121)	(0.118)	(0.113)	(0.112)	(0.110)
WTO SPS STC	-0.0471	-0.0365	-0.0336	-0.0435	-0.0355	-0.0328	-0.0418
	(0.0839)	(0.0863)	(0.0863)	(0.0829)	(0.0878)	(0.0871)	(0.0831)
WTO SPS notifications	0.000135	0.000152	0.000159	0.000168	0.000154	0.000160	0.000176
	(0.000170)	(0.000176)	(0.000180)	(0.000187)	(0.000160)	(0.000158)	(0.000166)

TABLE 26 SPS: Results from OLS regressions on standards-based integration at the dyad level (*cont.*)

	(1)	(2)	(3)	(4)	(5)	(6)	(7)
VARIABLES	Membership	Participation	Participation	Participation	Participants	Participants	Participants
Food exports	0.00586	0.00559	0.00580*	0.00622*	0.00567*	0.00585*	0.00604*
	(0.00355)	(0.00339)	(0.00345)	(0.00339)	(0.00337)	(0.00346)	(0.00339)
Food imports	-0.0276**	-0.0227**	-0.0214*	-0.0275**	-0.0231**	-0.0217*	-0.0274**
	(0.0118)	(0.0115)	(0.0117)	(0.0114)	(0.0115)	(0.0116)	(0.0116)
GDP	0.0533	0.0307	0.0314	0.0719	0.0211	0.0209	0.0618
	(0.0408)	(0.0370)	(0.0378)	(0.0437)	(0.0382)	(0.0387)	(0.0431)
GDP asymmetry	-0.00223	-0.000353	0.00158	2.89e-05	-0.000244	0.00231	0.000534
	(0.00285)	(0.00271)	(0.00315)	(0.00328)	(0.00258)	(0.00324)	(0.00340)
EU	-0.592	-0.657	-0.661	-0.586	-0.632	-0.601	-0.521
	(0.566)	(0.565)	(0.563)	(0.580)	(0.585)	(0.582)	(0.595)
US	-2.462***	-2.430***	-2.440***	-2.517***	-2.374***	-2.350***	-2.417***
	(0.573)	(0.572)	(0.571)	(0.572)	(0.575)	(0.573)	(0.573)
PTA parties	0.154***	0.155***	0.154***	0.149***	0.151***	0.148***	0.145***
	(0.0359)	(0.0359)	(0.0357)	(0.0359)	(0.0359)	(0.0357)	(0.0359)
WTO mission	0.0158	0.0171	0.0177	0.0166	0.0215	0.0223	0.0201
	(0.0126)	(0.0126)	(0.0126)	(0.0131)	(0.0158)	(0.0158)	(0.0161)

TABLE 26 SPS: Results from OLS regressions on standards-based integration at the dyad level (*cont.*)

	(1)	(2)	(3)	(4)	(5)	(6)	(7)
VARIABLES	Membership	Participation	Participation	Participation	Participants	Participants	Participants
Polity	−0.00753	−0.0110	−0.00916	0.000851	−0.0141	−0.0139	−0.00447
	(0.0220)	(0.0230)	(0.0230)	(0.0229)	(0.0223)	(0.0224)	(0.0219)
Distance	0.134*	0.104	0.101	0.131*	0.0626	0.0592	0.0960
	(0.0696)	(0.0697)	(0.0689)	(0.0670)	(0.0807)	(0.0804)	(0.0767)
						(0.00299)	(0.00367)
Constant	−1.885	−1.361	−1.157	−1.694	−0.805	−0.617	−1.338
	(1.145)	(1.122)	(1.114)	(1.133)	(1.216)	(1.219)	(1.206)
Observations	942	942	942	942	942	942	942
	0.637	0.633	0.634	0.643	0.634	0.636	0.643
Time	Yes	Yes	Yes	Yes	Yes	Yes	Yes
Region	Yes	Yes	Yes	Yes	Yes	Yes	Yes
Model	OLS	OLS	CLS	OLS	OLS	OLS	OLS

Robust standard errors clustered at the PTA level in parentheses.
*p<.05; **p<.01; ***p<.001

TABLE 27 SPS: Results from probit regressions on standards-based integration at the PTA level

	(1)	(2)	(3)	(4)	(5)	(6)	(7)	(8)	(9)	(10)
VARIABLES	Membership	Chair	Chair	Chair	Participation	Participation	Participation	Participants	Participants	Participants
Membership	−0.0155***			−0.0151***			−0.0100**			−0.0144***
	(0.00427)			(0.00393)			(0.00469)			(0.00445)
Chair		−0.0143***	−0.0147***	−0.0138***						
		(0.00400)	(0.00401)	(0.00359)						
Chair asymmetry			0.00117	0.00162						
			(0.00142)	(0.00129)						
Participation					−0.00199***	−0.00198***	−0.00155***			
					(0.000531)	(0.000541)	(0.000573)			
Participation asymmetry						0.00199	0.00167			
						(0.00130)	(0.00135)			
Participants								−0.000177*	−0.000177*	−0.000146
								(0.000103)	(0.000104)	(9.98e−05)
Participants asymmetry									0.00170	0.00135
									(0.00128)	(0.00128)
WTO SPS disputes	0.0342	0.0195	0.0191	0.0311	0.0449*	0.0418	0.0462*	0.0190	0.0188	0.0315
	(0.0235)	(0.0234)	(0.0234)	(0.0231)	(0.0256)	(0.0255)	(0.0245)	(0.0244)	(0.0242)	(0.0237)
WTO SPS STC	0.00247	0.0106*	0.0105*	0.00748	0.00788	0.00821	0.00597	0.0113	0.0118	0.00794
	(0.00604)	(0.00633)	(0.00631)	(0.00624)	(0.00593)	(0.00592)	(0.00595)	(0.00735)	(0.00745)	(0.00723)

TABLE 27 SPS: Results from probit regressions on standards-based integration at the PTA level (*cont.*)

	(1)	(2)	(3)	(4)	(5)	(6)	(7)	(8)	(9)	(10)
VARIABLES	Membership	Chair	Chair	Chair	Participation	Participation	Participation	Participants	Participants	Participants
WTO SPS	−0.000269	−0.000124	−0.000158	−0.000297	−0.000242	−0.000208	−0.000298	−0.000170	−0.000172	−0.000288
notifications	(0.000374)	(0.000363)	(0.000368)	(0.000349)	(0.000389)	(0.000397)	(0.000383)	(0.000376)	(0.000382)	(0.000359)
Food exports	0.00536	0.00319	0.00308	0.00412	0.00496	0.00496	0.00537	0.00382	0.00369	0.00471
	(0.00354)	(0.00364)	(0.00364)	(0.00332)	(0.00342)	(0.00345)	(0.00334)	(0.00376)	(0.00378)	(0.00350)
Food imports	−0.0398***	−0.0385***	−0.0402***	−0.0355***	−0.0334***	−0.0335**	−0.0329**	−0.0390***	−0.0385***	−0.0352***
	(0.0129)	(0.0129)	(0.0132)	(0.0120)	(0.0129)	(0.0133)	(0.0130)	(0.0140)	(0.0140)	(0.0133)
GDP	−0.0687*	−0.123***	−0.132***	−0.0802**	−0.0106	−0.00226	0.00723	−0.111***	−0.111***	−0.0643
	(0.0391)	(0.0353)	(0.0367)	(0.0370)	(0.0456)	(0.0463)	(0.0451)	(0.0376)	(0.0382)	(0.0396)
GDP	0.000649	0.00165	0.00175	−0.000239	−0.000156	−0.00111	−0.00170	0.00193	0.00113	−0.000493
asymmetry	(0.00148)	(0.00130)	(0.00129)	(0.00139)	(0.00145)	(0.00151)	(0.00155)	(0.00138)	(0.00142)	(0.00149)
EU	0.430**	0.935***	0.882***	0.610**	0.400	0.385	0.298	0.763***	0.692**	0.483**
	(0.218)	(0.309)	(0.313)	(0.270)	(0.260)	(0.256)	(0.226)	(0.277)	(0.284)	(0.245)
US	−0.509**	−0.0934	−0.0922	−0.0637	−0.646***	−0.697***	−0.618***	−0.433*	−0.483*	−0.418*
	(0.219)	(0.233)	(0.229)	(0.219)	(0.224)	(0.235)	(0.216)	(0.245)	(0.255)	(0.237)
PTA parties	−0.00879	0.00403	0.00485	−0.00628	−0.00478	−0.00347	−0.00909	0.00193	0.00273	−0.00716
	(0.0136)	(0.0154)	(0.0154)	(0.0136)	(0.0141)	(0.0138)	(0.0135)	(0.0151)	(0.0149)	(0.0138)
WTO mission	−0.00256	0.0103	0.0110	0.0147*	−0.00867	−0.00957	−0.00609	0.00911	0.00857	0.0105
	(0.00748)	(0.00806)	(0.00797)	(0.00819)	(0.00783)	(0.00778)	(0.00734)	(0.0111)	(0.0114)	(0.0117)

TABLE 27 SPS: Results from probit regressions on standards-based integration at the PTA level (*cont.*)

	(1)	(2)	(3)	(4)	(5)	(6)	(7)	(8)	(9)	(10)
VARIABLES	Membership	Chair	Chair	Chair	Participation	Participation	Participation	Participants	Participants	Participants
Polity	−0.0163	−0.0133	−0.0149	−0.0116	−0.00561	−0.00594	−0.00625	−0.0168	−0.0168	−0.0131
	(0.0105)	(0.0104)	(0.00987)	(0.00967)	(0.0114)	(0.0111)	(0.0111)	(0.0111)	(0.0106)	(0.0106)
Distance	0.136***	0.0687**	0.0635*	0.0974***	0.0940***	0.0975***	0.121***	0.0826**	0.0801**	0.117***
	(0.0334)	(0.0331)	(0.0327)	(0.0339)	(0.0308)	(0.0310)	(0.0317)	(0.0337)	(0.0332)	(0.0349)
Observations	178	178	178	178	178	178	178	178	178	178
Time	Yes	Yes	Yes	Yes	Yes	Yes	Yes	Yes	Yes	Yes
Region	Yes	Yes	Yes	Yes	Yes	Yes	Yes	Yes	Yes	Yes
Model	Probit	Probit	Probit	Probit	Probit	Probit	Probit	Probit	Probit	Probit

Robust standard errors clustered at the PTA level in parentheses.
*p<.05; **p<.01; ***p<.001

TABLE 28 SPS: Results from probit regressions on standards-based integration at the dyad level

	(1)	(2)	(3)	(4)	(5)	(6)	(7)
VARIABLES	Membership	Participation	Participation	Participation	Participants	Participants	Participants
Membership	-0.00533***			-0.00513***			-0.00480***
	(0.00152)			(0.00142)			(0.00141)
Participation		-0.000837***	-0.000906***	-0.000690***			
		(0.000265)	(0.000266)	(0.000239)			
Participation asymmetry			-0.000576	-0.00199*			
			(0.000974)	(0.00113)			
Participants					-2.77e-05***	-2.74e-05***	-1.79e-05**
					(9.08e-06)	(9.01e-06)	(8.22e-06)
Participants asymmetry						0.000104	-0.000888
						(0.000898)	(0.000986)
WTO SPS disputes	0.00269	0.0169	0.0160	0.0115	0.0189	0.0190	0.0142
	(0.0433)	(0.0463)	(0.0462)	(0.0439)	(0.0443)	(0.0443)	(0.0422)
WTO SPS STC	0.0494	0.0689*	0.0714*	0.0648*	0.0591*	0.0589*	0.0526
	(0.0360)	(0.0374)	(0.0373)	(0.0356)	(0.0351)	(0.0351)	(0.0338)
WTO SPS notifications	0.000221***	0.000249***	0.000251***	0.000244***	0.000200***	0.000200***	0.000210***
	(7.42e-05)	(8.05e-05)	(8.02e-05)	(7.26e-05)	(7.63e-05)	(7.63e-05)	(7.20e-05)

TABLE 28 SPS: Results from probit regressions on standards-based integration at the dyad level (*cont.*)

	(1)	(2)	(3)	(4)	(5)	(6)	(7)
VARIABLES	**Membership**	**Participation**	**Participation**	**Participation**	**Participants**	**Participants**	**Participants**
Food exports	0.00173*	0.00147	0.00141	0.00154	0.00166*	0.00168*	0.00169*
	(0.000991)	(0.000989)	(0.000997)	(0.000956)	(0.000964)	(0.000985)	(0.000986)
Food imports	-0.0136***	-0.0133***	-0.0131***	-0.0136***	-0.0132***	-0.0132***	-0.0140***
	(0.00461)	(0.00460)	(0.00464)	(0.00457)	(0.00467)	(0.00472)	(0.00474)
GDP	0.0107	0.00584	0.00596	0.0170	-0.00302	-0.00294	0.00875
	(0.0160)	(0.0156)	(0.0160)	(0.0165)	(0.0137)	(0.0138)	(0.0161)
GDP asymmetry	-0.000827	-0.000578	-0.000400	-0.00101	6.40e-05	1.13e-05	-0.000738
	(0.00104)	(0.00103)	(0.00115)	(0.00123)	(0.000954)	(0.00114)	(0.00123)
EU	-0.0580	-0.0936	-0.0976	-0.0802	-0.107	-0.107	-0.0815
	(0.116)	(0.124)	(0.124)	(0.113)	(0.124)	(0.124)	(0.114)
US	-0.669***	-0.698***	-0.699***	-0.679***	-0.603***	-0.605***	-0.609***
	(0.168)	(0.179)	(0.178)	(0.164)	(0.166)	(0.167)	(0.157)
PTA parties	0.0180***	0.0177***	0.0175***	0.0163***	0.0166***	0.0166***	0.0159***
	(0.00578)	(0.00586)	(0.00580)	(0.00564)	(0.00593)	(0.00586)	(0.00568)
WTO mission	0.00241	0.00315	0.00329*	0.00298	0.00524**	0.00521**	0.00426*
	(0.00182)	(0.00192)	(0.00198)	(0.00189)	(0.00213)	(0.00214)	(0.00218)
Polity	-0.00356	-0.00333	-0.00312	-0.00147	-0.00582	-0.00581	-0.00379
	(0.00464)	(0.00485)	(0.00489)	(0.00469)	(0.00484)	(0.00483)	(0.00463)

TABLE 28 SPS: Results from probit regressions on standards-based integration at the dyad level (*cont.*)

	(1)	(2)	(3)	(4)	(5)	(6)	(7)
VARIABLES	Membership	Participation	Participation	Participation	Participants	Participants	Participants
Distance	0.0164	−0.0102	−0.0112	0.00432	−0.0219	−0.0219	−0.00138
	(0.0162)	(0.0180)	(0.0179)	(0.0166)	(0.0212)	(0.0211)	(0.0196)
Observations	745	745	745	745	745	745	745
Time	Yes	Yes	Yes	Yes	Yes	Yes	Yes
Region	Yes	Yes	Yes	Yes	Yes	Yes	Yes
Model	Probit	Probit	Probit	Probit	Probit	Probit	Probit

Robust standard errors clustered at the PTA level in parentheses.
*p<.05; **p<.01; ***p<.001

TABLE 29 SPS: Results from logit regressions on standards-based integration at the PTA level

	(1)	(2)	(3)	(4)	(5)	(6)	(7)	(8)	(9)	(10)
VARIABLES	Membership	Chair	Chair	Chair	Participation	Participation	Participation	Participants	Participants	Participants
Membership	−0.0152***			−0.0147***			−0.00985*			−0.0142***
	(0.00457)			(0.00436)			(0.00518)			(0.00494)
Chair		−0.0142***	−0.0145***	−0.0132***						
		(0.00499)	(0.00513)	(0.00418)						
Chair asymmetry			0.00124	0.00150						
			(0.00159)	(0.00141)						
Participation					−0.00192***	−0.00190***	−0.00146**			
					(0.000568)	(0.000581)	(0.000622)			
Participation asymmetry						0.00200	0.00169			
						(0.00159)	(0.00167)			
Participants								−0.000175	−0.000177	−0.000136
								(0.000116)	(0.000120)	(0.000113)
Participants asymmetry									0.00174	0.00133
									(0.00156)	(0.00157)
WTO SPS disputes	0.0387	0.0248	0.0242	0.0348	0.0506	0.0436	0.0487	0.0246	0.0216	0.0351
	(0.0278)	(0.0285)	(0.0287)	(0.0293)	(0.0316)	(0.0322)	(0.0313)	(0.0289)	(0.0290)	(0.0293)

TABLE 29 SPS: Results from logit regressions on standards-based integration at the PTA level (*cont.*)

	(1)	(2)	(3)	(4)	(5)	(6)	(7)	(8)	(9)	(10)
VARIABLES	Membership	Chair	Chair	Chair	Participation	Participation	Participation	Participants	Participants	Participants
WTO SPS STC	0.00185	0.0105	0.0105	0.00715	0.00689	0.00748	0.00527	0.0105	0.0114	0.00711
	(0.00685)	(0.00826)	(0.00830)	(0.00803)	(0.00713)	(0.00710)	(0.00725)	(0.00879)	(0.00943)	(0.00884)
WTO SPS	−0.000255	−0.000172	−0.000214	−0.000327	−0.000269	−0.000225	−0.000302	−0.000178	−0.000180	−0.000273
notifications	(0.000409)	(0.000430)	(0.000437)	(0.000436)	(0.000440)	(0.000453)	(0.000446)	(0.000400)	(0.000409)	(0.000401)
Food exports	0.00599	0.00328	0.00320	0.00419	0.00521	0.00523	0.00568	0.00432	0.00427	0.00531
	(0.00407)	(0.00458)	(0.00469)	(0.00432)	(0.00404)	(0.00415)	(0.00404)	(0.00452)	(0.00459)	(0.00421)
Food imports	−0.0398***	−0.0384**	−0.0402***	−0.0349**	−0.0343**	−0.0349**	−0.0338**	−0.0397**	−0.0401**	−0.0360**
	(0.0140)	(0.0152)	(0.0155)	(0.0138)	(0.0146)	(0.0156)	(0.0150)	(0.0161)	(0.0167)	(0.0153)
GDP	−0.0660	−0.120***	−0.129***	−0.0803*	−0.0110	−0.00252	0.00487	−0.107***	−0.108**	−0.0648
	(0.0405)	(0.0423)	(0.0437)	(0.0422)	(0.0480)	(0.0494)	(0.0476)	(0.0415)	(0.0432)	(0.0431)
GDP	0.000508	0.00152	0.00163	−0.000224	−0.000255	−0.00113	−0.00166	0.00171	0.000976	−0.000466
asymmetry	(0.00163)	(0.00144)	(0.00140)	(0.00160)	(0.00154)	(0.00158)	(0.00161)	(0.00148)	(0.00148)	(0.00158)
EU	0.417*	0.972*	0.924*	0.586*	0.400	0.378	0.288	0.767**	0.693*	0.459*
	(0.217)	(0.524)	(0.549)	(0.321)	(0.303)	(0.293)	(0.236)	(0.352)	(0.364)	(0.259)
US	−0.522**	−0.101	−0.101	−0.0689	−0.632**	−0.684**	−0.618**	−0.436	−0.487*	−0.438
	(0.249)	(0.258)	(0.251)	(0.252)	(0.254)	(0.276)	(0.260)	(0.269)	(0.292)	(0.290)
PTA parties	−0.00884	0.00566	0.00665	−0.00543	−0.00380	−0.00271	−0.00884	0.00281	0.00364	−0.00725
	(0.0136)	(0.0173)	(0.0175)	(0.0145)	(0.0147)	(0.0143)	(0.0141)	(0.0161)	(0.0158)	(0.0143)

TABLE 29 SPS: Results from logit regressions on standards-based integration at the PTA level (*cont.*)

	(1)	(2)	(3)	(4)	(5)	(6)	(7)	(8)	(9)	(10)
VARIABLES	**Membership**	**Chair**	**Chair**	**Chair**	**Participation**	**Participation**	**Participation**	**Participants**	**Participants**	**Participants**
WTO mission	−0.00235	0.00880	0.00935	0.0142	−0.00839	−0.00908	−0.00571	0.00901	0.00845	0.00985
	(0.00769)	(0.0103)	(0.0104)	(0.00926)	(0.00896)	(0.00874)	(0.00789)	(0.0121)	(0.0126)	(0.0132)
Polity	−0.0185	−0.0147	−0.0158	−0.0122	−0.00893	−0.00788	−0.00852	−0.0183	−0.0170	−0.0140
	(0.0137)	(0.0133)	(0.0123)	(0.0128)	(0.0144)	(0.0139)	(0.0143)	(0.0139)	(0.0135)	(0.0140)
Distance	0.130***	0.0635	0.0584	0.0934**	0.0881***	0.0926***	0.115***	0.0771**	0.0748*	0.111***
	(0.0361)	(0.0433)	(0.0440)	(0.0377)	(0.0335)	(0.0346)	(0.0346)	(0.0393)	(0.0390)	(0.0379)
Observations	178	178	178	178	178	178	178	178	178	178
Time	Yes	Yes	Yes	Yes	Yes	Yes	Yes	Yes	Yes	Yes
Region	Yes	Yes	Yes	Yes	Yes	Yes	Yes	Yes	Yes	Yes
Model	Logit	Logit	Logit	Logit	Logit	Logit	Logit	Logit	Logit	Logit

Robust standard errors clustered at the PTA level in parentheses.
*p<.05; **p<.01; ***p<.001

TABLE 30 SPS: Results from logit regressions on standards-based integration at the dyad level

	(1)	(2)	(3)	(4)	(5)	(6)	(7)
VARIABLES	Membership	Participation	Participation	Participation	Participants	Participants	Participants
Membership	−0.00508***			−0.00497***			−0.00465***
	(0.00175)			(0.00160)			(0.00160)
Participation		−0.000712**	−0.000779***	−0.000567**			
		(0.000281)	(0.000285)	(0.000253)			
Participation asymmetry			−0.000556	−0.00178			
			(0.00100)	(0.00117)			
Participants					−2.53e−05***	−2.58e−05***	−1.59e−05*
					(9.40e−06)	(9.56e−06)	(8.26e−06)
Participants asymmetry						−0.000176	−0.00101
						(0.000887)	(0.000966)
WTO SPS disputes	0.00873	0.0209	0.0201	0.0120	0.0263	0.0261	0.0169
	(0.0593)	(0.0581)	(0.0579)	(0.0570)	(0.0528)	(0.0527)	(0.0547)
WTO SPS STC	0.0437	0.0628	0.0652	0.0601	0.0485	0.0488	0.0467
	(0.0488)	(0.0547)	(0.0540)	(0.0491)	(0.0464)	(0.0461)	(0.0455)

TABLE 30 SPS: Results from logit regressions on standards-based integration at the dyad level (*cont.*)

	(1)	(2)	(3)	(4)	(5)	(6)	(7)
VARIABLES	Membership	Participation	Participation	Participation	Participants	Participants	Participants
WTO SPS	0.000237***	0.000265***	0.000268***	0.000258***	0.000225**	0.000226**	0.000230***
notifications	(8.73e-05)	(9.55e-05)	(9.46e-05)	(8.43e-05)	(8.82e-05)	(8.82e-05)	(8.34e-05)
Food exports	0.00171	0.00155	0.00148	0.00155	0.00168	0.00165	0.00165
	(0.00104)	(0.00112)	(0.00113)	(0.00106)	(0.00105)	(0.00107)	(0.00107)
Food imports	-0.0143**	-0.0134**	-0.0131**	-0.0137**	-0.0133**	-0.0132**	-0.0141**
	(0.00635)	(0.00563)	(0.00575)	(0.00639)	(0.00548)	(0.00560)	(0.00650)
GDP	0.00418	0.00234	0.00261	0.0109	-0.00603	-0.00620	0.00332
	(0.0192)	(0.0207)	(0.0212)	(0.0210)	(0.0172)	(0.0173)	(0.0200)
GDP asymmetry	-7.73e-05	6.99e-05	0.000231	-0.000254	0.000590	0.000678	6.93e-05
	(0.00109)	(0.00110)	(0.00117)	(0.00132)	(0.00102)	(0.00111)	(0.00127)
EU	0.0231	0.0213	0.0185	-0.00719	0.0108	0.0117	-0.00276
	(0.145)	(0.174)	(0.175)	(0.150)	(0.171)	(0.172)	(0.150)
US	-0.683***	-0.714***	-0.714***	-0.682***	-0.641***	-0.638***	-0.630***
	(0.176)	(0.187)	(0.185)	(0.168)	(0.180)	(0.179)	(0.167)

TABLE 30 SPS: Results from logit regressions on standards-based integration at the dyad level (*cont.*)

VARIABLES	(1) Membership	(2) Participation	(3) Participation	(4) Participation	(5) Participants	(6) Participants	(7) Participants
PTA parties	0.0182***	0.0188***	0.0187***	0.0169***	0.0178***	0.0177***	0.0164***
	(0.00555)	(0.00572)	(0.00565)	(0.00562)	(0.00566)	(0.00560)	(0.00558)
WTO mission	0.00196	0.00214	0.00225	0.00249	0.00414	0.00419	0.00366
	(0.00220)	(0.00258)	(0.00263)	(0.00237)	(0.00258)	(0.00258)	(0.00245)
Polity	−0.00305	−0.00319	−0.00297	−0.00143	−0.00530	−0.00531	−0.00328
	(0.00458)	(0.00477)	(0.00479)	(0.00461)	(0.00460)	(0.00460)	(0.00448)
Distance	0.0181	−0.00817	−0.00946	0.00637	−0.0183	−0.0185	0.00239
	(0.0164)	(0.0191)	(0.0192)	(0.0180)	(0.0219)	(0.0220)	(0.0203)
Observations	745	745	745	745	745	745	745
Time	Yes	Yes	Yes	Yes	Yes	Yes	Yes
Region	Yes	Yes	Yes	Yes	Yes	Yes	Yes
Model	Logit	Logit	Logit	Logit	Logit	Logit	Logit

Robust standard errors clustered at the PTA level in parentheses.
*p<.05; **p<.01; ***p<.001

TABLE 31 TBT: Results from ordered logit regressions on standards-based integration at the PTA level

VARIABLES	(1) Membership	(2) Participation	(3) Participation	(4) Participation
Membership	0.0889**			0.0975**
	(0.0367)			(0.0456)
Participation		-0.000871	0.000174	0.00103
		(0.000951)	(0.00121)	(0.00132)
Participation asymmetry			0.0285*	0.0312**
			(0.0154)	(0.0153)
WTO TBT disputes	-0.173	-0.0871	-0.114	-0.238
	(0.140)	(0.136)	(0.136)	(0.150)
WTO TBT STC	-0.0327	-0.0271	-0.0274	-0.0305
	(0.0216)	(0.0205)	(0.0206)	(0.0209)
WTO TBT notifications	0.00791	0.00759	0.00707	0.00731
	(0.00530)	(0.00566)	(0.00535)	(0.00548)
Exports	0.0185***	0.0154***	0.0143**	0.0174***
	(0.00615)	(0.00561)	(0.00582)	(0.00635)
Imports	-0.0120	-0.0143	-0.0235	-0.0221
	(0.0201)	(0.0210)	(0.0223)	(0.0218)
GDP	-0.0463	0.596	0.370	-0.163
	(0.452)	(0.420)	(0.538)	(0.589)
GDP asymmetry	-0.00971	-0.0261***	-0.0427***	-0.0276**
	(0.00922)	(0.00904)	(0.0109)	(0.0118)
EU	3.808*	2.632	3.242	4.297*
	(1.977)	(2.029)	(2.143)	(2.377)
US	-15.55***	-16.45***	-17.23***	-16.57***
	(1.852)	(1.709)	(1.776)	(1.951)
PTA parties	0.132	0.0398	0.105	0.223
	(0.139)	(0.134)	(0.137)	(0.152)
WTO mission	-0.160**	-0.128*	-0.123*	-0.159*
	(0.0734)	(0.0737)	(0.0718)	(0.0854)
Polity	-0.0157	-0.0689	-0.0367	0.0261
	(0.117)	(0.115)	(0.104)	(0.117)
Distance	-0.411	-0.295	-0.188	-0.331
	(0.294)	(0.284)	(0.299)	(0.318)

TABLE 31 TBT: Results from ordered logit regressions on standards-based integration at the PTA level (*cont.*)

VARIABLES	(1) Membership	(2) Participation	(3) Participation	(4) Participation
Observations	200	200	200	200
Time	Yes	Yes	Yes	Yes
Region	Yes	Yes	Yes	Yes
Model	OLogit	OLogit	OLogit	OLogit

Robust standard errors clustered at the PTA level in parentheses.
*p<.05; **p<.01; ***p<.001

TABLE 32 TBT: Results from ordered logit regressions on standards-based integration at the dyad level

VARIABLES	(1) Membership	(2) Participation	(3) Participation	(4) Participation
Membership	0.0723***			0.0743***
	(0.0240)			(0.0260)
Participation		0.000584	0.000723	0.000228
		(0.000984)	(0.000965)	(0.00117)
Participation			0.00604	0.00858
asymmetry			(0.00492)	(0.00559)
WTO TBT	-1.739**	-1.897**	-1.928**	-1.770*
disputes	(0.876)	(0.889)	(0.917)	(0.907)
WTO TBT STC	-0.463	-0.363	-0.369	-0.476
	(0.342)	(0.276)	(0.282)	(0.344)
WTO TBT	-0.00118**	-0.000799	-0.000766	-0.00114*
notifications	(0.000583)	(0.000562)	(0.000571)	(0.000655)
Exports	0.0108**	0.00624	0.00627	0.0110**
	(0.00465)	(0.00461)	(0.00461)	(0.00477)
Imports	-0.0133	-0.00768	-0.00886	-0.0149
	(0.0105)	(0.0103)	(0.0101)	(0.0107)
GDP	-0.400***	-0.117	-0.143	-0.442***
	(0.140)	(0.115)	(0.120)	(0.158)

TABLE 32 TBT: Results from ordered logit regressions on standards-based integration at the dyad level (*cont.*)

	(1)	(2)	(3)	(4)
VARIABLES	Membership	Participation	Participation	Participation
GDP asymmetry	0.0159	−0.0102	−0.0108*	0.0159
	(0.0102)	(0.00641)	(0.00649)	(0.0104)
EU	8.861***	7.884***	7.917***	8.992***
	(2.410)	(2.077)	(2.057)	(2.527)
US	−22.67***	−23.26***	−22.19***	−22.82***
	(2.561)	(2.448)	(2.446)	(2.559)
PTA parties	0.157	0.105	0.106	0.161
	(0.131)	(0.123)	(0.124)	(0.140)
WTO mission	−0.146***	−0.105*	−0.106*	−0.149***
	(0.0545)	(0.0548)	(0.0547)	(0.0574)
Polity	−0.0114	−0.000445	−0.00952	−0.0259
	(0.0709)	(0.0693)	(0.0733)	(0.0763)
Distance	−0.133	−0.0410	−0.0325	−0.121
	(0.113)	(0.167)	(0.163)	(0.169)
Observations	942	942	942	942
Time	Yes	Yes	Yes	Yes
Region	Yes	Yes	Yes	Yes
Model	OLogit	OLogit	OLogit	OLogit

Robust standard errors clustered at the PTA level in parentheses.
*p<.05; **p<.01; ***p<.001

TABLE 33 TBT: Results from OLS regressions on standards-based integration at the PTA level

	(1)	(2)	(3)	(4)
VARIABLES	Membership	Participation	Participation	Participation
Membership	0.0235**			0.0226*
	(0.0118)			(0.0124)
Participation		−0.000267	−9.39e−05	6.75e−05
		(0.000324)	(0.000370)	(0.000377)
Participation			0.00538	0.00543
asymmetry			(0.00438)	(0.00438)
WTO TBT	−0.0575	−0.0486	−0.0547	−0.0640
disputes	(0.0495)	(0.0493)	(0.0507)	(0.0502)
WTO TBT STC	−0.00987	−0.00791	−0.00835	−0.00936
	(0.00921)	(0.00869)	(0.00843)	(0.00867)
WTO TBT	0.00293*	0.00287	0.00311*	0.00328*
notifications	(0.00169)	(0.00179)	(0.00179)	(0.00175)
Exports	0.00577**	0.00470*	0.00424*	0.00501*
	(0.00255)	(0.00241)	(0.00245)	(0.00261)
Imports	−0.00496	−0.00519	−0.00613	−0.00593
	(0.00520)	(0.00522)	(0.00537)	(0.00539)
GDP	−0.0406	0.133	0.0425	−0.112
	(0.0962)	(0.0854)	(0.122)	(0.134)
GDP asymmetry	−0.00362	−0.00835***	−0.0106***	−0.00622
	(0.00344)	(0.00312)	(0.00384)	(0.00416)
EU	1.316*	1.132	1.243	1.392*
	(0.771)	(0.788)	(0.813)	(0.812)
US	−0.0124	−0.263	−0.0804	0.158
	(0.528)	(0.560)	(0.606)	(0.578)
PTA parties	0.0294	−0.00705	0.00676	0.0415
	(0.0456)	(0.0435)	(0.0432)	(0.0468)
WTO mission	−0.0432*	−0.0319	−0.0260	−0.0340
	(0.0242)	(0.0247)	(0.0254)	(0.0267)
Polity	−0.00899	−0.0101	−0.00113	−0.000217
	(0.0292)	(0.0297)	(0.0297)	(0.0293)
Distance	−0.170**	−0.152*	−0.133	−0.154*
	(0.0850)	(0.0864)	(0.0911)	(0.0910)
			(0.00438)	(0.00438)

TABLE 33 TBT: Results from OLS regressions on standards-based integration at the PTA level (*cont.*)

	(1)	(2)	(3)	(4)
VARIABLES	Membership	Participation	Participation	Participation
Constant	2.581	−1.184	0.754	4.120
	(2.515)	(2.215)	(2.887)	(3.131)
Observations	200	200	200	200
	0.504	0.497	0.503	0.510
Time	Yes	Yes	Yes	Yes
Region	Yes	Yes	Yes	Yes
Model	OLS	OLS	OLS	OLS

Robust standard errors clustered at the PTA level in parentheses.
*p<.05; **p<.01; ***p<.001

TABLE 34 TBT: Results from OLS regressions on standards-based integration at the dyad level

	(1)	(2)	(3)	(4)
VARIABLES	Membership	Participation	Participation	Participation
Membership	0.0119**			0.0118**
	(0.00500)			(0.00499)
Participation		0.000242*	0.000270*	0.000247*
		(0.000140)	(0.000149)	(0.000140)
Participation asymmetry			0.00128	0.00160
			(0.00131)	(0.00139)
WTO TBT disputes	−0.0751	−0.104	−0.105	−0.101*
	(0.0476)	(0.0631)	(0.0635)	(0.0548)
WTO TBT STC	−0.0305	−0.0474	−0.0479	−0.0499
	(0.0410)	(0.0423)	(0.0425)	(0.0423)
WTO TBT notifications	−0.000230	−0.000221*	−0.000218*	−0.000224*
	(0.000144)	(0.000129)	(0.000130)	(0.000131)
Exports	0.000967	0.000414	0.000412	0.00127
	(0.00147)	(0.00149)	(0.00149)	(0.00147)
Imports	−0.00134	−0.00117	−0.00122	−0.00154
	(0.00185)	(0.00174)	(0.00174)	(0.00185)

TABLE 34 TBT: Results from OLS regressions on standards-based integration at the dyad level (*cont.*)

	(1)	(2)	(3)	(4)
VARIABLES	**Membership**	**Participation**	**Participation**	**Participation**
GDP	−0.0227	0.0138	0.0103	−0.0279
	(0.0247)	(0.0233)	(0.0230)	(0.0260)
GDP asymmetry	0.000120	−0.00341	−0.00379*	0.000348
	(0.00178)	(0.00211)	(0.00223)	(0.00184)
EU	1.935***	1.962***	1.972***	1.972***
	(0.437)	(0.453)	(0.456)	(0.460)
US	−1.626***	−1.699***	−1.688***	−1.628***
	(0.549)	(0.576)	(0.577)	(0.548)
PTA parties	0.0265	0.0190	0.0189	0.0273
	(0.0306)	(0.0319)	(0.0319)	(0.0306)
WTO mission	−0.0200	−0.0163	−0.0164	−0.0251
	(0.0183)	(0.0188)	(0.0187)	(0.0194)
Polity	−0.00126	0.00172	0.00165	−0.00194
	(0.0168)	(0.0165)	(0.0165)	(0.0169)
Distance	−0.0934**	−0.0550	−0.0529	−0.0723*
	(0.0418)	(0.0411)	(0.0410)	(0.0400)
			(0.00131)	(0.00139)
Constant	1.234	0.407	0.405	1.062
	(0.840)	(0.831)	(0.829)	(0.871)
Observations	942	942	942	942
	0.808	0.805	0.806	0.809
Time	Yes	Yes	Yes	Yes
Region	Yes	Yes	Yes	Yes
Model	OLS	OLS	OLS	OLS

Robust standard errors clustered at the PTA level in parentheses.
*p<.05; **p<.01; ***p<.001

TABLE 35 TBT: Results from probit regressions on standards-based integration at the PTA level

	(1)	(2)	(3)	(4)
VARIABLES	Membership	Participation	Participation	Participation
Membership	0.00755**			0.00876**
	(0.00345)			(0.00380)
Participation		−7.50e−05	5.58e−05	0.000125
		(0.000102)	(0.000100)	(0.000106)
Participation asymmetry			0.00344***	0.00376***
			(0.00106)	(0.00115)
WTO TBT disputes	−0.00771	−0.00424	−0.000628	−0.00724
	(0.0145)	(0.0144)	(0.0132)	(0.0137)
WTO TBT STC	−0.00998***	−0.00862***	−0.0108***	−0.0121***
	(0.00293)	(0.00301)	(0.00289)	(0.00298)
WTO TBT notifications	0.00157***	0.00139***	0.00156***	0.00181***
	(0.000475)	(0.000468)	(0.000492)	(0.000516)
Exports	0.00394***	0.00341***	0.00353***	0.00402***
	(0.000921)	(0.000911)	(0.00105)	(0.00105)
Imports	−0.00331*	−0.00318*	−0.00431**	−0.00448**
	(0.00170)	(0.00168)	(0.00177)	(0.00177)
GDP	−0.0106	0.0477	0.0157	−0.0407
	(0.0378)	(0.0333)	(0.0394)	(0.0492)
GDP asymmetry	−0.000612	−0.00231**	−0.00416***	−0.00250**
	(0.000998)	(0.000897)	(0.00114)	(0.00123)
EU	0.0268	0.0171	−0.0109	−0.0319
	(0.159)	(0.162)	(0.162)	(0.161)
PTA parties	0.0277**	0.0134	0.0305**	0.0496***
	(0.0127)	(0.0123)	(0.0137)	(0.0155)
WTO mission	−0.0181**	−0.0149*	−0.0120	−0.0139
	(0.00789)	(0.00820)	(0.0111)	(0.0111)
Polity	−0.00470	−0.00676	−0.00472	−0.00283
	(0.00998)	(0.00977)	(0.00891)	(0.00925)
Distance	−0.0717***	−0.0578**	−0.0615*	−0.0818**
	(0.0273)	(0.0264)	(0.0326)	(0.0353)
Observations	148	148	148	148
Time	Yes	Yes	Yes	Yes

TABLE 35 TBT: Results from probit regressions on standards-based integration at the PTA level (*cont.*)

	(1)	(2)	(3)	(4)
VARIABLES	**Membership**	**Participation**	**Participation**	**Participation**
Region	Yes	Yes	Yes	Yes
Model	Probit	Probit	Probit	Probit

Robust standard errors clustered at the PTA level in parentheses.
*p<.05; **p<.01; ***p<.001

TABLE 36 TBT: Results from probit regressions on standards-based integration at the dyad level

	(1)	(2)	(3)	(4)
VARIABLES	**Membership**	**Participation**	**Participation**	**Participation**
Membership	0.00300***			0.00305***
	(0.00101)			(0.00101)
Participation		−2.49e−06	6.88e−06	−2.91e−05
		(5.77e−05)	(5.72e−05)	(6.23e−05)
Participation asymmetry			0.000400	0.000153
			(0.000539)	(0.000507)
WTO TBT disputes	−0.0929**	−0.105**	−0.105**	−0.0909**
	(0.0412)	(0.0416)	(0.0417)	(0.0406)
WTO TBT STC	−0.0467*	−0.0427*	−0.0422*	−0.0402*
	(0.0281)	(0.0232)	(0.0226)	(0.0208)
WTO TBT notifications	−4.98e−05**	−4.08e−05*	−3.98e−05*	−5.30e−05**
	(2.17e−05)	(2.32e−05)	(2.32e−05)	(2.28e−05)
Exports	0.000540	0.000380	0.000347	0.000501
	(0.000355)	(0.000409)	(0.000420)	(0.000366)
Imports	−0.00101*	−0.000983	−0.000984	−0.000956
	(0.000573)	(0.000628)	(0.000638)	(0.000585)
GDP	−0.0134	0.00145	−0.000643	−0.0147
	(0.00862)	(0.00930)	(0.00925)	(0.00905)

TABLE 36 TBT: Results from probit regressions on standards-based integration at the dyad level (*cont.*)

	(1)	(2)	(3)	(4)
VARIABLES	**Membership**	**Participation**	**Participation**	**Participation**
GDP asymmetry	−0.000770	−0.00237***	−0.00246***	−0.000908
	(0.000680)	(0.000632)	(0.000712)	(0.000762)
EU	0.502***	0.465***	0.471***	0.464***
	(0.120)	(0.137)	(0.142)	(0.155)
PTA parties	−0.000772	−0.00382	−0.00379	−0.00100
	(0.00544)	(0.00597)	(0.00594)	(0.00544)
WTO mission	−0.00902	−0.00717	−0.00682	−0.00758
	(0.00553)	(0.00723)	(0.00749)	(0.00693)
Polity	0.000569	0.000631	0.000524	0.000651
	(0.00443)	(0.00447)	(0.00441)	(0.00427)
Distance	−0.0202**	−0.0170*	−0.0162	−0.0219**
	(0.00846)	(0.00994)	(0.00986)	(0.00860)
Observations	625	625	625	625
Time	Yes	Yes	Yes	Yes
Region	Yes	Yes	Yes	Yes
Model	Probit	Probit	Probit	Probit

Robust standard errors clustered at the PTA level in parentheses.
*p<.05; **p<.01; ***p<.001

TABLE 37 TBT: Results from logit regressions on standards-based integration at the PTA level

	(1)	(2)	(3)	(4)
VARIABLES	Membership	Participation	Participation	Participation
Membership	0.00828**			0.00936**
	(0.00382)			(0.00390)
Participation		-0.000106	3.50e-05	0.000102
		(0.000129)	(0.000114)	(0.000119)
Participation asymmetry			0.00335***	0.00372***
			(0.00107)	(0.00116)
WTO TBT disputes	-0.00989	-0.00689	-0.000367	-0.00795
	(0.0159)	(0.0157)	(0.0135)	(0.0144)
WTO TBT STC	-0.00977***	-0.00800**	-0.0106***	-0.0119***
	(0.00311)	(0.00323)	(0.00324)	(0.00333)
WTO TBT notifications	0.00164***	0.00148***	0.00164***	0.00188***
	(0.000485)	(0.000510)	(0.000549)	(0.000570)
Exports	0.00391***	0.00333***	0.00348***	0.00391***
	(0.000996)	(0.000962)	(0.00114)	(0.00110)
Imports	-0.00302	-0.00298	-0.00427**	-0.00430**
	(0.00216)	(0.00210)	(0.00211)	(0.00209)
GDP	-0.0131	0.0560	0.0233	-0.0354
	(0.0426)	(0.0392)	(0.0446)	(0.0560)
GDP asymmetry	-0.000611	-0.00247***	-0.00425***	-0.00246**
	(0.001000)	(0.000918)	(0.00108)	(0.00117)
EU	0.0537	0.0195	-0.00469	-0.0448
	(0.176)	(0.175)	(0.177)	(0.181)
PTA parties	0.0278**	0.0131	0.0305**	0.0517***
	(0.0128)	(0.0135)	(0.0154)	(0.0171)
WTO mission	-0.0183*	-0.0146	-0.0121	-0.0127
	(0.00953)	(0.00987)	(0.0124)	(0.0125)
Polity	-0.00497	-0.00853	-0.00673	-0.00403
	(0.0119)	(0.0116)	(0.00970)	(0.00999)
Distance	-0.0755**	-0.0597**	-0.0666**	-0.0904**
	(0.0315)	(0.0294)	(0.0339)	(0.0365)

TABLE 37 TBT: Results from logit regressions on standards-based integration at the PTA level (*cont.*)

	(1)	(2)	(3)	(4)
VARIABLES	**Membership**	**Participation**	**Participation**	**Participation**
Observations	148	148	148	148
Time	Yes	Yes	Yes	Yes
Region	Yes	Yes	Yes	Yes
Model	Logit	Logit	Logit	Logit

Robust standard errors clustered at the PTA level in parentheses.
*p<.05; **p<.01; ***p<.001

TABLE 38 TBT: Results from logit regressions on standards-based integration at the dyad level

	(1)	(2)	(3)	(4)
VARIABLES	**Membership**	**Participation**	**Participation**	**Participation**
Membership	0.00275**			0.00283***
	(0.00107)			(0.00106)
Participation		−6.13e−06	−2.10e−07	−3.64e−05
		(5.30e−05)	(5.31e−05)	(5.65e−05)
Participation asymmetry			0.000242	1.40e−05
			(0.000553)	(0.000499)
WTO TBT disputes	−0.0857**	−0.0928**	−0.0926**	−0.0826**
	(0.0420)	(0.0418)	(0.0419)	(0.0417)
WTO TBT STC	−0.0553*	−0.0510**	−0.0505**	−0.0489*
	(0.0336)	(0.0248)	(0.0242)	(0.0272)
WTO TBT notifications	−5.66e−05**	−4.88e−05*	−4.83e−05	−6.00e−05**
	(2.49e−05)	(2.94e−05)	(2.95e−05)	(2.58e−05)
Exports	0.000459	0.000289	0.000268	0.000440
	(0.000401)	(0.000420)	(0.000428)	(0.000398)
Imports	−0.000873	−0.000803	−0.000804	−0.000824
	(0.000612)	(0.000669)	(0.000673)	(0.000616)

TABLE 38 TBT: Results from logit regressions on standards-based integration at the dyad level (*cont.*)

	(1)	(2)	(3)	(4)
VARIABLES	**Membership**	**Participation**	**Participation**	**Participation**
GDP	−0.0166*	−0.00416	−0.00541	−0.0172*
	(0.00860)	(0.00923)	(0.00903)	(0.00898)
GDP asymmetry	−0.000556	−0.00207***	−0.00213***	−0.000656
	(0.000678)	(0.000633)	(0.000711)	(0.000745)
EU	0.486***	0.451***	0.454***	0.451***
	(0.115)	(0.111)	(0.114)	(0.120)
PTA parties	0.000661	−0.00160	−0.00158	0.000559
	(0.00517)	(0.00556)	(0.00554)	(0.00512)
WTO mission	−0.00720	−0.00514	−0.00493	−0.00609
	(0.00647)	(0.00724)	(0.00735)	(0.00693)
Polity	−0.000395	−0.000134	−0.000202	−0.000231
	(0.00444)	(0.00433)	(0.00430)	(0.00430)
Distance	−0.0202***	−0.0169*	−0.0163*	−0.0224***
	(0.00769)	(0.00987)	(0.00985)	(0.00845)
Observations	625	625	625	625
Time	Yes	Yes	Yes	Yes
Region	Yes	Yes	Yes	Yes
Model	Logit	Logit	Logit	Logit

Robust standard errors clustered at the PTA level in parentheses.
*p<.05; **p<.01; ***p<.001

CHAPTER 6

Conclusion and Future Research

Over the past decades, tariff rates have fallen dramatically. At the same time, non-tariff measures, including technical barriers to trade (TBT) and sanitary and phytosanitary (SPS) measures, have replaced tariffs as core international trade policy tools. The World Trade Organization (WTO) strongly encourages its members to base their TBT and SPS measures on international standards as a means to facilitate trade. Similarly, many preferential trade agreements (PTAs) refer to international standards to reduce the trade-impeding costs of regulatory heterogeneity and to facilitate trade among their signatories.

Despite the importance of international standards for the regulation of international trade, relatively little is known about the organizations that develop these standards. Furthermore, while the dialectical relationship of the multilateral and preferential trade policy regimes is well understood in the literature, far less research investigates their linkages with related regimes such as the work of international standardization organizations.

The principal objective of this book is to contribute to closing this literature gap by exploring the linkages between international standardization and the regulation of international trade. More precisely, this book aims to explore the linkages between the international standardization regime, and the multilateral and preferential trade policy regimes.

The international standardization regime is empirically represented by two international standardization organizations — the Codex Alimentarius (Codex) and the International Organization for Standardization (ISO). The multilateral trade policy regime is empirically represented by two WTO Agreements in which international standards play an important role — the SPS Agreement and the TBT Agreement. The preferential trade policy regime is represented by the SPS and TBT chapters of PTAs.

The central proposition of this book is that the institutional design of multilateral trade agreements matters for countries' incentives to participate in international standardization organizations. Countries' participation in international standardization organizations, in turn, matters for the institutional design of the preferential trade agreements. To explore these linkages, this book is organized in six Chapters.

Chapter 1 provides an introduction into international standards, international standardization organizations and, in particular, the role of Codex and ISO in multilateral and preferential trade agreements.

 | DOI:10.1163/9789004691841_007

Chapter 2 outlines the concepts and debates which present the foundation for this book. More specifically, the Chapter provides a brief review of the relevant literature on international regime complexity, regime-shifting and forum-shopping, and institutional design and indirect governance. Based on this, the Chapter outlines the principal propositions on which the empirical Chapters 4 and 5 are based.

Chapter 3 provides a detailed and comparative account of Codex's and ISO's history, structure, procedures, and controversies. The Chapter also describes the two original datasets on countries' participation in ISO and Codex that were collected for this book and upon which the empirical Chapters 4 and 5 are based. A descriptive analysis indicates that both international standardization organizations are dominated by relatively a small group of countries. While the United States is particularly well represented and influential at Codex, European countries are particularly well represented and influential at ISO. Over the past years, China has significantly increased its participation and influence in both international standardization organizations.

Chapter 4 explores the linkage between the multilateral trade policy regime and the international standardization regime. The institutional design of multilateral trade agreements is the independent variable of interest, and countries' participation in international standardization organizations is the dependent variable of interest. Empirically, the multilateral trade policy regime is represented by the WTO's TBT and SPS Agreements. The international standardization regime is empirically represented by the two international standardization organizations Codex and ISO. Both WTO Agreements strongly encourage WTO members to base their national TBT and SPS measures on international standards. However, while the SPS Agreement explicitly endorses Codex as *the* international standardization organization in the area of food safety, the TBT Agreement includes no explicit reference to ISO as the relevant organization to develop TBT-related international standards. The principal argument is that the explicit endorsement of Codex by the SPS Agreement increases countries' political and economic stakes in Codex standards, reduces countries' ability to engage in forum-shopping and/or regime-shifting, and ultimately increases their incentives to actively participate in Codex to influence the design of standards in their political and economic interests. The absence of an explicit endorsement of ISO in the TBT Agreement, by contrast, is expected to result in a more subdued effect on countries' participation in ISO. The results of the empirical analysis provide supportive evidence for this argument. While countries' participation in Codex is positively and statistically significantly associated with countries' accession to the WTO, and therefore their commitments under the WTO Agreements, this association is smaller in size and statistically less robust in the case of ISO.

Chapter 5 explores the linkage between the international standardization regime and the preferential trade policy regime. Countries' participation in international standardization organizations is the independent variable of interest, and the institutional design of preferential trade agreements is the dependent variable of interest. Empirically, the international standardization regime is represented by the two international standardization organizations Codex and ISO. The preferential trade regime is empirically represented by the TBT and SPS chapters of 200 PTAs signed between the WTO's establishment in 1995, and 2016. The principal argument is that PTA parties have political and economic interests to base their cooperation on international standards to reduce the trade-impeding costs of cross-country regulatory heterogeneity and to facilitate trade among themselves. However, due to distributional conflicts, countries' incentives to agree on cooperation based on international standards is stronger if these international standards are designed in their political and economic interests and, consequently, would only result in minimal adjustment costs for their respective domestic industries. More precisely, it is argued that the more countries have participated in the international standard-setting processes of ISO and Codex, the more they have been able to shape the design of standards in their political and economic interests, and the more likely they are to refer to international standards as a basis for cooperation in the TBT and SPS chapters of their PTAs, respectively. Since, however, only the SPS Agreement explicitly endorses a particular international standardization organization, this positive relationship is expected to be stronger for Codex and SPS chapters than for ISO and TBT chapters. The empirical analysis provides mixed evidence for this argument. Surprisingly, countries' participation in the international standard-setting processes in Codex is negatively, and statistically significantly, associated with the probability of countries referring to international standards in the SPS chapters of their PTAs. The relationship between countries' participation in the international standard-setting processes of ISO is found to be positive, but not statistically significantly, related to the probability that TBT chapters base cooperation on international standards.

This Chapter 6 summarizes the research questions and findings of this book, and suggests some avenues for future research. And indeed, as global supply chains become more complex and as technology and trade become more interlinked, international standards are likely to become even more politically and economically salient. In 2021, the United States (US) and the European Union (EU) launched the Trade and Technology Council (TTC) to lead a values-based global digital transformation (European Commission,

2021). One of the main goals of the TTC is the cooperation on the development of compatible and international standards. To work towards this goal, a working group on technology standards cooperation (including AI and Internet of Things, among other emerging technologies) is established. The establishment of the TTC has two closely intertwined objectives. First, the TTC is supposed to address some of the transatlantic divergences discussed in various parts of this book. Second, the TTC is an "attempt to push back against China and promote democratic values" (Politico, 2021).

Over the past years, the increasing politicization of information and communication technology (ICT) has been observable in the international trade policy regimes as well as in the international standardization regime. In the multilateral trade policy regime, for instance, it is well-known that China, the EU, and the US have had and continue to have rather different views on digital trade and e-commerce in the WTO (Wunsch-Vincent, 2004, 2006; Fleuter, 2016; Gao, 2018).[1] While the progress of digital trade-related discussions at the WTO has been fairly limited since its Declaration on Global Electronic Commerce more than 20 years ago, recent developments in Geneva indicate that the WTO is likely to take on a more active role (Cheng and Brandi, 2019; Mitchell and Mishra, 2019).[2]

Still, due to the lack of progress in digital trade-related negotiations, many of the previously mentioned divergences have already spilled over to the preferential trade policy regime. Indeed, since the early 2000s, PTAs increasingly include provisions or entire chapters related to digital trade. China, the EU, and the US follow rather different institutional design approaches when it comes to the governance of digital trade, data, and related technologies in their PTAs. (Herman, 2010; Wunsch-Vincent and Hold, 2016; Monteiro and Teh, 2017; Wu, 2017; Aaronson and Leblond, 2018; Gao, 2018; Burri and Polanco, 2020; Willemyns, 2020; Abendin and Duan, 2021; Elsig and Klotz, 2021a,b, 2022) This divergence reflects the different domestic approaches that China, the EU, the US, but also other countries, have when it comes ICT, digital trade, and data-related policies (Ferracane et al., 2018; González and Ferencz, 2018; Sen, 2018; Casalini and González, 2019; Casalini et al., 2019; Ferencz, 2019;

1 The WTO defines electronic commerce, or e-commerce, as the "production, distribution, marketing, sale or delivery of goods and services by electronic means" (WTO, 1998, p. 1). While there exists no single definition of digital trade, "[...] there is a growing consensus that it encompasses digitally enabled transactions in trade in goods and services which can be either digitally or physically delivered involving consumers, firms and governments" (González and Jouanjean, 2019, p. 3). In this Section, the terms are used interchangeably.

2 On January 25, 2019, 76 WTO members signed a Joint Statement on E-commerce.

Ferencz and Gonzales, 2019; Bradford, 2020; UNCTAD, 2020; van der Marel and Ferracane, 2021; Klotz, 2023).

The politicization of technology is also evident in the international standardization regime (Financial Times, 2019). While the international standardization organizations in the area of ICT, notably the International Telecommunication Union, have historically been dominated by the EU and the US, Chinese actors are becoming increasingly represented and influential (Kanevskaia, 2023; Klotz, 2023). Furthermore, it is important to note that the ICT standard-setting landscape is, as one observer describes it, "balkanized" (Liu, 2018), meaning that there is an increasing number of organizations active in this field that go beyond the "Big Three" — ISO, IEC, and the ITU. Indeed, other increasingly important actors in this area include the Internet Corporation for Assigned Names and Numbers (ICANN), the Institute of Electrical and Electronics Engineers (IEEE), the Internet Engineering Task Force (IETF), the Internet Governance Forum (IGF), the United Nations Commission on International Trade Law (UNCITRAL), and the World Summit on the Information Society (WSIS).

Some PTAs already include explicit references to the ITU (McDaniels et al., 2018), others refer to UNCITRAL (Burri and Polanco, 2020). In line with this book, future research may explore what drives these explicit references. Is, for instance, the probability of including these references related to PTA parties' participation in these organizations? Do countries which now drive the discussions in ICT-related standardization organizations advocate for these standards as a basis for cooperation in their PTAs because it serves their interests? Importantly, will the WTO members ever agree on an e-commerce related Agreement and, if so, will they endorse an international standardization organization to develop the related standards? This book argues that these questions are closely intertwined but leaves it to future research to further explore the linkages between international standardization and trade regulation.

Bibliography

Aaronson, S. A. and Leblond, P. (2018). Another Digital Divide: The Rise of Data Realms and its Implications for the WTO. *Journal of International Economic Law*, 21(2):245–272 (see page: 236).

Abbott, F. M. (1997). The Intersection of Law and Trade in the WTO System: Economics and the Transition to a Hard Law System. In Orden, D. and Roberts, D., editors, *Understanding Technical Barriers to Agricultural Trade*. IATRC Proceedings Issue, Tucson, AZ (see pages: 39, 126).

Abbott, F. M. (2000). NAFTA and the Legalization of World Politics: A Case Study. *International Organization*, 54(3):519–547 (see pages: 39, 126).

Abbott, K. M. (2003). US-EU Disputes over Technical Barriers to Trade and the 'Hushkits' Dispute. In Petersmann, E.-U. and Pollack, M. A., editors, *Transatlantic Economic Disputes: The EU, the US, and the WTO*. Oxford University Press, Oxford (see pages: 69, 73, 74, 137, and 173).

Abbott, K. W. and Faude, B. (2022). Hybrid institutional complexes in global governance. *The Review of International Organizations*, 17:263291 (see page: 38).

Abbott, K. W., Genschel, P., Snidal, D., and Zangl, B. (2015). Orchestration: Global Governance through Intermediaries. In Abbott, K. W., Genschel, P., Snidal, D., and Zangl, B., editors, *International Organizations as Orchestrators*. Cambridge University Press, Cambridge (see pages: 40, 48, 49, and 133).

Abbott, K. W., Genschel, P., Snidal, D., and Zangl, B. (2016). Two Logics of Indirect Governance: Delegation and Orchestration. *British Journal of Political Science*, 46:719–729 (see pages: 40, 48).

Abbott, K. W., Genschel, P., Snidal, D., and Zangl, B. (2020). Competence versus Control: The Governors Dilemma. *Regulation & Governance*, 14(4):619–636 (see pages: 40, 48).

Abbott, K. W., Keohane, R. O., Moravcsik, A., Slaughter, A.-M., and Snidal, D. (2000). The Concept of Legalization. *International Organization*, 54(3):401–419 (see pages: 39, 48, 132, 133, 142, and 143).

Abbott, K. W., Levi-Faur, D., and Snidal, D. (2017). Theorizing Regulatory Intermediaries: The RIT Model. *The ANNALS of the American Academy of Political and Social Science*, 670(1):14–35 (see page: 40).

Abbott, K. W. and Snidal, D. (1998). Why States Act through Formal International Organizations. *The Journal of Conflict Resolution*, 42(1):3–32 (see pages: 33, 57).

Abbott, K. W. and Snidal, D. (2000). Hard and Soft Law in International Governance. *International Organization*, 54(3):421–456 (see pages: 39, 49, 50, 126, 133, and 142).

Abbott, K. W. and Snidal, D. (2001). International 'Standards' and International Governance. *Journal of European Public Policy*, 8(3):345–370 (see pages: 51, 57, 199, and 200).

Abbott, K. W. and Snidal, D. (2009). Strengthening International Regulation Through Transnational New Governance: Overcoming the Orchestration Deficit. *Vanderbilt Journal of Transnational Law*, 42:501–578 (see page: 40).

Abendin, S. and Duan, P. (2021). Global E-Commerce Talks at the WTO: Positions on Selected Issues of the United States, European Union, China, and Japan. *World Trade Review*, 20(5):707–724 (see page: 236).

Aisbett, E. and Silberberger, M. (2021). Tariff liberalization and product standards: Regulatory chill and race to the bottom? *Regulation & Governance*, 15(3):987–1006 (see page: 125).

Alemanno, A. (2007). *Trade in Food: Regulatory and Judicial Approaches in the EC and the WTO*. Cameron May Ltd, London (see pages: 49, 58, 132, 134, and 142).

Allee, T. and Elsig, M. (2014). Why Do Some International Institutions Contain Strong Dispute Settlement Provisions? New Evidence from Preferential Trade Agreements. *The Review of International Organizations*, (11):89–120 (see pages: 35, 167, and 178).

Allee, T. and Elsig, M. (2019). Are the Contents of International Treaties Copied and Pasted? Evidence from Preferential Trade Agreements. *International Studies Quarterly*, 63(3):603–613 (see pages: 36, 167, and 168).

Allee, T., Elsig, M., and Lugg, A. (2017a). Is the European Union Deal with Canada New or Recycled? A Text-as-Data Approach. *Global Policy*, 8(2):246–252 (see pages: 36, 167, and 168).

Allee, T., Elsig, M., and Lugg, A. (2017b). The Ties between the World Trade Organization and Preferential Trade Agreements: A Textual Analysis. *Journal of International Economic Law*, 20(2):333–363 (see pages: 35, 167, and 168).

Allee, T. and Lugg, A. (2016). Who Wrote the Rules for the Trans-Pacific Partnership? *Research and Politics*, pages 1–9 (see pages: 36, 167, and 168).

Alschner, W., Seiermann, J., and Skougarevskiy, D. (2018). Text of Trade Agreements (ToTA)A Structured Corpus for the TextasData Analysis of Preferential Trade Agreements. *Journal of Empirical Legal Studies*, 15(3):648–666 (see page: 166).

Alter, K. J. (2022). The promise and perils of theorizing international regime complexity in an evolving world. *The Review of International Organizations*, 17:375396 (see page: 37).

Alter, K. J. and Meunier, S. (2009). The Politics of International Regime Complexity. *Perspectives on Politics*, 7(1):13–24 (see pages: 36, 37).

Alter, K. J. and Raustiala, K. (2018). The Rise of International Regime Complexity. *Annual Review of Law and Social Science*, 14:329–349 (see pages: 36, 37).

Ansell, C. and Vogel, D. (2006). *What's the Beef? The Contested Governance of European Food Safety*. MIT Press, Cambridge, MA (see pages: 39, 49, 50, 56, 126, 133, and 142).

Arcuri, A. (2015). Global Food Safety Standards: The Evolving Regulatory Epistemology at the Intersection of the SPS Agreement and the Codex Alimentarius Commission. In Delimatsis, P., editor, *The Law, Economics and Politics of International*

Standardisation. Cambridge University Press, Cambridge (see pages: 49, 50, 56, 64, 133, 142, and 173).

Athey, S. and Imbens, G. W. (2018). Design-based Analysis in Difference-In-Differences Settings with Staggered Adoption. *NBER Working Paper*, (24963):1–38 (see page: 147).

Avant, D. D., Finnemore, M., and Sell, S. K. (2010). Who Governs the Globe? In Avant, D. D., Finnemore, M., and Sell, S. K., editors, *Who Governs the Globe?* Cambridge University Press, Cambridge (see pages: 49, 50, 133, and 142).

Baccini, L. (2019). The Economics and Politics of Preferential Trade Agreements. *Annual Review of Political Science*, 22:75–92 (see pages: 35, 166).

Baccini, L., Dür, A., and Elsig, M. (2015a). The Politics of Trade Agreement Design: Revisiting the Depth-Flexibility Nexus. *International Studies Quarterly*, 59(4):765–775 (see pages: 35, 167, 185, and 186).

Baccini, L., Dür, A., and Haftel, Y. Z. (2015b). Imitation and Innovation in International Governance: The Diffusion of Trade Agreement Design. In Dür, A. and Elsig, M., editors, *Trade Cooperation: The Purpose, Design and Effects of Preferential Trade Agreements*. Cambridge University Press, Cambridge (see pages: 36, 168, and 186).

Baier, S. L. and Bergstrand, J. H. (2004). Economic Determinants of Free Trade Agreements. *Journal of International Economics*, 64(1):29–63 (see pages: 35, 166, 185, and 186).

Bailer, S. (2017). Bargaining Resources and Strategies in Climate Change Negotiations. *SNIS Working Paper*, pages 1–27 (see pages: 47, 52, and 142).

Bailer, S. and Weiler, F. (2015). A Political Economy of Positions in Climate Change Negotiations: Economic, Structural, Domestic, and Strategic Explanations. *The Review of International Organizations*, 10(1):43–66 (see pages: 47, 52, and 142).

Baldwin, R. E. (1993). A Domino Theory of Regionalism. *National Bureau of Economic Research (NBER) Working Paper Series*, (4465):1–23 (see page: 35).

Baldwin, R. E. (2000). Regulatory Protectionism, Developing Nations, and a Two-Tier World Trade System. Brookings Trade Forum. pp. 237–293 (see page: 171).

Barton, J. H., Goldstein, J. L., Josling, T. E., and Steinberg, R. H. (2006). *The Evolution of the Trade Regime: Politics, Law, and Economics of the GATT and the WTO*. Princeton University Press, Princeton, NJ (see page: 43).

Bergkamp, L. and Kogan, L. (2013). Trade, the Precautionary Principle, and Post-Modern Regulatory Process. *European Journal of Risk Regulation*, 4(4):493–507 (see page: 47).

Berman, A. (2017). Industry, Regulatory Capture and Transnational Standard Setting. *American Society of International Law*, 111:112–118 (see pages: 46, 47, 68, 141, and 142).

Bernstein, S. and Hannah, E. (2008). Non-state Global Standard Setting and the WTO: Legitimacy and the Need for Regulatory Space. *Journal of International Economic Law*, 11(3):575–608 (see pages: 50, 73, 138, and 143).

Besen, S. M. and Farrell, J. (1994). Choosing How to Compete: Strategies and Tactics in Standardization. *Journal of Economic Perspectives*, 8(2):117–131 (see page: 46).

Bijlmakers, S. and van Calster, G. (2015). You'd be surprised how much it costs to look this cheap! A case study of ISO26000 on social responsibility. In Delimatsis, P., editor, *The Law, Economics and Politics of International Standardisation*. Cambridge University Press, Cambridge (see pages: 22, 45).

Blind, K. (2015). From standards to quality infrastructure: A review of impact studies and an outlook. In Delimatsis, P., editor, *The Law, Economics and Politics of International Standardisation*. Cambridge University Press, Cambridge (see pages: 21, 46, and 141).

Boutrif, E. (2003). The New Role of Codex Alimentarius in the Context of WTO/SPS Agreement. *Food Control*, 14:81–88 (see pages: 56, 133).

Bradford, A. (2020). *The Brussels Effect: How the European Union Rules the World*. Oxford University Press, Oxford (see page: 236).

Bradley, C. A. and Kelley, J. G. (2008). The Concept of International Delegation. *Law and Contemporary Problems*, 71(1):1–36 (see pages: 33, 39, 49, 57, and 132).

Braithwaite, J. and Drahos, P. (2000). *Global Business Regulation*. Cambridge University Press, Cambridge (see pages: 46, 49, 55, 56, 57, 68, 128, 129, 132, 133, 134, 141, and 142).

Brown, R. L. (2010). Measuring Delegation. *The Review of International Organizations*, 5:141–175 (see page: 39).

BSI (2018). The benefits of standards for international trade. Online. London: British Standards Institution (see page: 21).

Burri, M. (2023). Trade Law 4.0: Are We There Yet? *Journal of International Economic Law*, 26(1):90100 (see page: 35).

Burri, M. and Polanco, R. (2020). Digital Trade Provisions in Preferential Trade Agreements: Introducing a New Dataset. *Journal of International Economic Law*, 23(1):187–220 (see pages: 167, 236, and 237).

Busch, M. L. (2007). Overlapping Institutions, Forum Shopping, and Dispute Settlement in International Trade. *International Organization*, 61(4):735–761 (see page: 37).

Büthe, T. (2008). The Globalization of Health and Safety Standards: Delegation of Regulatory Authority in the SPS-Agreement of 1994 Agreement Establishing the World Trade Organization. *Law and Contemporary Problems*, 71(1):219–255 (see pages: 49, 50, 56, 64, 128, 129, 130, 131, 132, 133, 134, and 142).

Büthe, T. (2009). The Politics of Food Safety in the Age of Global Trade: The Codex Alimentarius Commission in the SPS Agreement of the WTO. In Coglianese, C., Finkel, A. M., and Zaring, D., editors, *Import Safety: Regulatory Governance in the Global Economy*. University of Pennsylvania Press, Philadelphia, PA (see pages: 49, 56, 64, 129, 130, 131, 132, 134, and 142).

Büthe, T. (2010). Engineering Uncontestedness? The Origins and Institutional Development of the International Electrotechnical Commission (IEC). *Business and Politics*, 12(3):1–64 (see pages: 50, 73, 138, and 143).

Büthe, T. (2010). The Power of Norms; the Norms of Power: Who Governs International Electrical and Electronic Technology? In Avant, D. D., Finnemore, M., and Sell, S. K., editors, *Who Governs the Globe?* Cambridge University Press, Cambridge (see pages: 46, 50, 73, 138, 141, and 143).

Büthe, T. (2015). Institutionalization and its Consequences. In Halliday, T. C. and Shaffer, G., editors, *Transnational Legal Orders*. Cambridge University Press, Cambridge (see pages: 49, 56, 58, 132, 134, and 142).

Büthe, T. and Harris, N. (2011). Codex Alimentarius Commission. In Hale, T. and Held, D., editors, *Handbook of Transnational Governance: Institutions and Innovations*. Polity, Cambridge and Malden, MA (see pages: 49, 57, 64, 134, and 142).

Büthe, T. and Mattli, W. (2010a). International Standards and Standard-Setting Bodies. In Coen, D., Grant, W., and Wilson, G., editors, *The Oxford Handbook of Business and Government*. Oxford University Press, Oxford (see pages: 50, 70, 73, 138, and 143).

Büthe, T. and Mattli, W. (2010b). Standards for Global Markets: Domestic and International Institutions for Setting International Product Standards. In Henrik Enderlein, S. W. and Zürn, M., editors, *Handbook on Multi-Level Governance*. Edward Elgar, Cheltenham Glos (UK) (see pages: 47, 50, 73, 138, 142, and 143).

Büthe, T. and Mattli, W. (2011). *The New Global Rulers: The Privatization of Regulation in the World Economy*. Princeton University Press, Princeton, NJ (see pages: 74, 173).

Büthe, T. and Witte, J. M. (2004). Product Standards in Transatlantic Trade and Investment. American Institute for Contemporary German Studies. Washington, DC (see page: 73).

Cadot, O., Disdier, A.-C., and Fontagné, L. (2015). Harmonizing non-tariff measures: Always a blessing? In Delimatsis, P., editor, *The Law, Economics and Politics of International Standardisation*. Cambridge University Press, Cambridge (see page: 125).

Cafaggi, F. (2012). The Architecture of Transnational Private Regulation. *Comparative Research in Law & Political Economy*, (20):1–28 (see page: 70).

Campbell, J. L. (2004). *Institutional Change and Globalization*. Princeton University Press, Princeton, NJ (see page: 41).

Capoccia, G. and Kelemen, R. D. (2007). The Study of Critical Junctures: Theory, Narrative, and Counterfactuals in Historical Institutionalism. *World Politics*, 59(3):341–369 (see page: 43).

Carrère, C., Olarreaga, M., and Raess, D. (2022). Labor clauses in trade agreements: Hidden protectionism? *The Review of International Organizations*, 17:453483 (see page: 167).

Cartwright, M. (2019). Preferential Trade Agreements and Power Asymmetries: The Case of Technological Protection Measures in Australia. *The Pacific Review*, 32(3):313–335 (see page: 185).

Casalini, F. and González, J. L. (2019). Trade and Cross-Border Data Flows. *Organisation for Economic Co-operation and Development* (OECD) *Trade Policy Papers*, (220):1–41 (see page: 236).

Casalini, F., González, J. L., and Moïsé, E. (2019). Approaches to Market Openness in the Digital Age. *Organisation for Economic Co-operation and Development* (OECD) *Trade Policy Papers*, (219):1–19 (see page: 236).

Casper, S. and Hancké, B. (1999). Global Quality Norms within National Production Regimes: ISO 9000 Standards in the French and German Car Industries. *Organization Studies*, 43(3):961–985 (see page: 75).

Cecere, G., Corrocher, N., Gossart, C., and Ozman, M. (2014). Lock-in and path dependence: an evolutionary approach to eco-innovations. *Journal of Evolutionary Economics*, 24:1037–1065 (see page: 48).

CEN/CENELEC (2020). International Cooperation: ISO and IEC. https://www.cencenelec.eu/intcoop/StandardizationOrg/Pages/default.aspx. Online. Accessed on 31 July 2020 (see page: 74).

Center for Systemic Peace (2020). The Polity Project. Center for Systemic Peace. Online. Accessed on 31 July 2020 (see pages: 146, 186).

CEPII (2020). GeoDist database. Online. Accessed on 19 April 2021 (see page: 186).

Cheng, C. (2019). Codex Alimentarius Commission. *Encyclopedia of Food Security and Sustainability*, 1:50–55 (see page: 60).

Cheng, C. and Klotz, S. (2023). Do Too Many Cooks Spoil the Broth? The Effect of Increasing Participation on the Codex Food Standard-Making Process. Working Paper, first presented at the International Political Economy Society in San Diego, CA, United States, in November 2019 (see page: 153).

Cheng, W. and Brandi, C. (2019). Governing Digital Trade — A New Role for the WTO. *Deutsches Institut fr Entwicklungspolitik* (DIE) *Briefing Paper*, (6):1–5 (see page: 235).

Chu, M. (2020). Horses for Courses: Chinas Accommodative Approach to Food Standard-setting in Response to the Internationalization of Regulation. *Regulation & Governance*, 14:514–530 (see pages: 46, 141).

Clapp, J. and Fuchs, D. (2009). *Corporate Power in Global Agrifood Governance*. MIT Press, Cambridge, MA (see pages: 49, 68, 134, and 142).

Clarke, D. and Schythe, K. T. (2020). Implementing the Panel Event Study. *IZA Working Paper*, (13524):1–32 (see pages: 146, 147).

Codex (1995). Report of the 21st Session of the Codex Alimentarius Commission, Rome, 3–8 July 1995. Codex Alimentarius Commission (see page: 136).

Codex (2018). Understanding Codex, 5th edition. Codex Alimentarius Commission (see page: 60).

Codex (2019). Procedural Manual (27th edition). Codex Alimentarius Commission (see pages: 60, 61).

Codex (2020). Codex Alimentarius. http://www.fao.org/fao-who-codexalimentarius/home/en/. Online. Accessed on 27 July 2020 (see pages: 56, 67).

Collier, R. B. and Collier, D. (1991). *Critical Junctures and Historical Legacies: Shaping the Political Arena: Critical Junctures, the Labor Movement, and Regime Dynamics in Latin America*. Princeton University Press, Princeton, NY (see page: 43).

Congressional Research Service (2014). U.S. and EU Motor Vehicle Standards: Issues for Transatlantic Trade Negotiations. Congressional Research Service (see page: 172).

Copelovitch, M. S. and Putnam, T. L. (2014). Design in Context: Existing International Agreements and New Cooperation. *International Organization*, 68(2):471–493 (see page: 42).

Cottier, T., Sieber-Gasser, C., and Wermelinger, G. (2015). The Dialectical Relationship of Preferential and Multilateral Trade Agreements. In Dür, A. and Elsig, M., editors, *Trade Cooperation: The Purpose, Design and Effects of Preferential Trade Agreements*. Cambridge University Press, Cambridge (see page: 35).

Croome, J. (1999). *Reshaping the World Trading System: A History of the Uruguay Round*. Kluwer Law International/ World Trade Organization, The Hague, London, and Boston, MA (see pages: 128, 129, 130, 131, and 137).

Dadush, U. and Prost, E. D. (2023). Preferential Trade Agreements, Geopolitics, and the Fragmentation of World Trade. *World Trade Review*, 22(2):278–294 (see page: 165).

Davis, C. L. (2003). *Food Fights over Free Trade: How International Institutions Promote Agricultural Trade Liberalization*. Princeton University Press, Princeton, NJ (see page: 128).

Dawson, R. J. (1995). The Role of the Codex Alimentarius Commission in Setting Food Standard and the SPS Agreement Implementation. *Food Control*, 6(5):261–265 (see pages: 56, 133).

Dawson, R. J. (1997). Impact of WTO on Codex Alimentarius and Its Implications for World Trade. In Orden, D. and Roberts, D., editors, *Understanding Technical Barriers to Agricultural Trade*. IATRC Proceedings Issue, Tucson, AZ (see pages: 56, 133).

de Senarclens, P. (1993). Regime Theory and the Study of International Organizations. *International Social Science Journal*, 45(4):453–462 (see page: 36).

de Vries, H. J. (2006). International Standardization as a Strategic Tool. Technical report, International Electronical Commission, Oslo (see pages: 46, 141).

de Vries, H. J. (2015). Standardisation: A developing field of research. In Delimatsis, P., editor, *The Law, Economics and Politics of International Standardisation*. Cambridge University Press, Cambridge (see page: 21).

Delimatsis, P. (2015a). Introduction: Continuity and Change in International Standarisation. In Delimatsis, P., editor, *The Law, Economics and Politics of International*

Standardisation. Cambridge University Press, Cambridge (see pages: 46, 49, and 133).

Delimatsis, P. (2015b). 'Relevant International Standards' and 'Recognised Standardisation Bodies' under the TBT Agreement. In Delimatsis, P., editor, *The Law, Economics and Politics of International Standardisation*. Cambridge University Press, Cambridge (see pages: 46, 50, 70, 73, 133, 138, 141, and 143).

Delimatsis, P. (2015c). *The Law, Economics and Politics of International Standardisation*. Cambridge University Press, Cambridge (see pages: 46, 50, 73, 127, 138, 141, and 143).

Delimatsis, P. (2018). Global Standard-Setting 2.0: How the WTO Spotlights ISO and Impacts the Transnational Standard-Setting Process. *Duke Journal of Comparative and International Law*, (273) (see page: 138).

Demortain, D. (2012). Enabling Global Principle-based Regulation: The Case of Risk Analysis in the Codex Alimentarius. *Regulation & Governance*, 6(2):207–224 (see page: 134).

Demortain, D. (2015). The Tools of Globalization: Ways of Regulating and the Structure of the International Regime for Pharmaceuticals. *Review of International Political Economy*, 22(6):1249–1275 (see page: 134).

DiMaggio, P. J. and Powell, W. W. (1983). The Iron Cage Revisited: Institutional Isomorphism and Collective Rationality in Organizational Fields. *American Sociological Review*, 48(2):147–160 (see page: 44).

Drezner, D. W. (2004). The Global Governance of the Internet: Bringing the State Back In. *Political Science Quarterly*, 119(3):477–498 (see page: 73).

Drezner, D. W. (2007). *All Politics is Global: Explaining International Regulatory Regimes*. Princeton University Press, Princeton, NJ (see pages: 64, 73, and 130).

Drezner, D. W. (2009). The Power and Peril of International Regime Complexity. *Perspectives on Politics*, 7(1):65–70 (see page: 37).

Duffield, J. S. (2003). The Limits of "Rational Design". *International Organization*, 57(3):743–758 (see page: 42).

Dupont, C. and Elsig, M. (2017). Performance and International Organisations' Borders. In Elsig, M., Hoekman, B., and Pauwelyn, J., editors, *Assessing the World Trade Organization: Fit for Purpose?* Cambridge University Press, Cambridge (see pages: 49, 133).

Duquet, S. and Geraets, D. (2012). Food Safety Standards and Informal International Lawmaking. In Berman, A., Duquet, S., Pauwelyn, J., Wessel, R. A., and Wouters, J., editors, *Informal International Lawmaking: Case Studies*. Torkel Opsahl Academic EPublisher, Florence (see pages: 58, 70).

Dür, A., Baccini, L., and Elsig, M. (2014). The Design of International Trade Agreements: Introducing a New Dataset. *The Review of International Organizations*, 9(3):353–375 (see pages: 24, 35, 165, 166, 167, and 178).

Dür, A. and Elsig, M. (2015). *Trade Cooperation: The Purpose, Design and Effects of Preferential Trade Agreements*. Cambridge University Press, Cambridge (see page: 166).

Eckhardt, J. and Wang, H. (2021). China's new generation trade agreements: Importing rules to lock in domestic reform? *Regulation & Governance*, 15(3):581–597 (see page: 166).

Egan, M. and Pelkmans, J. (2015). TTIPs Hard Core: Technical barriers to trade and standards. Technical Report 117, Centre for European Policy Studies, Brussels. Special Report (see pages: 36, 168, 172, and 186).

EilstrupSangiovanni, M. and Westerwinter, O. (2022). The global governance complexity cube: Varieties of institutional complexity in global governance. *The Review of International Organizations*, 17:233262 (see page: 37).

Elsig, M. (2015). Orchestration on a Tight Leash: State Oversight of the WTO. In Abbott, K. W., Genschel, P., Snidal, D., and Zangl, B., editors, *International Organizations as Orchestrators*. Cambridge University Press, Cambridge (see pages: 49, 50, 73, 133, 137, 138, and 143).

Elsig, M. and Dupont, C. (2012). European Union Meets South Korea: Bureaucratic Interests, Exporter Discrimination and the Negotiations of Trade Agreements. *Journal of Common Market Studies*, 50(3):492–507 (see page: 199).

Elsig, M. and Klotz, S. (2019). Behind-the-Border Measures and the New Generation of Trade Agreements: Technical Barriers To Trade And Sanitary And Phytosanitary Measures Compared. In Francois, J. and Hoekman, B., editors, *Behind-the-Border Policies: Assessing and Addressing Non-Tariff Measures*. Cambridge University Press, Cambridge (see pages: 36, 168, 169, and 186).

Elsig, M. and Klotz, S. (2021a). Data flow-related provisions in preferential trade agreements: Trends and patterns of diffusion. In Burri, M., editor, *Big Data and Global Trade Law*. Cambridge University Press, Cambridge (see page: 236).

Elsig, M. and Klotz, S. (2021b). Digital Trade Rules in Preferential Trade Agreements: Is There a WTO Impact? *Global Policy*, 12(S4):25–36 (see page: 236).

Elsig, M. and Klotz, S. (2022). Initiator conditions and the diffusion of digital trade-related provisions in PTAs. *International Interactions*, 48(2):292–308 (see page: 236).

Espitia, A., Pardo, S., Piermartini, R., and Rocha, N. (2020). Technical Barriers to Trade. In Mattoo, A., Rocha, N., and Ruta, M., editors, *Handbook of Deep Trade Agreements*. World Bank Group, Washington, DC (see pages: 24, 170, 177, 178, and 186).

European Commission (2007). Chile Country Strategy Paper. European Commission (see page: 171).

European Commission (2016). TTIP Car Safety Analysis in the EU and US in relation to US and EU Regulatory Standards on Crash Testing. European Commission (see page: 172).

European Commission (2021). EU-US launch Trade and Technology Council to lead values-based global digital transformation. European Commission (see page: 235).

European Council (1981). Council Directive of 31 July 1981 concerning the Prohibition of certain Substances having a Hormonal Action and of any Substances having a Thyrostatic Action (81/602/EEC). Official Journal of the European Communities (see page: 135).

European Parliament (1987). Resolution on the Ban on Hormones (Doc. B2-1701/87) and on the Ban on Hormones in Meat (Doc. B2-1702/87). Official Journal of the European Communities (see page: 135).

FAO (2020). Codex E-Learning Course: Lesson 2. How Codex Committees function. http://www.fao.org/fao-who-codexalimentarius/resources/elearning-course/en/. Online. Accessed on 29 July 2020 (see page: 61).

FAO and WTO (2017). Trade and Food Standards. Technical report, Food and Agriculture Organization of the United Nations and World Trade Organization, Rome and Geneva (see page: 57).

Farquhar, B. J. (2005). Governance in the International Organization for Standardization (ISO) and the International Electrotechnical Commission (IEC). Consumers International (see page: 76).

Farrell, H. (2018). The Shared Challenges of Institutional Theories: Rational Choice, Historical Institutionalism, and Sociological Institutionalism. In Glückler, J., Suddaby, R., and Lenz, R., editors, *Knowledge and Institutions*. Springer, Cham (see pages: 41, 42, 43, and 44).

Ferencz, J. (2019). The OECD Digital Services Trade Restrictiveness Index. *Organisation for Economic Co-operation and Development (OECD) Trade Policy Papers*, (221):1–22 (see page: 236).

Ferencz, J. and Gonzales, F. (2019). Barriers to trade in digitally enabled services in the G20. *Organisation for Economic Co-operation and Development (OECD) Trade Policy Papers*, (232):1–18 (see page: 236).

Ferracane, M. F., Lee-Makiyama, H., and van der Marel, E. (2018). Digital Trade Restrictiveness Index. Technical report, European Centre for International Political Economy (ECIPE), Brussels (see page: 236).

Financial Times (2019). Technology: how the US, EU and China compete to set industry standards. Financial Times. Brussels (see page: 236).

Finnemore, M. (1996). Norms, culture, and world politics: insights from sociology's institutionalism. *International Organization*, 50(2):325–347 (see pages: 41, 44).

Finnemore, M. and Sikkink, K. (2001). Taking Stock: The Constructivist Research Program in International Relations and Comparative Politics. *Annual Review of Political Science*, 4:391–416 (see page: 41).

Finnemore, M. and Toope, S. J. (2001). Alternatives to "Legalization": Richer Views of Law and Politics. *International Organization*, 55:411–430 (see page: 38).

Fioretos, O. (2011). Historical Institutionalism in International Relations. *International Organization*, 65(2):367–399 (see pages: 41, 43, and 44).

Fioretos, O., Falleti, T. G., and Sheingate, A. (2016). *The Oxford Handbook of Historical Institutionalism*. Oxford University Press, Oxford (see page: 41).

Fleuter, S. (2016). The Role of Digital Products Under the WTO: A New Framework for GATT and GATS Classification. *Chicago Journal of International Law*, 17(1):1–26 (see page: 235).

Fliess, B., Gonzales, F., Kim, J., and Schonfeld, R. (2010). The Use of International Standards in Technical Regulation. *Organisation for Economic Co-operation and Development (OECD) Trade Policy Papers*, (102):1–150 (see page: 45).

Fontanelli, F. (2011). ISO and Codex Standards and International Trade Law: What Gets Said Is Not What's Heard. *International & Comparative Law Quarterly*, 60(4):895–932 (see page: 133).

Fuchs, D. and Kalfagianni, A. (2010). The Causes and Consequences of Private Food Governance. *Business and Politics*, 12(3):1–34 (see pages: 49, 68, 134, and 142).

Fulponi, L., Shearer, M., and Almeida, J. (2011). Regional Trade Agreements — Treatment of Agriculture. *Organisation for Economic Co-operation and Development (OECD) Food, Agriculture and Fisheries Papers*, (44):1–72 (see page: 169).

Gao, H. (2018). Digital or Trade? The Contrasting Approaches of China and US to Digital Trade. *Journal of International Economic Law*, 21(2):297–321 (see pages: 235, 236).

Garrett, E. S., Jahncke, M. L., and Cole, E. A. (1998). Effects of Codex and GATT. *Food Control*, 9(2):177–182 (see pages: 56, 133).

GATT (1947). General Agreement on Tariffs and Trade. Preamble (see page: 124).

Ghodsi, M. and Stehrer, R. (2022). Non-Tariff Measures and the Quality of Imported Products. *World Trade Review*, 21(1):71–92 (see page: 125).

Goldstein, J., Kahler, M., Keohane, R. O., and Slaughter, A.-M. (2000). Introduction: Legalization and World Politics. *International Organization*, 54(3):385–399 (see page: 38).

Goldstein, J., Kahler, M., Keohane, R. O., and Slaughter, A.-M. (2001). Response to Finnemore and Toope. *International Organization*, 55(3):759–760 (see page: 38).

Goldstein, J. and Martin, L. L. (2000). Legalization, Trade Liberalization, and Domestic Politics: A Cautionary Note. *International Organization*, 54(3):603–632 (see pages: 39, 126).

Goldstein, J. L. and Steinberg, R. H. (2009). Regulatory Shift: The Rise of Judicial Liberalization at the WTO. In Mattli, W. and Woods, N., editors, *The Politics of Global Regulation*. Princeton University Press, Princeton, NJ (see page: 43).

González, J. L. and Ferencz, J. (2018). Digital Trade and Market Openness. *Organisation for Economic Co-operation and Development* (OECD) *Trade Policy Papers*, (217):1–62 (see page: 236).

González, J. L. and Jouanjean, M.-A. (2019). Digital Trade: Developing a framework for analysis. *Organisation for Economic Co-operation and Development* (OECD) *Trade Policy Papers*, (205):1–25 (see page: 235).

Graz, J.-C. (2019). *The Power of Standards: Hybrid Authority and the Globalisation of Services*. Cambridge University Press, Cambridge (see page: 73).

Graz, J.-C. and Hauert, C. (2014). Beyond the Transatlantic Divide: The Multiple Authorities of Standards in the Global Political Economy of Services. *Business and Politics*, 16(1):113–150 (see page: 73).

Graz, J.-C. and Hauert, C. (2019). Translating Technical Diplomacy: The Participation of Civil Society Organisations in International Standardisation. *Global Society*, 33(2):163–183 (see page: 75).

Guler, I., Guillén, M. F., and Macpherson, J. M. (2002). Global Competition, Institutions, and the Diffusion of Organizational Practices: The International Spread of ISO 9000 Quality Certificates. *Administrative Science Quarterly*, 47(2):207–232 (see page: 75).

Haftel, Y. Z. and Lenz, T. (2022). Measuring institutional overlap in global governance. *The Review of International Organizations*, 17:323347 (see page: 36).

Halabi, S. (2015). The Codex Alimentarius Commission, Corporate Influence, and International Trade: A Perspective on FDA's Global Role. *American Journal of Law and Medicine*, 41:406–421 (see pages: 47, 68).

Hall, P. A. and Taylor, R. C. (1996). Political Science and the Three New Institutionalisms. *Political Studies*, 44(5):936–957 (see pages: 41, 44).

Halliday, T. C., Pacewicz, J., and Block-Lieb, S. (2013). Who governs? Delegations and Delegates in Global Trade Lawmaking. *Regulation & Governance*, 7(3):279–298 (see pages: 47, 52, and 142).

Havinga, T. and Verbruggen, P. (2017). Understanding Complex Governance Relationships in Food Safety Regulation: The RIT Model as a Theoretical Lens. *The ANNALS of the American Academy of Political and Social Science*, 670(1):58–77 (see page: 40).

Hawkins, D. G., Lake, D. A., Nielson, D. L., and Tierney, M. J. (2006). Delegation under anarchy: states, international organizations, and principal-agent theory. In Hawkins, D. G., Lake, D. A., Nielson, D. L., and Tierney, M. J., editors, *Delegation and Agency in International Organizations*. Cambridge University Press, Cambridge (see page: 39).

Heires, M. (2008). The International Organization for Standardization (ISO). *New Political Economy*, 13(3):357–367 (see pages: 46, 51, 70, 74, 141, and 173).

Helfer, L. R. (1999). Forum Shopping for Human Rights. *University of Pennsylvania Law Review*, 148:285–399 (see page: 37).

Helfer, L. R. (2004). Regime Shifting: The TRIPS Agreement and New Dynamics of International Intellectual Property Lawmaking. *Yale Journal of International Law*, 29(1):26–45 (see page: 37).

Helfer, L. R. (2009). Shifting in the International Intellectual Property System. *Perspectives on Politics*, 7(1):39–44 (see page: 37).

Herman, L. (2010). Multilateralising Regionalism: The Case of E-Commerce. *Organisation for Economic Co-operation and Development* (OECD) *Trade Policy Papers*, (99):1–25 (see page: 236).

Heydon, K. and Woolcock, S. (2009). *The Rise of Bilateralism, Comparing American, European and Asian Approaches to Preferential Trade Agreements*. United Nations University Press, Shibuya City (see pages: 170, 171, and 185).

Hoekman, B. (2014). Sustaining Multilateral Trade Cooperation in a Multipolar World Economy. *The Review of International Organizations*, (9):241–260 (see page: 35).

Hofmann, C., Osnago, A., and Ruta, M. (2019). The Content of Preferential Trade Agreements. *World Trade Review*, 18(3):365–398 (see pages: 35, 166, and 167).

Horn, H., Mavroidis, P. C., and Sapir, A. (2010). Beyond the WTO? An Anatomy of EU and US Preferential Trade Agreements. *The World Economy*, pages 1565–1588 (see pages: 35, 36, 167, 168, 171, and 185).

Horn, H., Mavroidis, P. C., and Sapir, A. (2011). EU and U.S. Preferential Trade Agreements: Deepening or Widening of WTO Commitments. In Bagwell, K. W. and Mavroidis, P. C., editors, *Preferential Trade Agreements: A Law and Economics Analysis*. Cambridge University Press, Cambridge (see pages: 36, 168, 171, and 185).

Horton, L. R. (2001). Risk Analysis and the Law: International Law, the World Trade Organization, Codex Alimentarius and National Legislation. *Food Additives & Contaminants*, 18(12):1057–1067 (see pages: 56, 133).

Hüller, T. and Maier, M. L. (2006). Fixing the Codex? Global Food-Safety Governance Under Review. In Joerges, C. and Petersmann, E.-U., editors, *Constitutionalism, Multilevel Trade Governance And Social Regulation*. Hart Publishing, Portland, OR (see pages: 47, 52, and 142).

Hurrell, A. (1993). International Society and the Study of Regimes: A Reflective Approach. In Rittberger, V. and Mayer, P., editors, *Regime theory and international relations*. Oxford University Press, Oxford (see page: 36).

Immergut, E. M. (1998). The Theoretical Core of the New Institutionalism. *Politics and Society*, 26(1):5–34 (see page: 41).

ISO (2012). ISO/IEC Directives, third edition. International Organization for Standardization (see page: 72).

ISO (2017). ISO and food. Technical report, International Organization for Standardization, Geneva (see page: 71).

ISO (2020a). International Organization for Standardization. https://www.iso.org/home.html. Online. Accessed on 28 July 2020 (see page: 75).

ISO (2020b). WTO ISO Standards Information Gateway. https://tbtcode.iso.org/sites/wto-tbt/list-of-standardizing-bodies.html. Online. Accessed on 31 July 2020 (see page: 69).

ITC (2016). SME Competitiveness Outlook: Meeting the standard for trade. Online. Geneva: International Trade Centre (see page: 22).

Jackson, L. A. and Jansen, M. (2010). Risk Assessment in the International Food Safety Policy Arena: Can the Multilateral Institutions encourage Unbiased Outcomes? *Food Policy*, page 538 (see page: 68).

Jackson, L. A. and Vitikala, H. (2016). Cross-cutting Issues in Regional Trade Agreements: Sanitary and Phytosanitary Measures. In Acharya, R., editor, *Regional Trade Agreements and the Multilateral Trading System*. Cambridge University Press, Cambridge (see page: 170).

Jansen, M. (2010). Developing Countries, Standards and the WTO. *The Journal of International Trade & Economic Development*, 19(1):163–185 (see page: 67).

Jansen, M. (2012a). Defining the Borders of the WTO Agenda. In Narlikar, A., Daunton, M., and Stern, R. M., editors, *The Oxford Handbook on the World Trade Organization*. Oxford University Press, Oxford (see pages: 50, 73, 128, 129, 138, and 143).

Jansen, M. (2012b). Internal Measures in the Multilateral Trading System: Where are the Borders of the WTO Agenda? In Cottier, T. and Elsig, M., editors, *Governing the World Trade Organization: Past, Present and Beyond Doha*. Cambridge University Press, Cambridge (see pages: 50, 73, 128, 129, 130, 138, and 143).

Jansen, M., Klotz, S., and Virdee, J. (2020). Regional Integration: The Next Wave. In Klasen, A., editor, *The Handbook of Global Trade Policy*. John Wiley and Sons, Hoboken, NJ (see page: 124).

Johnson, R. (2015). The U.S.-EU Beef Hormone Dispute. Congressional Research Service (see page: 134).

Jordana, J. (2017). Transgovernmental Networks as Regulatory Intermediaries: Horizontal Collaboration and the Realities of Soft Power. *The ANNALS of the American Academy of Political and Social Science*, 670(1):245–262 (see page: 40).

Jupille, J., Mattli, W., and Snidal, D. (2013). *Institutional Choice and Global Commerce*. Cambridge University Press, Cambridge (see page: 44).

Kanevskaia, O. (2023). *The Law and Practice of Global ICT Standardization*. Cambridge University Press, Cambridge (see page: 236).

Karttunen, M. B. (2020). *Transparency in the WTO SPS and TBT Agreements: The Real Jewel in the Crown*. Cambridge University Press, Cambridge (see pages: 45, 141).

Katznelson, I. and Weingast, B. R. (2005). Intersections Between Historical and Rational Choice Institutionalism. In Katznelson, I. and Weingast, B. R., editors, *Preferences and Situations: Points of Intersection Between Historical and Rational Choice Institutionalism*. Russell Sage Foundation, New York, NY (see page: 41).

Keohane, R. O. (1988). International Institutions: Two Approaches. *International Studies Quarterly*, 32(4):379–396 (see pages: 33, 38, and 44).

Kim, M. (2018). The 'Standard' in the GATT/WTO TBT Agreements: Origin, Evolution and Application. *Journal of World Trade*, 52(5):765–788 (see page: 137).

Kim, S. and Hofmann, T. (2018). Designing Credible Commitment: The Political Economy of Dispute Settlement Design in PTAs. In Velut, J.-B., Dalingwater, L., Boullet, V., and Peyronel, V., editors, *Understanding Mega Free Trade Agreements: The Political and Economic Governance of New Cross-Regionalism*. Routledge, Abingdon-on-Thames (see pages: 183, 185).

Kim, S. E., Urpelainen, J., and Yang, J. (2019). Environmental Effects of GATT/WTO Membership: An Empirical Evaluation. *International Interactions*, 45(5):917–932 (see page: 145).

Kingsbury, B. (1998). The Concept of Compliance as a Function of Competing Conceptions of International Law. *Michigan Journal of International Law*, 19(2):345–372 (see page: 36).

Kingsbury, B., Krisch, N., and Stewart, R. B. (2005). The Emergence of Global Administrative Law. *Law and Contemporary Problems*, 68(15):15–62 (see pages: 57, 69).

Kleimann, D. (2014). Beyond Market Access? The Anatomy of ASEAN's Preferential Trade Agreements. *Journal of World Trade*, 48(2):629–682 (see pages: 169, 170).

Klotz, S. (2023). Who drives the international standardisation of telecommunication and digitalisation? Introducing a new data set. *Global Policy*, 14(3):558–568 (see page: 236).

Klotz, S. and Appleton, A. (2024). TBT and SPS in PTAs: The Recent Past and the Near Future. In Claussen, K., Elsig, M., and Polanco, R., editors, *The Concept Design of a 21st Century Preferential Trade Agreement*. Cambridge University Press, Cambridge (see pages: 168, 169, and 186).

Koenig-Archibugi, M. and Macdonald, K. (2017). The Role of Beneficiaries in Transnational Regulatory Processes. *The ANNALS of the American Academy of Political and Social Science*, 670(1):36–57 (see page: 40).

Kollman, K. and Prakash, A. (2001). Green by Choice? Cross-National Variations in Firms' Responses to EMS-Based Environmental Regimes. *World Politics*, 53(3):399–430 (see page: 75).

Koremenos, B., Lipson, C., and Snidal, D. (2001). The Rational Design of International Institutions. *International Organization*, 55(4):761–799 (see pages: 33, 41).

Koremenos, B. and Snidal, D. (2003). Moving Forward, One Step at a Time. *International Organization*, 57:431–444 (see page: 42).

Krasner, S. D. (1983). Structural Causes and Regime Consequences: Regimes as Intervening Variables. *International Organization*, 36(2):185–205 (see pages: 36, 38).

Krasner, S. D. (1991). Global Communications and National Power: Life on the Pareto Frontier. *Political Science Quarterly*, 43(3):336–366 (see pages: 46, 141).

Lang, A. and Scott, J. (2009). The Hidden World of WTO Governance. *The European Journal of International Law*, 20(3):575–614 (see page: 57).

Larouche, P. and van Overwalle, G. (2015). Interoperability standards, patents and competition policy. In Delimatsis, P., editor, *The Law, Economics and Politics of*

International Standardisation. Cambridge University Press, Cambridge (see pages: 46, 141).

Lasalle-de Salins, M. (2011). *Lobbying de l'Agroalimentaire et Normes Internationales: Le Cas du Codex Alimentarius*. Éditions Quæ, Versailles Cedex, France (see page: 68).

Lavenex, S. and Jurje, F. (2021). Opening-up labor mobility? Rising powers' rulemaking in trade agreements. *Regulation & Governance*, 15(3):598–615 (see page: 167).

Lechner, L. (2016). The Domestic Battle over the Design of Non-trade Issues in Preferential Trade Agreements. *Review of International Political Economy*, 23(5):840–871 (see page: 167).

Lee, E. (2005). The World Health Organization's Global Strategy on Diet, Physical Activity, and Health: Turning Strategy into Action. *Food and Drug Law Journal*, 60:569–595 (see page: 133).

Lejárraga, I. (2013). Multilateralising Regionalism: Strengthening Transparency Disciplines in Trade. *Organisation for Economic Co-operation and Development* (OECD) *Trade Policy Papers*, (152):1–48 (see pages: 169, 171, and 184).

Lejárraga, I. (2014). Deep Provisions in Regional Trade Agreements: How Multilateral-friendly? *Organisation for Economic Co-operation and Development* (OECD) *Trade Policy Papers*, (168):1–44 (see pages: 169, 171, and 184).

Lesser, C. (2007). Do Bilateral and Regional Approaches for Reducing Technical Barriers to Trade Converge Towards the Multilateral Trading System? *Organisation for Economic Co-operation and Development* (OECD) *Trade Policy Working Papers*, (58):1–75 (see pages: 170, 185, and 186).

Lester, S. and Barbee, I. (2013). The Challenge of Cooperation: Regulatory Trade Barriers in the Transatlantic Trade and Investment Partnership. *Journal of International Economic Law*, 16(4):847–867 (see pages: 36, 168).

Levi-Faur, D. (2005). The Global Diffusion of Regulatory Capitalism. *The Annals of the American Academy of Political and Social Science*, 598:12–32 (see page: 134).

Levi-Faur, D. and Starobin, S. M. (2014). Transnational Politics and Policy: From Two-way to Three-way Interactions. *Jerusalem Papers in Regulation & Governance Working Paper*, (62):1–38 (see page: 40).

Levinson, M. (2016). *The Box: How the Shipping Container Made the World Smaller and the World Economy Bigger*. Princeton University Press, Princeton, NJ (see page: 22).

Lewis, M. K. (2011). The Politics and Indirect Effects of Asymmetrical Bargaining Power in Free Trade Agreements. In Broude, T., Busch, M. L., and Porges, A., editors, *The Politics of International Economic Law*. Cambridge University Press, Cambridge (see page: 185).

Lewis, M. K. (2023). International Trade Agreements: Laboratories of Innovation or Propellers of Fragmentation? *Journal of International Economic Law*, 26(1):110123 (see page: 35).

Lim, S. and Prakash, A. (2018). Inter-Governmental Regimes and Recruitment to Private Regimes: GATT/WTO and the ISO, 1951–2005. *Global Policy*, 9(3):352–364 (see pages: 75, 139).

Lin, C.-F. (2011). Global Food Safety: Exploring Key Elements for an International Regulatory Strategy. *Virginia Journal of International Law*, 51(3):637–696 (see pages: 56, 133).

Lindahl, H. (2015). ISO standards and authoritative collective action: Conceptual and normative issues. In Delimatsis, P., editor, *The Law, Economics and Politics of International Standardisation*. Cambridge University Press, Cambridge (see pages: 22, 46, 50, 70, 73, and 138).

Liu, H.-W. (2018). International Standards in Flux: A Balkanized ICT Standard-Setting Paradigm and its Implications for the WTO. *Journal of International Economic Law*, 17(3):551–600 (see page: 236).

Livermore, M. A. (2006). Authority and Legitimacy in Global Governance: Deliberation, Institutional Differentiation, and the Codex Alimentarius. *New York University Law Review*, 81:766–801 (see pages: 49, 50, 56, 133, 134, and 142).

Liyang Sun and Sarah Abraham (2020). Estimating Dynamic Treatment Effects in Event Studies with Heterogeneous Treatment Effects. Online. Accessed on 19 April 2021 (see page: 147).

Lytton, T. D. (2017). The Taming of the Stew: Regulatory Intermediaries in Food Safety Governance. *The ANNALS of the American Academy of Political and Social Science*, 670(1):78–92 (see page: 40).

Mahoney, J. (2000). Path Dependence in Historical Sociology. *Theory and Society*, 29(4):507–548 (see pages: 42, 43).

Manger, M. S. (2009). *Investing in Protection: The Politics of Preferential Trade Agreements between North and South*. Cambridge University Press, Cambridge (see pages: 35, 166).

Mansfield, E. D. and Milner, H. V. (1999). The New Wave of Regionalism. *International Organization*, 53(3):589–627 (see page: 35).

Mansfield, E. D. and Milner, H. V. (2012). *Votes, Vetoes, and the Political Economy of International Trade Agreements*. Princeton University Press, Princeton, NJ (see page: 35).

Mansfield, E. D. and Pevehouse, J. C. W. (2022). Nationalism, Populism, and Trade Agreements. *International Studies Review*, 24(2):viac016 (see page: 166).

Mansfield, E. D. and Reinhardt, E. (2003). Multilateral Determinants of Regionalism: The Effects of GATT/WTO on the Formation of Preferential Trading Arrangements. *International Organization*, 57(4):829–862 (see page: 35).

Marceau, G. and Trachtman, J. P. (2014). A Map of the World Trade Organization Law of Domestic Regulation of Goods: The Technical Barriers to Trade Agreement, the Sanitary and Phytosanitary Measures Agreement, and the General Agreement on Tariffs and Trade. *Journal of World Trade*, 48(2):351–432 (see pages: 58, 127, and 128).

Margulis, M. E. (2018). Negotiating from the Margins: How the UN Shapes the Rules of the WTO. *Review of International Political Economy*, 25(3):364–391 (see page: 130).

Margulis, M. E. (2021). Intervention by international organizations in regime complexes. *The Review of International Organizations*, 16:871902 (see page: 131).

Marx, J. (2010). Path Dependency and Change in International Relations: Institutional Dynamics in the Field of Intellectual Property Rights. *Historical Social Research*, 35(3):175–199 (see page: 37).

Masson-Matthee, M. D. (2007). *The Codex Alimentarius Commission and its Standards*. TMC Asser Press, The Hague (see pages: 56, 57, and 60).

Matthews, A. (2016). Food Safety Regulation in TTIP: Much Ado About Nothing? *European Journal of Risk Regulation*, 7(2):256–261 (see page: 172).

Mattli, W. (2001a). International Governance for Voluntary Standards: A Gametheoretic Perspective. In Bermann, G. A., Herdegenand, M., and Lindseth, P. L., editors, *Transatlantic Regulatory Cooperation: Legal Problems and Political Prospects*. Oxford University Press, Oxford (see pages: 73, 74, 137, and 173).

Mattli, W. (2001b). The Politics and Economics of International Institutional Standards Setting: An introduction. *Journal of European Public Policy*, 8(3):328–344 (see pages: 73, 74, and 173).

Mattli, W. and Büthe, T. (2003). Setting International Standards: Technological Rationality or Primacy of Power? *World Politics*, 56(1):1–42 (see pages: 46, 74, 141, and 173).

Mattli, W. and Seddon, J. (2015). The Power of the Penholder: The Missing Politics in Global Regulatory Governance Analysis. In Delimatsis, P., editor, *The Law, Economics and Politics of International Standardisation*. Cambridge University Press, Cambridge (see pages: 46, 141).

Mattli, W. and Woods, N. (2009). In Whose Benefit? In Mattli, W. and Woods, N., editors, *The Politics of Global Regulation*. Princeton University Press, Princeton, NJ (see page: 70).

Mattoo, A., Rocha, N., and Ruta, M. (2020). *Handbook of Deep Trade Agreements*. World Bank Group, Washington, DC (see page: 166).

Maur, J.-C. and Shepherd, B. (2011). Product Standards. In Chauffour, J.-P. and Maur, J.-C., editors, *Preferential Trade Agreement Policies for Development: A Handbook*. World Bank, Washington, DC (see page: 171).

Mavroidis, P. C. (2003). The Trade Disputes Concerning Health Policy Between the EC and the US. In Petersmann, E.-U. and Pollack, M. A., editors, *Transatlantic Economic Disputes: The EU, the US, and the WTO*. Oxford University Press, Oxford (see page: 134).

Mavroidis, P. C. and Wolfe, R. (2017). Private Standards and the WTO: Reclusive No More. *World Trade Review*, 16(1):1–24 (see pages: 46, 50, 73, 138, 141, and 143).

McDaniels, D. and Karttunen, M. (2016). Trade, Testing and Toasters: Conformity Assessment Procedures and the TBT Committee. *World Trade Organization (WTO) Staff Working Paper*, (9):1–23 (see page: 184).

McDaniels, D., Molina, A. C., and Wijkström, E. N. (2018). A Closer Look At WTO's Third Pillar: How WTO Committees Influence Regional Trade Agreements. *Journal of International Economic Law*, 21(4):815–843 (see pages: 24, 74, 171, 184, and 236).

Melillo, M. (2022). Standards of Scientific Evidence in Preferential Trade Agreements. *Journal of International Economic Law*, 25(3):369389 (see page: 170).

Meyer, J. W., Boli, J., Thomas, G. M., and Ramirez, F. O. (1997). World Society and the Nation-State. *American Journal of Sociology*, 103(1):144–181 (see page: 44).

Meyer, N., Fenyes, T., Breitenbach, M., and Idsardi, E. (2010). Bilateral and Regional Trade Agreements and Technical Barriers to Trade: An African Perspective. *Organisation for Economic Co-operation and Development (OECD) Trade Policy Papers*, (96):1–49 (see page: 170).

Milewicz, K., Hollway, J., Peacock, C., and Snidal, D. (2018). Beyond Trade: The Expanding Scope of the Non-trade Agenda in Trade Agreements. *Journal of Conflict Resolution*, 62(4):743–773 (see page: 167).

Milner, H. V. (1998). Rationalizing Politics: The Emerging Synthesis of International, American, and Comparative Politics. *International Organization*, 52(4):759–786 (see page: 41).

Mitchell, A. D. and Mishra, N. (2019). Regulating Cross-Border Data Flows in a Data-Driven World: How WTO Law Can Contribute. *Journal of International Economic Law*, (22):389–416 (see page: 235).

Molina, A. C. and Khoroshavina, V. (2015). TBT Provisions in Regional Trade Agreements: To what Extent do they go beyond the WTO TBT Agreement? *World Trade Organization (WTO) Staff Working Paper*, (9):1–24 (see pages: 170, 186).

Molina, A. C. and Khoroshavina, V. (2018). How Regional Trade Agreements Deal with Disputes Concerning their TBT Provisions? *World Trade Organization (WTO) Staff Working Paper*, (9):1–22 (see page: 170).

Monteiro, J.-A. and Teh, R. (2017). Provisions on Electronic Commerce in Regional Trade Agreements. *World Trade Organization Working Paper*, (11):1–75 (see page: 236).

Morikawa, M. and Morrison, J. (2004). Who Develops ISO Standards? A Survey of Participation in ISO's International Standards Development Processes. Technical report, Pacific Institute for Studies in Development, Environment, and Security, Oakland, CA (see page: 75).

Morin, J.-F., Dür, A., and Lechner, L. (2018). Mapping the Trade and Environment Nexus: Insights from a New Data Set. *Global Environmental Politics*, 18(1):122–139 (see page: 167).

Morin, J.-F. and Surbeck, J. (2020). Mapping the New Frontier of International IP Law: Introducing a TRIPs-plus Dataset. *World Trade Review*, 19(1):109–122 (see page: 167).

Murphy, C. N. and Yates, J. (2009). *The International Organization for Standardization (ISO): Global Governance through Voluntary Consensus (Global Institutions)*. Routledge, England (see pages: 70, 71, and 73).

Naiki, Y. (2009). Accountability and Legitimacy in Global Health and Safety Governance: The World Trade Organization, the SPS Committee, and International Standard-Setting Organizations. *Journal of World Trade*, 43(6):1255–1279 (see pages: 128, 137).

Newman, A. L. and Zaring, D. (2013). Regulatory Networks: Power, Legitimacy, and Compliance. In Dunoff, J. L. and Pollack, M. A., editors, *Interdisciplinary Perspectives on International Law and International Relations: The State of the Art*. Cambridge University Press, Cambridge (see page: 58).

North, D. C. (1990). *Institutions, Institutional Change and Economic Performance*. Cambridge University Press, Cambridge (see page: 41).

O'Connel, M. E. (2000). The Role of Soft Law in a Global Order. In Shelton, D., editor, *Commitment and Compliance: The Role of Non-binding Norms in the International Legal System*. Oxford University Press, Oxford (see page: 46).

Onderco, M. (2019). Variation in Delegation Size in Multilateral Diplomacy. *The British Journal of Politics and International Relations*, 21(2):421–438 (see pages: 47, 52, and 142).

Oswald, O. R. S. and Eckhardt, J. (2023). New champions of preferential trade? Two-level games in China's and India's shifting commercial strategies. *Review of International Political Economy*, 30:654–677 (see page: 166).

Pauwelyn, J. (2006). Non-Traditional Patterns of Global Regulation: Is the WTO 'Missing the Boat'? In Joerges, C. and Petersmann, E.-U., editors, *Constitutionalism, Multilevel Trade Governance And Social Regulation*. Hart Publishing, Portland, OR (see page: 127).

Peacock, C., Milewicz, K., and Snidal, D. (2019). Boilerplate in International Trade Agreements. *International Studies Quarterly*, 63(4):923–937 (see pages: 36, 167).

Pernet, A. O. (2015). The Development Dimension of the Codex Alimentarius Standard-setting Process. In Delimatsis, P., editor, *The Law, Economics and Politics of International Standardisation*. Cambridge University Press, Cambridge (see pages: 57, 67, and 133).

Peters, A., Koechlin, L., Förster, T., and Zinkernagel, G. F. (2009). *Non-State Actors as Standard Setters*. University of Cambridge, Cambridge (see page: 68).

Piermartini, R. and Budetta, M. (2009). A Mapping of Regional Rules on Technical Barriers to Trade. In Estevadeordal, A., Suominen, K., and Teh, R., editors, *Regional Rules in the Global Trading System*. Cambridge University Press, Cambridge (see pages: 170, 185, and 186).

Pierson, P. (2000). Increasing Returns, Path Dependence, and the Study of Politics. *The American Political Science Review*, 94(2):251–267 (see page: 42).

Poli, S. (2004). The European Community and the Adoption of International Food Standards within the Codex Alimentarius Commission. *European Law Journal*, 10(5):613–630 (see pages: 56, 58, 64, and 133).

Politico (2021). US and Europe to forge tech alliance amid China's rise. Politico (see page: 235).

Pollack, M. A. (2006). Rational Choice and EU Politics. In Jørgensen, K. E., Pollack, M. A., and Rosamond, B., editors, *Handbook of European Union Politics*. Sage, London (see page: 41).

Pollack, M. A. and Shaffer, G. C. (2009). *When Cooperation Fails: The International Law and Politics of Genetically Modified Foods*. Oxford University Press, Oxford (see pages: 47, 49, 56, 64, 134, and 142).

Posada, K. C., Ganne, E., and Piermartini, R. (2022). The Role of WTO Committees through the Lens of Specific Trade Concerns Raised in the TBT Committee. *World Trade Review*, 21(4):411–431 (see page: 184).

Post, D. L. (2005). Standards and Regulatory Capitalism: The Diffusion of Food Safety Standards in Developing Countries. *The ANNALS of the American Academy of Political and Social Science*, 598(1):168–183 (see pages: 47, 56, 64, and 133).

Post, D. L. (2006). The Precautionary Principle and Risk Assessment in International Food Safety: How the World Trade Organization Influences Standards. *Risk Analysis*, 26(5):1259–1273 (see pages: 56, 64, and 133).

Potoski, M. and Prakash, A. (2005a). Covenants with weak swords: ISO 14001 and facilities' environmental performance. *Journal of Policy Analysis and Management*, 24(4):745–769 (see page: 75).

Potoski, M. and Prakash, A. (2005b). Green Clubs and Voluntary Governance: ISO 14001 and Firms' Regulatory Compliance. *American Journal of Political Science*, 49(2):235–248 (see page: 75).

Prakash, A. and Potoski, M. (2006a). Racing to the Bottom? Globalization, Environmental Governance and ISO 14001. *American Journal of Political Science*, 50(2):347–361 (see page: 75).

Prakash, A. and Potoski, M. (2006b). *The Voluntary Environmentalists: Green Clubs, ISO 14001, and Voluntary Environmental Regulation*. Cambridge University Press, Cambridge (see page: 75).

Prakash, A. and Potoski, M. (2007). Investing Up: FDI and the Cross-National Diffusion of ISO 14001. *International Studies Quarterly*, 51(3):723–744 (see page: 75).

Prakash, A. and Potoski, M. (2010). The International Organization for Standardization as a global governor: a club theory perspective. In Avant, D. D., Finnemore, M., and Sell, S. K., editors, *Who Governs the Globe?* Cambridge University Press, Cambridge (see pages: 49, 50, 133, and 142).

Puig, G. V. and Dalke, E. D. (2016). Nature and Enforceability of WTO-plus SPS and TBT Provisions in Canada's PTAs: From NAFTA to CETA. *World Trade Review*, 15(1):51–83 (see pages: 169, 170).

Raess, D. and Sari, D. (2018). Labor Provisions in Trade Agreements (LABPTA): Introducing a New Dataset. *Global Policy*, 9(4):451–466 (see page: 167).

Raustiala, K. and Victor, D. G. (2004). The Regime Complex for Plant Genetic Resources. *International Organization*, 58(2):277–309 (see pages: 36, 37, and 38).

Rixen, T. and Viola, L. (2016). Historical Institutionalism and International Relations: Towards Explaining Change and Stability in International Institutions. In Rixen, T., Viola, L. A., and Zürn, M., editors, *Historical Institutionalism and International Relations*. Oxford University Press, Oxford (see pages: 41, 42, and 43).

Roberts, D. (1998). Preliminary Assessment of the Effects of the WTO Agreement on Sanitary and Phytosanitary Trade Regulations. *Journal of International Economic Law*, 1(3):377–405 (see page: 128).

Roberts, D., Orden, D., and Josling, T. (2004). Sanitary and Phytosanitary Barriers to Agricultural Trade: Progress, Prospects, and Implications for Developing Countries. In Ingco, M. D. and Winters, L. A., editors, *Agriculture and the New Trade Agenda: Creating a Global Trading Environment for Development*. Cambridge University Press, Cambridge (see page: 134).

Roberts, D. and Unnevehr, L. (2005). Resolving Trade Disputes Arising from Trends in Food Safety Regulation: The Role of the Multilateral Governance Framework. *World Trade Review*, 4(3):469–497 (see page: 64).

Rosendorff, B. P. and Milner, H. V. (2001). The Optimal Design of International Trade Institutions: Uncertainty and Escape. *International Organization*, 55(4):829–857 (see pages: 35, 167).

Rosman, L. (1993). Public Participation in International Pesticide Regulation: When the Codex Commission Decides, Who Will Listen? *Virginia Environmental Law Journal*, 12(2):329–365 (see pages: 56, 132).

Rountree, G. H. (1999). Raging Hormones: A Discussion of the World Trade Organization's Decision in the European Union-United States Beef Dispute. *Georgia Journal of International and Comparative Law*, 27(3):607–634 (see page: 134).

Rudloff, B. and Simons, J. (2004). Comparing EU Free Trade Agreements: Sanitary and Phytosanitary Standards. *European Centre for Development Policy Management (ECDPM) InBrief*, (6):1–6 (see page: 169).

Santeramo, F. G. and Lamonaca, E. (2022). Standards and regulatory cooperation in regional trade agreements: What the effects on trade? *Applied Economic Perspectives and Policy*, 44(4):1682–1701 (see page: 125).

Scarbrough, F. E. (2005). Codex — What's All the Fuss? *Food and Drug Law Journal*, 65:631–638 (see page: 64).

Schepel, H. (2015). Between standards and regulation: On the concept of 'de facto mandatory standards' after Tuna II and Fra.bo. In Delimatsis, P., editor, *The Law, Economics and Politics of International Standardisation*. Cambridge University Press, Cambridge (see pages: 22, 46).

Schmidt, V. A. (1999). Approaches to the Study of European Politics. This Forum was first published in the ECSA Review, Spring 1999 (XII: 2), pp. 2–9 (see pages: 41, 44).

Schroder, H. Z. (2009). Definition of the Concept 'International Standard' in the TBT Agreement. *Journal of World Trade*, 43(6):1223–1254 (see page: 127).

Schroder, H. Z. (2011). *Harmonization, Equivalence and Mutual Recognition of Standards in WTO law*. Wolters Kluwer, The Netherlands (see page: 127).

Schroeder, H., Boykoff, M. T., and Spiers, L. (2012). Equity and State Representations in Climate Negotiations. *Nature Climate Change*, 2:834–836 (see pages: 47, 52, and 142).

Sen, N. (2018). Understanding the Role of the WTO in International Data Flows: Taking the Liberalization or the Regulatory Autonomy Path? *Journal of International Economic Law*, (21):1–26 (see page: 236).

Sewell, W. H. (1996). Three Temporalities: Toward an Eventful Sociology. In McDonald, T. J., editor, *The Historic Turn in the Human Sciences*. University of Michigan Press, Ann Arbor, MI (see page: 43).

Shaffer, G. C. and Pollack, M. A. (2013). Hard and Soft Law. In Dunoff, J. L. and Pollack, M. A., editors, *Interdisciplinary Perspectives on International Law and International Relations: The State of the Art*. Cambridge University Press, Cambridge (see pages: 39, 49, 50, 126, 133, and 142).

Silverglade, B. (2000). The WTO Agreement of Sanitary and Phytosanitary Measures: Weakening Food Safety Regulations to Facilitate Trade? *Food and Drug Law Journal*, 55(4):517–524 (see page: 134).

Simmons, B. A. and Martin, L. L. (2012). International Organizations and Institutions (Second Edition). In Carlsnaes, W., Risse, T., and Simmons, B. A., editors, *Handbook of International Relations*. SAGE Publications, Thousand Oaks, CA (see pages: 34, 38).

Sklair, L. (2002). The Transnational Capitalist Class and Global Politics: Deconstructing the Corporate: State-Connection. *International Political Science Review*, 23(2):159–174 (see pages: 49, 134, and 142).

Skogstad, G. (2001). Internationalization, Democracy, and Food Safety Measures: The (Il)Legitimacy of Consumer Preferences? *Global Governance*, 7(3):293–316 (see pages: 129, 130).

Smith, J. M. (2000). The Politics of Dispute Settlement Design: Explaining Legalism in Regional Trade Pacts. *International Organization*, 54(1):137–180 (see page: 185).

Smythe, E. (2009). In Whose Interests? Transparency and Accountability in the Global Governance of Food: Agribusiness, the Codex Alimentarius and the World Trade

Organization. In Clapp, J. and Fuchs, D., editors, *Corporate Power in Global Agrifood Governance*. MIT Press, Cambridge, MA (see pages: 49, 57, 133, 134, and 142).

Snidal, D. (2002). Rational Choice and International Relations. In Carlsnaes, W., Risse, T., and Simmons, B., editors, *Handbook of International Relations* (*First Edition*). SAGE Publications, Thousand Oaks, CA (see pages: 41, 42).

Snidal, D. (2012). Rational Choice and International Relations (Second Edition). In Carlsnaes, W., Risse, T., and Simmons, B., editors, *Handbook of International Relations*. SAGE Publications, Thousand Oaks, CA (see pages: 41, 42).

Stanton, G. (2004). A Review of the Operation of the Agreement on Sanitary and Phytosanitary Measures. In Ingco, M. D. and Winters, L. A., editors, *Agriculture and the New Trade Agenda: Creating a Global Trading Environment for Development*. Cambridge University Press, Cambridge (see page: 128).

Stanton, G. H. (1997). Implications of the WTO Agreement on Sanitary and Phytosanitary Measures. In Orden, D. and Roberts, D., editors, *Understanding Technical Barriers to Agricultural Trade*. IATRC Proceedings Issue, Tucson, AZ (see pages: 128, 129, and 130).

Steinberg, R. H. (2002). In the Shadow of Law or Power? Consensus-Based Bargaining and Outcomes in the GATT/WTO. *International Organization*, 56(2):339–374 (see page: 37).

Stewart, T. P. and Johanson, D. S. (1998). The SPS Agreement of the World Trade Organization and International Organizations: The Roles Of the Codex Alimentarius Commission, the International Plant Protection Convention, and the International Office of Epizootics. *Syracuse Journal of International Law and Commerce*, 26(1):1–27 (see pages: 49, 132, 134, and 142).

Stoler, A. L. (2011). TBT and SPS Measures, in Practice. In Chauffour, J.-P. and Maur, J.-C., editors, *Preferential Trade Agreement Policies for Development: A Handbook*. World Bank, Washington, DC (see pages: 170, 171, and 185).

Stone, S. and Casalini, F. (2020). Sanitary and Phytosanitary Measures. In Mattoo, A., Rocha, N., and Ruta, M., editors, *Handbook of Deep Trade Agreements*. World Bank Group, Washington, DC (see pages: 24, 170, 177, and 178).

Strange, S. (1982). Cave! Hic Dragones: A Critique of Regime Analysis. *International Organization*, 36(2):479–496 (see page: 36).

Streeck, W. and Thelen, K. (2005). *Beyond Continuity: Institutional Change in Advanced Political Economies*. Oxford University Press, Oxford (see page: 43).

Suppan, S. (2004). Consumers Internationals Decision-Making in the Global Market: Codex Briefing Paper. Institute for Agriculture and Trade Policy (see page: 68).

Sykes, A. O. (1999). Regulatory Protectionism and the Law of International Trade. *University of Chicago Law Review*, 66(1):1–46 (see page: 134).

Tate, J. (2003). National Varieties of Standardization. In Hall, P. A. and Soskice, D., editors, *Varieties of Capitalism: The Institutional Foundations of Comparative Advantage*. Oxford University Press, Oxford (see pages: 74, 173).

Thiermann, A. (1997). Implementation of the World Trade Organization's Agreement on Sanitary and Phytosanitary Measures: The US Perspective. In Orden, D. and Roberts, D., editors, *Understanding Technical Barriers to Agricultural Trade*. IATRC Proceedings Issue, Tucson, AZ (see page: 128).

Thompson, A. (2010). Rational Design in Motion: Uncertainty and Flexibility in the Global Climate Regime. *European Journal of International Relations*, 16(2):269–296 (see page: 42).

Ti-Ting, L. (2012). Technical Barriers to Trade Provisions in Regional Trade Agreements. *Society of International Economic Law(SIEL)*, (12):629–682 (see pages: 170, 186).

Trachtman, J. P. (2003). Toward Open Recognition? Standardization and Regional Integration under Article XXIV of GATT. *Journal of International Economic Law*, 6(2):459–492 (see page: 128).

UNCTAD (2019). International Classification of Non-tariff measures. Technical report, United Nations Conference on Trade and Development (UNCTAD), Geneva (see page: 125).

UNCTAD (2020). Global Cyberlaw Tracker. Geneva: United Nations Conference on Trade and Development (see page: 236).

USTR (2020). 2020 National Trade Estimate Report on Foreign Trade Barriers. Office of the United States Trade Representative (USTR). Washington, DC (see pages: 73, 74, and 172).

van der Marel, E. and Ferracane, M. F. (2021). Do Data Policy Restrictions Inhibit Trade in Services? *Review of World Economics*, (0):1–50 (see page: 236).

Veggeland, F. (2015). Hard and Soft Governance in World Food Trade: The Use of Dispute Settlement and Equivalence in Conflict-resolution. Paper presented in the Panel Food System Governance (No.P145), ECPR General Conference 26–29 August 2015 (see page: 134).

Veggeland, F. and Borgen, S. O. (2005). Negotiating International Food Standards: The World Trade Organization's Impact on the Codex Alimentarius Commission. *Governance: An International Journal of Policy, Administration, and Institutions*, 18(4):675–708 (see pages: 47, 49, 50, 65, 67, 129, 133, 134, 139, and 142).

Veggeland, F. and Sørbye, S. E. (2015). Transatlantic Governance in Food Trade: Dispute settlement and equivalence as trade-facilitating tools. Technical report, Norwegian Institute of International Affairs, Oslo (see pages: 134, 172, and 186).

Victor, D. G. (2000). The Sanitary and Phytosanitary Agreement of the World Trade Organization: An Assessment after Five Years. *New York University Journal of International Law and Politics*, 32:865–937 (see pages: 46, 49, 134, 141, and 142).

Victor, D. G. (2004). WTO Efforts to Manage Differences in National Sanitary and Phytosanitary Policies. In Vogel, D. and Kagan, R. A., editors, *Dynamics of Regulatory Change: How Globalization Affects National Regulatory Policies*, pages 167–206. University of California, Berkeley, CA (see pages: 131, 133, and 134).

Villarreal, A. B. (2018). *International Standardization and the Agreement on Technical Barriers to Trade*. Cambridge University Press, Cambridge (see page: 127).

Vogel, D. (1995). *Trading Up: Consumer and Environmental Regulation in a Global Economy*. Harvard University Press, Cambridge, MA and London (see pages: 134, 135).

Vogel, D. (2012). *The Politics of Precaution: Regulating Health, Safety, and Environmental Risks in Europe and the United States*. Princeton University Press, Princeton, NJ (see page: 47).

von Lampe, M. and Jeong, H. (2013). Design and Implementation of Food-Import Related Regulations: Experiences from Some Regional Trade Agreements? *Organisation for Economic Co-operation and Development (OECD) Food, Agriculture and Fisheries Papers*, (62):1–38 (see page: 169).

Weiler, F. (2012). Determinants of Bargaining Success in the Climate Change Negotiations. *Climate Policy*, 12(5):552–574 (see pages: 47, 52, and 142).

Wijkström, E. N. and McDaniels, D. (2013). International Standards and the WTO TBT Agreement: Improving Governance for Regulatory Alignment. *World Trade Organization (WTO) Staff Working Paper*, (6):1–30 (see pages: 171, 184).

Willemyns, I. (2020). Agreement Forthcoming? A Comparison of EU, US, and Chinese RTAs in Times of Plurilateral E-Commerce Negotiations. *Journal of International Economic Law*, 23(1):221244 (see page: 236).

Winickoff, D. E. and Bushey, D. M. (2009). Science and Power in Global Food Regulation: The Rise of the Codex Alimentarius. *Science, Technology, & Human Values*, 35(3):356–381 (see page: 133).

Winn, J. K. (2009). Globalization and Standards: The Logic of Two-Level Games. *Journal of Law and Policy for the Information Society*, 5(2):185–218 (see pages: 74, 173).

World Bank (2020). World Bank Open Data. World Bank. Online. Accessed on 31 July 2020 (see pages: 146, 185).

Wouters, J. and Geraets, D. (2012). Private Food Standards and the World Trade Organization: Some Legal Considerations. *World Trade Review*, 11(3):479–489 (see page: 127).

WTO (1995). Agreement on Technical Barriers to Trade. Online. Geneva: World Trade Organization/General Agreement on Tariffs and Trade (see page: 22).

WTO (1995). Negotiating History of the Coverage of the Agreement on Technical Barriers to Trade with Regard to Labelling Requirements, Voluntary Standards, and Process and Production Methods Unrelated to Product Characteristics. World Trade Organization. WT/CTE/W/10. G/TBT/W/11. 29 August 1995 (see page: 137).

WTO (1998). Work Programme on Electronic Commerce: Adopted by the General Council on 25 September 1998. Online. Geneva: World Trade Organization/General Agreement on Tariffs and Trade (see page: 235).

WTO (2000). Second Triennial Review of the Operation and Implementation of the Agreement on Technical Barriers to Trade (G/BTB/9). World Trade Organization. Online. Accessed on 31 July 2020 (see page: 74).

WTO (2011a). Market Access for Non-agricultural Products — International Standards in Support of Trade and Economic Development: Strengthening the Contribution of the Committee Decision — A proposal from the United States. Negotiating Group on Market Access, TN/MA/W/141. 29 March 2011 (see page: 171).

WTO (2011b). Market Access for Non-agricultural Products, International Standardisation — Communication from the delegations of the European Union, India, Indonesia, Norway, Philippines, Switzerland and Thailand. Negotiating Group on Market Access, TN/MA/W/142. 12 April 2011 (see page: 171).

WTO (2011). World Trade Report 2011 — The WTO and Preferential Trade Agreements: From Co-existence to Coherence. Technical report, World Trade Organization, Geneva (see pages: 36, 168, 171, and 186).

WTO (2020a). Disputes by Agreement. World Trade Organization. Online. Accessed on 31 July 2020 (see page: 183).

WTO (2020b). Sanitary and Phytosanitary Information Management System. World Trade Organization. Online. Accessed on 31 July 2020 (see page: 184).

WTO (2020). The GATT Years: From Havana to Marrakesh. Technical report, World Trade Organisation, Geneva (see page: 125).

WTO (2020a). Understanding the WTO Agreement on Sanitary and Phytosanitary Measures. World Trade Organization. Online. Accessed on 31 July 2020 (see page: 127).

WTO (2020b). Understanding the WTO Agreement on Technical Barriers to Trade. World Trade Organization. Online. Accessed on 31 July 2020 (see page: 127).

Wu, M. (2017). Digital Trade-Related Provisions in Regional Trade Agreements: Existing Models and Lessons for the Multilateral Trade System. Technical report, RTA Exchange: International Centre for Trade and Sustainable Development (ICTSD) and the Inter-American Development Bank (IDB), Geneva (see page: 236).

Wunsch-Vincent, S. (2004). WTO, E-commerce, and Information Technologies: From the Uruguay Round through the Doha Development Agenda. Technical report, Markle Foundation and United Nations Information and Communication Technologies (UN ICT), New York, NY (see page: 235).

Wunsch-Vincent, S. (2006). *The WTO, the Internet and Trade in Digital Products*. Hart Publishing, Portland, OR (see page: 235).

Wunsch-Vincent, S. and Hold, A. (2016). Towards coherent rules for digital trade: Building on efforts in multilateral versus preferential trade negotiations. In Burri, M.

and Cottier, T., editors, *Trade Governance in the Digital Age*. Cambridge University Press, Cambridge (see page: 236).

Wüthrich, S. and Elsig, M. (2021). Challenged in Geneva: WTO Litigation Experience and the Design of Preferential Trade Agreements. *Business and Politics*, 13(3):344–363 (see pages: 178, 183, and 186).

Young, A. R. (2016). Not Your Parents' Trade Politics: The Transatlantic Trade and Investment Partnership Negotiations. *Review of International Political Economy*, 23(3):345–378 (see page: 172).

Index

Printed in the United States
by Baker & Taylor Publisher Services